Tracing Your Scottish Ancestry

Kathleen B Cory. FSA Scot.

Tracing Your Scottish Ancestry

Third Edition

Revised and Updated by Leslie Hodgson

Third edition published in 2004
by arrangement with Polygon, an imprint of Birlinn Ltd.,
Edinburgh, Scotland.
First edition published by Polygon in 1990.
Second edition published by Polygon in 1996.

Third edition published in the United States by
Genealogical Publishing Co., Inc.
1001 N. Calvert St., Baltimore, MD 21202
Library of Congress Catalogue Number 2003116455
International Standard Book Number 0-8063-1748-5

Contents

Preface

Note to third edition (from a note left by K.B.C.)

So here we are! A third edition of *Tracing Your Scottish Ancestry*. A great many things have changed since I wrote the introduction to the first edition twelve years ago. In those days few people possessed a personal computer. In these days few people do not. In those days few people were familiar with a web site (except perhaps Robert the Bruce). In these days few people are not.

One sad event was the death in March 1993 of Professor Gordon Donaldson, who as Historiographer Royal for Scotland, kindly and patiently (yes!) steered me through whirlpools of Scottish history. I don't think his masterly Foreword possibly could be bettered, so I have included it once again in this third edition.

I am delighted that so many people world-wide continue to find *Tracing Your Scottish Ancestry* a useful aid to their Scottish genealogy.

Kathleen B. Cory, 2002

★ ★ ★ ★ ★ ★ ★ ★

Since the second reprint of 1999 of the second edition of *Tracing Your Scottish Ancestry*, much has changed that has affected its contents. Kathleen was very aware of these changes and was actively gathering material for a proposed third edition when she died suddenly in late August 2002.

Her two surviving daughters, Mrs Alison Kozowyk and Mrs Maggie Murray, asked me to take on the task of carrying on her work for publication. This I have done with trepidation because I am not used to the publishing world, and because I am very aware of how popular and admired is her book.

A new chapter has been included to acknowledge the relationship between genealogy and local history. This has taken some paragraphs from the Introduction to the second edition, and some paragraphs from the two chapters dealing with the records in both New Register House and the National Archives of Scotland (formerly the Scottish Record Office). Some new material has been included in those three sections, and also in the chapter on Other Sources.

One of the greatest changes – and still on-going – is the amount of material now available for access by/with computers. IT is advancing in leaps and bounds, and indexes for both the Old Parish Registers and statutory registers, and for testaments/wills, are now available on the world-wide web. Also, digitised images of certificates and testaments/wills have been created for access by computer by people far away from Scotland. In some ways this is to be regretted, because soon people with Scottish ancestors will have no over-riding desire to visit the land of those ancestors. These advances have been incorporated into this edition.

The restructuring of local government in 1996 has involved the reorganisation of local archives and library services for local records. Some of the depositories have moved because of this, others have been created and others have had name changes. There has also been a growth in family-history societies – from fourteen to twenty-seven. Many people now make enquiries by e-mail, and read introductions about bodies, societies and organisations on web pages. These three events have necessitated the complete rewriting of Appendix II: List of useful addresses.

Because new books are being published, and existing ones are being revised and up-dated, Appendix IV: Book list, has also had to be rewritten.

I hope all these, and the other additions and rearrangements, reflect Kathleen's intentions and meet with the approval of her daughters. It has been a privilege to contribute to her memory in this way.

Leslie Hodgson
2004

Foreword

BY THE LATE PROFESSOR EMERITUS GORDON DONALDSON, CBE
HM Historiographer in Scotland

Ancestor hunting has been very much a growth industry in recent years and is by no means confined to Scotland. Yet its scale may have been exceptional there, perhaps because of the enormous emigration from Scotland which began on some scale in the seventeenth century and reached its peak after World War II. Scattered in every part of the globe there are many millions – several years ago the figure was put by a wild guess at 20,000,000 – which would now surely be an underestimate of people of Scottish extraction. Therefore numbers alone are enough to explain the vast amount of activity related to Scottish ancestry.

Yet searching for ancestors has a long history behind it. We hear plenty about searchers of records in the nineteenth century – many of course engaged for legal purposes in connection with property, but sometimes pursuing pedigree simply to satisfy people's curiosity about their ancestry. In the late nineteenth and early twentieth centuries two Edinburgh families earned their bread and butter for three successive generations by searching records, mainly for genealogical purposes.

There was something of a slump just after World War II, and some searchers gave up at that point because they saw no future in the business. How wrong they were. Private searchers have multiplied in the second half of the twentieth century and there are assuredly far more now than ever before. Nor are they confined to the traditional centre in Edinburgh, for modern methods of reproduction of record material have made it possible for genealogists to operate successfully even in remote parts of the country. But the business has gone far beyond private searchers and has extended into corporate activities of various kinds. The Scottish Genealogy Society was founded in 1953, the Scots Ancestry Research Society in 1945, and several local family-history groups have sprung up, one of which has been so enterprising as to open a shop in a main street of a Scottish city.

Apart from the private searchers and the societies, the business has been taken up in another way. Ancestry hunting has become something like 'part of the package' for visitors from overseas. Facilities are offered at a popular recreation centre and in at least one well-known hotel. If all this means that there is much competition, it also makes it the more important that anyone proposing to trace his family line must be well equipped and not attempt

searching without first learning from the experience of those practised in
the work.

The emphasis of the searcher has changed in recent times. In the nineteenth
century, and perhaps after it, a lot of people sought ancestors because they
were optimistically looking for a link with some noble family or the bearer of
some famous name. A lot of searching was specifically aimed at establishing
a right to property or to a title. Cases heard in the House of Lords, involving
a claim to a peerage or a dispute over a peerage, proliferated in the nineteenth
century and were entirely rare in the twentieth. Some of them involved vast
research. Indeed, anyone who thinks that it is easy to pursue pedigree, even
among the relatively well-documented members of a noble family, might
glance at the complexities of a case like that of the Dudhope Viscountcy in
1952: the last holder of the title had died in 1668 and the claimant had not
only to prove his descent, generation by generation, from a common ancestor
who was killed at the Battle of Harlaw in 1411, but also to demonstrate that
the many intermediate lines had died out.

More recently the seeking of title, property or even distinguished ancestry
has become less important, and most people who search for their ancestors
do not much mind – indeed they may be positively pleased, if only in a kind of
inverted snobbery – should their search lead to humble or even disreputable
characters.

Some of the searcher's problems are the same whether his ancestor be noble
or humble. In earlier records there are inevitable difficulties of handwriting
and language (often Latin or old Scots). I was amused at the understatement
of someone who was looking with puzzled bewilderment at an early record
and remarked, 'It must need something of a flair to read that'. Perseverance
and practice are all-important.

But much hard work is necessary before one ever sees an original document
or record. The searcher has to identify material which might be relevant, to
discover what guides in the way of indexes and lists are available, to learn
where the records are preserved. On such matters Mrs Cory not only furnishes
wise guidance but gives the appropriate 'class references' which are necessary
to direct the searcher to and through the multitudes of record volumes. She
reminds her readers of certain sources which are far from obvious and which
have been ignored by other writers on the subject. She gives examples of how
to set about a search, but it is not only beginners who will learn a lot from her
pages, containing as they do so many hints and tips drawn from her extensive
experience.

When you have discovered which records are relevant to your search, when
you have found where those records are, when you have used an index – if there
is an index – to lead you to the entry or entries in which you are interested,
when you have at last reached the original document, have read the entry and
deciphered it, with its handwriting and spelling, you still have the problem
of interpreting it. What deductions can be made about matters on which the
record itself is not explicit?

It is in this field that many of the more subtle pitfalls are awaiting, some of them peculiar to Scottish genealogy and arising from common presuppositions, errors or myths, often simply from ignorance of the origins and development of surnames. Names ending in '-son' or beginning with 'Mac-' reflect old practice whereby people were designated not by surnames but by patronymics. Thus Robert's son John was John Robertson, his son might be Andrew Johnson, his son Peter Anderson and so on. Likewise, Neil, son of Donald, was Neil MacDonald. At some stage, we must suppose, a son of a John Robertson decided to call himself not Andrew Johnson but Andrew Robertson, and from that generation Robertson became a surname. The same applied with most of the 'Mac-' names, though some of them appear from an early stage to have carried the connotation 'descendant of' rather than literally 'son of'.

Some indication of a fundamental misunderstanding is perhaps given by the very way in which Scots are apt to speak of their surnames. A man says, 'I'm a Robertson', almost as if Robertsons constitute some unique subspecies of humankind. That at once suggests an assumption that every Robertson is related to other bearers of that name. This is preposterous. The very most that a bearer of the name Robertson can deduce from his surname is that in some generation or other in the past he probably had an ancestor called Robert. It is no more than *probable,* for men changed their surnames because they moved from one part of the country to another, because they changed landlords or employers, perhaps even because they changed their occupation. To believe even that there was necessarily ever an ancestor called Robert is going beyond what the evidence warrants.

To assume that there is necessarily any kinship among 'Robertsons' is to be carried beyond rational thinking. But it is on such irrationality that a great deal which passes in common currency is based. Not only do Robertsons seem to believe that they constitute a sub-species: they also believe that they all came from a little place in Perthshire called Struan. Which at once summons up the picture of the most tremendous industry at Struan over the centuries, in the manufacture and export of Robertsons. Generation by generation, we must suppose, they marched out, kilts no doubt waggling and pipes skirling, to take possession of other parts of the country which meantime had obligingly remained empty awaiting their arrival. This is the kind of belief by which Scots bring down ridicule on their heads. Yet people who are otherwise quite rational seem to believe that kind of thing.

So while many people who engage in ancestor-hunting in Scotland seek no more than to learn what reliable records reveal about their ancestry, a good many are misled into other quests on which records give no information. They want to be connected with some kind of 'clan'. Now, clans (which were military, economic and social communities) ceased to be a reality generations ago: when they were realities few of their members had surnames at all, and members who had a surname did not necessarily share it with other members of the clan. There is of course no reason why people of the same surname should not form an association if it gives them any satisfaction to do so, but that association should not be confused with an historic clan. The idea that anyone, just because he chances to have a particular name, is automatically a member of a particular organisation is absurd. Some people want to argue some connection with a 'chief' – and some 'chiefs' are not averse to having 'clansmen', whose contributions can sometimes be relied on to patch up the roof of the 'chief's' ancestral home. Some want a 'clan connection' because they believe that 'entitles' them to wear cloth of a particular pattern, a so-called 'clan tartan'. Experience shows that the only qualification for the acquisition of a 'clan tartan' (nearly always a nineteenth-century invention) is the same qualification as for the acquisition of any other piece of cloth, namely, ability to pay for it. That is where the emphasis should be laid, because of course the whole tartan cult is a commercial enterprise – it is business, big business, for the tartan-makers, and no doubt it yields many a fee to hard-working genealogists. It is a sobering thought that anyone turning up in the Lowlands four hundred years ago clothed in anything recognisable as 'Highland dress' would probably have been shot on sight!

Our Robertson may be lucky enough to trace his own original Robert, the descent from whom gave him his name – but even so he should remember that had the change to a surname come a generation earlier or later his name might have been not Robertson but, say, Anderson or Johnson. However, as the adoption of a fixed surname may have taken place as far back as the fifteenth century the chances of a twentieth-century Robertson identifying his 'Robert' are not very good. Sometimes, though, the change took place more recently. It did so in my own case. I was aware that in Shetland (whence my paternal ancestry derives) there were Donaldsons who had arrived from Scotland, already with that name, before 1600, and that there were also Donaldsons or Danielsons who had used patronymics until, in some generation or other, an individual's patronymic Danielson was retained by his family as a surname. I thought I belonged to the first category, and indeed I did, but only through the curious coincidence that one of my patronymic ancestors happened to marry a Donaldson descended from Scottish immigrants. What mattered more was the discovery that my great-great-grandfather, William Donaldson or Danielson (baptised 1770), was the son of Daniel Theodoreson, who was the son of Theodore Danielson, and so back in patronymic succession to Matthew Thomasson about 1600. Readers of those pages will appreciate that I have good reasons to be thankful for skilled genealogical research.

Yet some would say that I am 'a Donaldson'. Worse than that, they might say that I am 'a MacDonald', that I am a member of 'The Clan Donald' and no doubt 'entitled' to wear the 'MacDonald Tartan'. What a load of nonsense! Of course the financial interests keep coming in. I recall some years ago receiving a request for funds for some object under the patronage of 'The Clan Donald'. I replied: 'If you can prove (a) that there is such a thing as The Clan Donald and (b) that I am a member of it, I shall gladly subscribe; but until you do I shall continue to deplore the way you distort historical truth for financial gain.' I heard no more.

Be warned!

Few people would be so foolish as to believe that all 'the Smiths' are descended from one and the same blacksmith, or that all 'the Littles' are descended from one and the same Little Richard or Richard Little, but when patronymics come in common sense flies out of the window.

These remarks are not intended to depreciate the historical importance of the surname or family name in Scottish society and politics, but the name was often used as a badge of party allegiance or affiliation rather than as proof of descent or kinship. I emphasise the numerous complexities to indicate the great danger of relying on casual assumptions about kinship and descent, based on nothing more than the surname. The case for serious study is strengthened, not weakened, because assumptions or guesses are no substitute for thorough research in original sources, for which Mrs Cory, who is well aware of all the manifold pitfalls, provides comprehensive guidance.

Gordon Donaldson
Fife, 1989

Acknowledgements

Extracts from the statutory registers, indexes of births, marriages and deaths, and census returns, held in New Register House, Edinburgh, are reproduced by permission of the Controller of the Stationery Office. The index to Sheriff Court Commissary records (Fig. 8), the letter to the General Assembly from Pennsylvania (Fig. 9), the government emigration regulations (Fig. 10), and the 'CH' extracts are reproduced courtesy of the National Archives of Scotland. The chart of the divisions and reunions of the Scottish Church 1690–1929 is from Professor J.H.S. Burleigh's *A Church History of Scotland*, and it is reproduced by kind permission of John K. Burleigh, Esq.

Margaret Dudgeon Young, a close personal friend of Kathleen, and her brother Archibald Henderson Young, are heartily thanked for allowing their family to be searched and used as the example in Part II of this book.

Also thanked are other personal friends of Kathleen for the checking of other material – Selina J. Corkerton, Alison E. Denholm and Daniella Shippey.

Invaluable advice and information have been given by the late Professor Gordon Donaldson, and also by Sir Malcolm Innes of Edingight, KCVO, Dr Athol Murray, Dr John Shaw, Mrs Jackie Ross and Mrs Margaret Whyte. Robin O. Blair, LVO, Lord Lyon King of Arms, is thanked for allowing the use of information from the Lyon Office heraldry leaflet, and for approving the chapters on Heraldry and Clans and Tartans.

Grateful thanks are repeated to Kathleen's daughters, the late Elizabeth S.B. Cory, Alison C.B. Kozowyk, and Margaret D.B. Murray, for keeping her at it and for the constructive comments made by them.

Charles J. Burnett, Ross Herald of Arms, is thanked for the opportunity he provided for the writing of this book in the first place.

Other friends and colleagues who responded to Kathleen for suggestions concerning material are again thanked. These are the late Miss A.S. Cowper, Mr & Mrs Angus Mitchell, and the Corkerton family who kindly allowed their entry to be used in the Voters' Roll as an example.

For this 3rd edition I am grateful to Charles Napier for obtaining and checking the entries for the members of the Scottish Association of Family History Societies, and to Tom Dewar for typing up Appendix II. Mrs Alan Borthwick has been a great help in answering questions about the lesser used records in New Register House.

K.C.

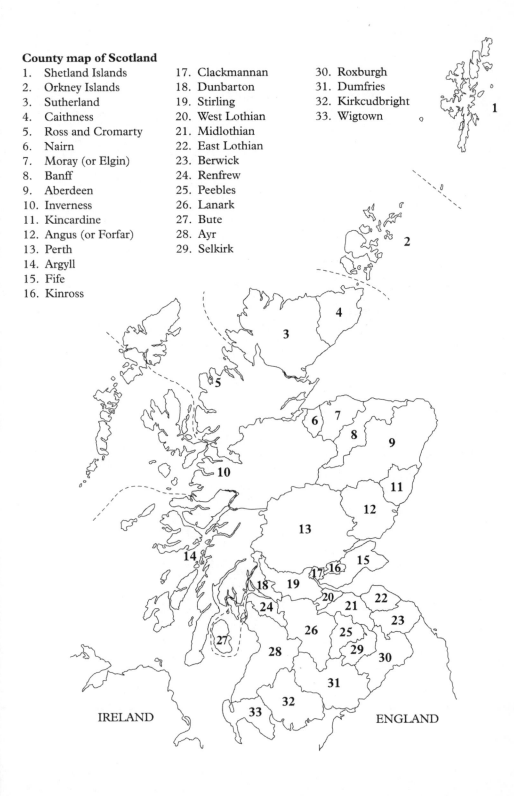

County map of Scotland

1. Shetland Islands
2. Orkney Islands
3. Sutherland
4. Caithness
5. Ross and Cromarty
6. Nairn
7. Moray (or Elgin)
8. Banff
9. Aberdeen
10. Inverness
11. Kincardine
12. Angus (or Forfar)
13. Perth
14. Argyll
15. Fife
16. Kinross
17. Clackmannan
18. Dunbarton
19. Stirling
20. West Lothian
21. Midlothian
22. East Lothian
23. Berwick
24. Renfrew
25. Peebles
26. Lanark
27. Bute
28. Ayr
29. Selkirk
30. Roxburgh
31. Dumfries
32. Kirkcudbright
33. Wigtown

IRELAND

ENGLAND

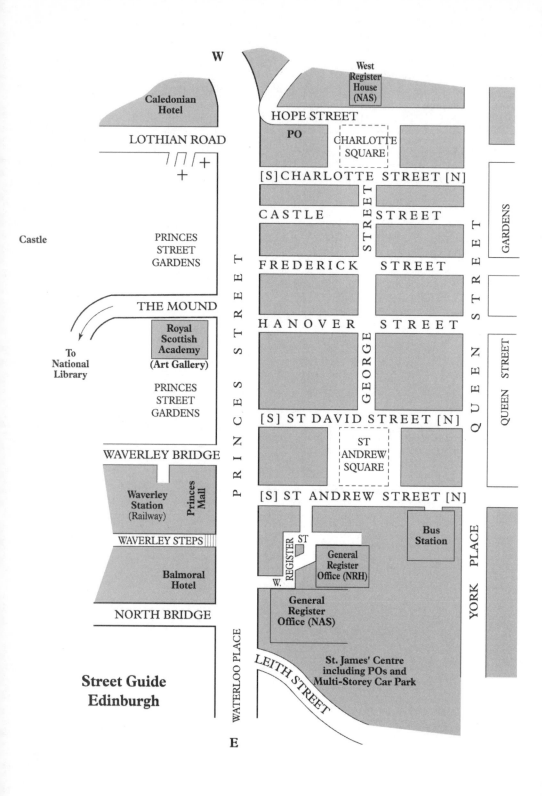

W

Caledonian Hotel

West Register House (NAS)

LOTHIAN ROAD

HOPE STREET

PO

CHARLOTTE SQUARE

Castle

PRINCES STREET GARDENS

[S] CHARLOTTE STREET [N]

CASTLE STREET

CASTLE STREET

FREDERICK STREET

THE MOUND

HANOVER STREET

Royal Scottish Academy (Art Gallery)

GEORGE STREET

QUEEN STREET

GARDENS

QUEEN STREET

To National Library

PRINCES STREET GARDENS

[S] ST DAVID STREET [N]

PRINCES STREET

ST ANDREW SQUARE

WAVERLEY BRIDGE

[S] ST ANDREW STREET [N]

Waverley Station (Railway)

Princes Mall

WAVERLEY STEPS

Balmoral Hotel

REGISTER ST

W.

Bus Station

YORK PLACE

General Register Office (NRH)

NORTH BRIDGE

General Register Office (NAS)

WATERLOO PLACE

LEITH STREET

St. James' Centre including POs and Multi-Storey Car Park

Street Guide Edinburgh

E

Part I

A GUIDE TO GENEALOGY IN SCOTLAND

Introduction

'Is it upon record, or else reported successively from age to age?' asked the Prince of Wales in Shakespeare's *Richard III*. Pooh Bah, the Lord High Everything Else, in Gilbert and Sullivan's *Mikado* had no such doubts. He knew his background: 'I can trace my ancestry back to a protoplasmal primordial atomic globule. Consequently, my family pride is something inconceivable. I cannot help it. I was born sneering.'

To whichever category you may feel you belong, I hope you will find this book interesting, informative and, in parts, entertaining.

That is how Kathleen introduced the first edition of her book in 1990.

Several books had been written about Scottish genealogy and record searching, but none, it then appeared, had combined a thorough explanation of the complexities of the records with step-by-step instructions on completing a search of your family history, using all the resources available, principally those in Scotland.

This book is based on the experience gained from genealogy lectures Kathleen gave in the United States of America, England, Australia, New Zealand and Canada. It is believed that it will succeed in answering most, if not all of the questions which had come her way over more than twenty years of being a genealogist searching people's Scottish family history.

The great advantage to be gained from working with post-1854 birth, marriage and death records in New Register House in Edinburgh, is that you can view each entry and so determine its relevance to your own search. This is *not* the case in England.

For those of you who have undertaken record searching in England and elsewhere, be advised that Scotland, and the records used for Scottish genealogy, is a whole new ball game!

To put you in the picture – on the death in 1603 of Queen Elizabeth of England, her nearest kinsman (through her aunt Princess Margaret) James VI, King of Scots, then also became King of England. King James I & VI moved his court down to London. Then in 1707, during the reign of Queen Anne, the parliaments of Scotland and England were merged so that the two countries were ruled by one monarch, and by one parliament.

Scotland has always retained, not only its own personality, but its own legal system, its own education system and its own church – the Presbyterian Church of Scotland. All this is reflected in the statutory records, the Old

1

Parish Registers, the land ownership records and other various sources for Scottish genealogy.

To lead you through this genealogical labyrinth and bring you out at the end with the Scottish ancestors you had been trying to search for, the aim is to explain the best way to get the most out of what is available.

Before you start your search you may like to read about Scotland's interesting social and local history, which would help you to understand why, and how, families moved around as much as they did. A list of useful books is included in Appendix IV: Book list.

In the text there is an attempt to describe the best method of approaching and questioning members of your family who may not be very co-operative. Remember that there is more to genealogy than just names, dates and places. Bearing this in mind, and trying to learn something of the background of her own family, Kathleen tape-recorded conversations she had with her mother when she was ninety-one. Her mother talked of her childhood in Hampshire, with her two sisters and her only brother who emigrated to Australia, returned with the Australian Army and died of wounds in 1917. This uncle Bill, who died long before Kathleen was born, left behind in Australia a young wife and baby daughter. Kathleen was in touch with his granddaughter, and was able to supply her with photographs and information about her great-grandparents.

Kathleen's mother remembered what London was like on Armistice Night in 1918 at the end of World War I, and recorded her impressions of the early motor-cars and airships, and the Royal Flying Corps before the Royal Air Force existed.

This tape can now be played by Kathleen's grandchildren in Oxfordshire and Canada, and they will probably put its contents onto their computers, together with photographs. Although they may not remember their great-grandmother, they are able to hear her voice and see what she looked like. Therefore 1895, the year of her birth, will not seem such a remote and meaningless date, and they can listen to someone whose memory ranges from the first car in her village (with a man holding a red flag, walking in front) to the first landing of a man on the moon!

The information which genealogists search for is to be found in primary sources, archival sources and in books. These sources are held by national, university and local authority archives and major libraries – and these repositories are *unlikely* to be replaced by the internet in the immediate future.

The internet is valuable in giving you an indication of where to look, and in helping you identify the books and records you need to consult. Most of the above-mentioned repositories have websites and on-line catalogues/lists and information on their holdings. See Appendix II for postal and e-mail addresses and websites. There are also now available, for purchase, many useful databases on CD-ROM, which are featured in the computer section of genealogical magazines.

Most of the information from the above sources provides important historical and context/background information concerning your ancestors.

Many family trees are available on the internet, and many are copied from secondary sources and hardly ever provide references to primary sources. In other words they cannot be relied on – there is much wishful-linking! Thanks to the guidance and advice given in genealogical magazines this situation is improving. Always include your references and sources so that people can be sure of the provenance, to see if they can actually connect into your family tree.

Nothing can replace looking at original documents and certificates, but hardly any are available on the internet. For Scotland there are available on the internet since April 2003, for a fee, digitised images of records of births (1856–1902), of marriages (1856–1927), and of deaths (1856–1952), census returns for 1891 and 1901, and testaments and wills 1500–1901. In England there are available on the internet wills of the Prerogative Court of Canterbury (1610–1858) – which include many Scots who moved south – and the 1901 census returns for England and Wales, and the indexes to the births, marriages and deaths registers (1837 to date). See Appendix VI for a short, but very useful list of websites from which you can access these indexes and digital images, together with another short list of websites which will lead you to thousands of other websites for genealogical and local-history information.

As Kathleen wrote in the second edition of this book: 'I again invite you to turn the pages and enter, or re-enter, the fascinating world of Scottish genealogy. Good luck and happy hunting!'

Leslie Hodgson, 2003

Note:

The former Scottish Record Office (SRO) is now the National Archives of Scotland (NAS).

In England the Public Record Office (PRO) in Kew merged in April 2003 with the Royal Commission on Historical Manuscripts (Historical Manuscripts Commission), Chancery Lane, London, to form the National Archives. The two sites continue to operate separately under the new name. For ease of distinction I have referred to this as (NA(E)) [National Archives in England].

1
Local History and Genealogy in Scotland

The local historian and the family historian, these days, have a great deal in common. There was a time when neither local history nor genealogy had a wide appeal, but more and more people are interested in knowing something about the background of their ancestors. They are keen to find out where their ancestors had lived, and in what conditions; where they went to church and school; their occupations, and how much they had earned; what they might have eaten as a staple diet and if that might have had any effect on their cause of death, trying to avoid the same trap themselves. In fact, a much wider spread of interest than just the names of their great-great-grandparents

Descendants of immigrants often come back to 'find their roots' (dreadful expression!) – but so often urban development has resulted in the visitor finding nothing but tower blocks and flyovers where whole areas have no bearing on the information so carefully gleaned from census returns. The streets are just not there any more. This is where the knowledge of the local historian is invaluable. Most local history societies possess photographic collections of places and people, and this, together with oral history, can often clothe the bare bones of names and addresses so far found.

As late as 1891 those people 'in service' (i.e. domestic servants) comprised the largest groups of the working population. About 1.5 million domestic servants (in England and Wales) were employed not just in large country houses but also in the suburban and town houses of the middle-class professionals (clergymen, lawyers, doctors, retired generals, etc.). Women outnumbered men by about two to one in employed domestic service. The situation was paralleled in Scotland.

From accounts of their lives it is amazing that they managed eventually to marry and have children – because married women were *not* employed in domestic service.

As elsewhere, local history societies abound in Scotland. The Scottish Local History Forum, as successor to a series of bodies interested in the promotion and development of local history in Scotland, was formally constituted in 1983. It encourages this interest by publishing a newsletter and by promoting conferences from time to time around Scotland. Information on local history societies, some of which are incorporated in family history societies, will be obtained from local record offices, libraries and family history societies. (see Appendix II: List of useful addresses).

It is important to try to widen the information found on a birth, marriage or death certificate, as well as census returns, and so finish up with a comprehensive picture of the family.

In Scotland, record searching for the purpose of genealogy falls into two parts:

1. births, marriages and deaths from 1855 to the present day;
2. births, marriages and deaths prior to 1855.

These two parts are bridged by the decennial census returns which are available to the public for the years 1841 to 1901 inclusive.

The above-mentioned records are held at the General Register Office for Scotland (GROS) at New Register House, Princes Street, Edinburgh, adjacent to the General Register House which houses the National Archives of Scotland. The street plan of central Edinburgh reproduced at the front of this book shows the locations of the main repositories.

New Register House holds the indexes to, and the registers of, births, marriages and deaths in Scotland from 1855 to the present day. The great advantage to be gained from working with post-1854 birth, marriage and death records in Scotland is that you may view each entry, and so determine its relevance to your own search. This is very different from working in the Family Records Centre, London, where each certificate has to be purchased, with no possibility of viewing it beforehand to establish its relevance.

The important date to remember as far as Scottish genealogy is concerned is 1855. It was in 1854 that Parliament decided to introduce statutory (or civil) registration of births, marriages and deaths in Scotland. This Act (17 & 18 Vict. Cap.80), was to take effect from 1 January 1855, and since that date it has been compulsory, by law, to register all births, marriages and deaths which take place in Scotland. I stress *Scotland* because statutory or civil registration had been introduced in England and Wales on 1 July 1837, some eighteen years earlier, but did not become compulsory until 1875.

It is not clear why Scotland lagged behind on this issue, but it certainly gave the Scottish authorities time to take note of the shortcomings in the English and Welsh recording system. When statutory registration was eventually introduced, then the information required was far and away more detailed and more comprehensive than that found in England and Wales. For example, a Scottish marriage certificate from 1855 onwards records the ages of the bride and bridegroom, whereas an English certificate often merely states 'of full age'. A Scottish certificate also records the maiden surname of the mother of both the bride and the groom, as well as their fathers' names and occupations, whereas over the border the equivalent certificate records only names and occupations of the fathers.

The greatest difference in the system can be seen in death certificates. A Scottish death certificate, unlike its English counterpart, gives a wealth of genealogical information, such as the name of the deceased's mother, her maiden surname and the name and occupation of the father, as well as, in most cases, the name of the spouse. This can be seen from the death certificate of my father, of which a copy is reproduced. (see Illustrations: Fig.2).

An interesting point to remember is, that in Scots law, a married woman retains her maiden surname. My name is Kathleen Beatrice Reed *or* Cory on all official documents such as testaments (wills), and when I die, should this be in Scotland, my death will be indexed under both surnames.

The link between 'modern' records (i.e. post-1854) and Old Parish Registers (i.e. pre-1855) is the census return. It is necessary to know in which parish the subject was born, in order to know through which Parish Registers to search for the appropriate entry. Only recently has the closure rule for the 1901 census been lifted. In New Register House the 1881 census for Scotland is on computer – both an index and a transcription – and the 1891 and 1901 census returns for Scotland are also on computer – both an index and a digitised image of the census register page.

As well as forming a link between the 'modern' records and the Old Parish Registers, the census returns hold a wealth of interesting material for both the local historian and the genealogist. By reading them carefully you can determine the lifestyle of the people. You can discover how many rooms a family lived in, and how many families lived in a block of flats or a tenement. Census returns also record occupations, as well as stating whether or not an individual was employed, unemployed or employing servants and/or apprentices. In rural areas they can state how many persons are employed on a particular farm.

New Register House also holds Old Parish Registers (baptisms, marriages and deaths/burials prior to statutory registration in 1855), which together with Kirk Session Minute Books (held in the National Archives of Scotland) contain many socially and historically interesting comments, such as this birth entry in Dunfermline in July 1690:

> *the 12 day about 9 hours in the morning being a Saturday John Christie precentor had ane manchild born to him and of his wife Joan Finlay baptized ye 15 instant by Mr Simon Cowper called James. The Godfayers was James King of Great Britain, France, and Ireland, defender of ye Faith, and James Finlay Grandfayer to the Child.*

Genealogically speaking the nugget of gold in this entry is that Joan Finlay was the daughter of James Finlay, and that her father was still alive in 1690 and may have left a testament or will. Historically speaking Mr. Simon Cowper, the minister, and John Christie, the father, appear not to be politically aware. HRH Prince James (1633–1701) was in Scotland in 1679 and 1680–2 when he was his brother's (King Charles II) High Commissioner to the Scottish Parliament, and when he succeeded to the throne in 1685 as King James VII and II the country was effusively loyal. However, as King James showed a determination to attain toleration for Roman Catholics, a convention held on 4 April 1689 declared that he had forfeited his throne!

Reading Old Handwriting

Having entered the realms of Old Parish Registers and in general, other records written prior to the 1800s (i.e. Kirk Session Minutes, testaments and

Sasines), it is useful to have at least a passing acquaintance with the old Scots tongue and the old Scots handwriting. For instance, you may come across 'the umquhile John MacDonald' which means nothing more than 'the late John MacDonald'.

Parish Registers were written in English, or at least, in Old Scots in the early years. They were not in Latin, nor, as some people think when they see the old-style handwriting, in Gaelic. For a list of words and contractions which you may find useful see Appendix I. A useful book on this subject is Grant G. Simpson's *Scottish Handwriting: 1150–1650: An introduction to the reading of documents* (see Appendix IV: Book list).

You will find the long 's' looking like an 'f', but without little horizontal line; the letter 't' was not always crossed; a capital 'F' was often written as 'ff'; 'z' and 'y' were interchangeable. The word 'possesses' looks like 'poffeffes'; the name 'Russell' looks like 'Ruffell'; and 'Finlay' is written as 'ffinlay'. You may find the place and surname 'Dalziel' spelled 'Dayell', and in some areas of Scotland it is pronounced 'Deyall'. Of course, what looks like 'ye' means 'the', as 'y' is an ancient character called a thorn and is the equivalent of 'th'. Also 'u' and 'v' are interchangeable and 'qu' is for 'w'.

Spelling variations must be expected, such as Dumfreis for Dumfries. The prefix 'Old' translates as 'Auld', so Oldhamstocks becomes written as Auldhamestokkis. St Quivox can be found as St Kevokiss, or Sanc-Kevokis, and Auchtergaven can be found as Ochtirgavin. Quheillands is Whillans, and Quhitlaw means Whitelaw.

Reading and understanding numbers may cause some difficulty, as they tend to be written in roman numerals for the years and items of money. Dates can present some problems at first; for example, 'jaj' is the sign for a thousand; it is a corruption of 'im' which was originally written as four vertical strokes: the first and last were elongated while the middle ones degenerated into 'a'. Four is often written as 'iiii' instead of 'iv', and the last 'i' of a sequence is usually written as 'j'. Hence viij = 8.

In the seventeenth century and earlier, sums of money were usually expressed in Scots currency. The value of Scots in relation to sterling dwindled over the decades, and by 1600 had become one twelfth, at which it remained. Sums were expressed in terms of pounds ($£$) or in merks which were worth 13s. 4d. (two thirds of £1 before decimalisation). Amounts of money are found written in testaments or wills, and also in accounts in the Parish Registers and Kirk Session Minutes. These entries show payments made to parishioners who were listed by name and receiving poor relief, and payment to tradesmen for repairing church property.

It was customary for churches to hire out mortcloths, and there were several grades and sizes: 'For the hire of the small mortcloth . . .' 'For the hire of the best mortcloth . . .'. When a couple gave intimation of marriage (proclamation of marriage or banns) they often had to consign a sum of money as a surety for good behaviour before the marriage, and a guarantee to marry within forty days of contracting. This sum of money was called a 'pawn', 'pand' or 'pledge', and most of it was retrievable on marriage, providing that the bridal couple had behaved themselves to the satisfaction of the elders of the Kirk and the minister, when a smaller amount was paid into the poor relief fund of the parish.

Amounts are shown as in the following examples:

li or lib (which can look like 'liv') = £.
s = shilling (20s = £1)
d = penny (12d = 1s; which was written 1/-)
ob = halfpenny (not often found)
summa = total (or sum)
xix li iiis. iiijd = £19 3s. 4d.

To help you in understanding and reading handwriting look at the website. See Appendix VI.

Term Days

Rents and interest on loans were due on term days, or quarter days. They were also the days when ministers' stipends were paid, and when servants, especially on farms, were hired and paid. These days were nearly always stated in deeds such as bonds, tacks and wills.

In Scotland the term days, dividing up the legal year, were:

Candlemas (2 February – originally the feast of the Purification of the Virgin Mary, usually involving candlelit processions);

Whitsun (15 May – originally the feast of Pentecost);

Lammas (1 August – traditionally a harvest festival); and

Martinmas (11 November – originally the feast of Saint Martin of Tours).

In the Old Style calendar (the Julian calendar introduced by Julius Caesar in 45 BC) the beginning of the year was 25 March. The New Style, or Gregorian, calendar, was introduced by Pope Gregory XIII in 1582 and the new year began on 1 January. For *all* the British Isles it was not until September 1752 that the Gregorian calendar became universal. For the hiring and removal of servants, the term days of Whitsun and Martinmas were fixed by statute in 1886 at 28 May and 28 November respectively.

Back to the Records

As well as statutory registrations of births, marriages and deaths, census returns and Old Parish Registers, New Register House holds Army, Navy and Air Force registers and a selection of miscellaneous records such as adoption records and consular returns, and many printed monumental inscriptions.

A further search into the realms of testaments, deeds, burgess records, and so on, necessitates a visit to the National Archives of Scotland (NAS) housed next door in HM General Register House.

HM General Register House was started in 1774 and was designed by Robert Adam as a repository for the principal legal registers and other historical records that were previously kept in the Laigh Parliament House (see under that name, and under 'Register House', in *A Dictionary of Scottish History*, by G. Donaldson and R.S. Morpeth). The main holdings include state papers and administrative records prior to the Union of the Parliaments in 1707, registers of the Court of Session, High Court of Justiciary, Sheriff, Commissary and other Courts, registers of Sasines and Deeds, local records, including local authority records, valuation rolls, church records, and gifts and deposits (private archives). Lists and other guides to the records are available for consultation in the Historical Search Room.

The National Archives of Scotland is on a split site – with a branch repository, the West Search Room, at West Register House, Charlotte Square, Edinburgh. This is a conversion (1968–71) of the former St George's Church designed by Robert Reid and founded in 1811. It is used for more modern records, and its main holdings include records of government departments and nationalised industries in Scotland, court processes, maps and plans, and registers of the Great Seal.

The records held in the National Archives are many and varied. The main ones used by the average genealogical searcher and local historian are testaments, deeds, sasines, Services of Heirs or Retours, Kirk Session Minutes and some non-established church records. More and more records are being returned to local authorities. It is advisable to find out beforehand where the records you may wish to consult are being held – General Register House *or* West Register House *or* local record offices/archives..

Registers of the Great Seal of Scotland are handwritten in Latin, and before circa 1750 you will find some sasines, and some testaments, hand-written in Latin and some in English/Old Scots within the same volume.

Sometimes, when you are searching the indexes and repertories, you will find a record that is housed at Thomas Thomson House, the centralised store and conservation centre on the west edge of Edinburgh. Unless you are familiar with the different types of records you will *not* know this until you order it. It takes twenty-four hours, after ordering, for the productions you require to be brought in for reading.

A recent innovation is the scanning and digitising of all testaments/wills up to 1901 onto computer. In the Historical Search Room annex (the Robertson Wing) there are terminals where you can read the indexes, and then bring up an image of the actual document. Some other records are on microfilm, but unfortunately the quality can be abysmal, making them extremely difficult (sometimes impossible) to read. You can purchase a copy of these for a small fee.

Descriptions of parishes and places, conditions within them, and an idea of their agricultural and industrial activity, and even wages earned during the times of your ancestors, can be found in Statistical Accounts. The first, compiled 1791–8 by Sir John Sinclair, was made when industry was just about to expand. The second, or New Statistical Account, was compiled mainly in the early 1840s. Another valuable source for similar information is Groome's *Ordnance Gazetteer*. See Appendix IV: Book list.

Snapshots of many places can be found in the written accounts of travels and diaries by the earlier visitors and tourists to Scotland; writers such as Thomas Pennant (1769), Johnson and Boswell (1773), Robert Heron (1799), Sarah Murray (1799), Dorothy Wordsworth (1803), Robert Southey (1819), and many more. The reports and journals of Scottish travellers also provide snapshots – for example: Revd Dr John Walker (1764 and 1771), James Hogg (1802–04), Sir Walter Scott (1814), Henry, Lord Cockburn (1837–54; published 1888), Alexander Smith (Skye; 1864), H.V. Morton (1929) and Edwin Muir (1935).

Maps can also add to your local-history knowledge of the parishes, villages, towns, farms and houses of your ancestors. These are more difficult to search out and look at. The Royal Scottish Geographical Society has published *The Early Maps of Scotland: to 1850* (vol.1, 1973; vol.2, 1983). Volume I contains information and lists; and the whereabouts of over 450 maps covering Scotland as a whole, and information on cartographers and map engravers. Volume 2 contains lists, and so on, of subsidiary maps and plans under such headings as canal, railway, agricultural, county and town maps. There are over 2,000 items recorded. Estate plans are not included.

The first national survey by the Ordnance Survey (OS) was completed in 1873, and subsequent editions have been produced. A certain edition of the OS maps is found in the South Reading Room of New Register House, and in the Historical Search Room at the NAS, and at the National Monuments Record for Scotland. (See Appendix II: List of useful addresses.)

If you really do want to pore over maps – quite fascinating really – then the place to go is the Map Library of the National Library of Scotland. (See Appendix II.)

Estate maps and plans will be found at the NAS, West Register House (see Appendix II). There is a descriptive list of plans in numerous volumes.

Some old town maps have been reprinted by Alan Godfrey, Gateshead, and can be purchased from most big bookshops and local-history societies.

2
Searching Records in the General Register Office (New Register House)

New Register House, the General Register Office for Scotland, is in Princes Street, Edinburgh, adjacent to the General Register House (National Archives of Scotland). A street plan of central Edinburgh, from which you can see where the main repositories are situated, is to be found at the beginning of this book. New Register House holds the indexes to, and the registers of births, marriages and deaths from 1855 to the present day. It also holds the Old Parish Registers (OPRs) of births, marriages and deaths to 1854 from the earliest extant date (this varies from parish to parish: see Appendix III); as well as census returns for 1841–1901 inclusive; some Army, Navy and Air Force registers; and a selection of miscellaneous records.

All the pre-1855 birth, marriage and death records, and all the census returns, are on microfilm. All the post-1854 birth, marriage and death records are on microfiche and most also on computer. Index books have been transferred onto computer, of which more later. The records are available to the public for inspection only on payment of a search fee. *No searching is free*: this includes searching the index to statutory registers of births, marriages and deaths from 1855, and searching census returns. Once you have bought a half-day, daily, weekly, four-weekly or quarterly search pass, it is only for your own use: you may not share it with anybody. For example, you may not use it in the morning, and hand it to somebody to use in the afternoon. An annual pass (which at the time of going to print is £1,500) may be shared by three persons. The purchaser of this pass may nominate two others, either of whom will be allowed to use his/her place when the purchaser is absent. The supervisor must be told at the beginning of each week when each person will be in, and financial arrangements are purely a private matter between the parties concerned. There is also an APEX pass at a reduced rate during the months November to January inclusive, for purchase fourteen days in advance of your visit. Telephone for more information.

New Register House is open from 9 a.m. until 4.30 p.m. from Monday to Friday. It is closed on Saturdays and on some local and public holidays. Evening visits are available for organised groups. These groups have to be a minumum number of eight persons and a maximum of twenty. The price is at present £160 irrespective of the number in the group. You are advised to write or telephone in advance to check this. (See Appendix II for addresses).

Accommodation is limited, and so, during the holiday months, when there is a large influx of visitors to Edinburgh, you should always write or telephone in advance to book yourself a seat/desk. If you are unable to do this, then you should arrive at least half an hour early to be sure of being admitted. It is important to arrive complete with a large pad, preferably A4 size, on which to write out all the information you find, and at least two *lead pencils*. The use of biros or pens is prohibited, as is the use of mobile phones, and smoking or eating anywhere in the building is forbidden. There are lavatories but no café, though there are several small eating-places nearby. Prior arrangements can be made to assist wheelchair searchers, and there is a lift available.

Each person sits at a small desk with a computer monitor, keyboard and mouse, and a microfiche reader.

SEARCHING THE RECORDS USING THE COMPUTER

Since 15 November 1993, the index to all births and marriages recorded in Scotland from 1533 to date, and all deaths recorded in Scotland from 1855 to date, has been entered on computer. As yet deaths prior to the introduction of statutory registration in 1855, which may be found in some Old Parish Registers, have not been indexed and entered on computer. The reason appears to be that the Mormon microfiche indexes have been used for this computer programme and as yet they have not included deaths, which are not as important to their religious beliefs. There is a slight snag to this using of the microfiche index to births/baptisms and marriages. Where there was an error or omission in the microfiche, then this has been transferred to the computer; however steps are taken to correct any error which is reported to a member of staff in New Register House.

In addition to the indexes, there are available digitised images of birth, marriage and death certificates 1855–1965.

Beware! Not all parish records prior to 1855 are complete, so the entry you seek may not be found on computer.

If you do not find a birth, marriage or death entry which was dated after 1855, then search the microfiche index for the year and the Registration District Number concerned. This index is to be found at the end of the box which holds the relevant microfiche. I have found entries on the microfiche index which were not on computer, but this only applies to statutory records and not to OPRs.

Remember that the absence of evidence does not necessarily mean evidence of absence – think about it!

The computer terminal screen at your desk in New Register House will have at the top – the title bar, the menu bar and the tool bar, in that order, and at the bottom the status bar. This status bar will have two icons on the left-hand side:

AS400 Lookup-Digros, and

Session A – [24x80]

When you first view the screen it will be either white with some lettering (in AS400 (etc.) mode) *or* black with green or white lettering (in Session A (etc.) mode). You change from one to the other by clicking on the icons using the mouse.

Session A – [24x80] – works more quickly than AS400 Lookup-Digros, but only the latter programme has digital images of post-1855 certificates and of the Census returns for 1891 and 1901. Sometimes it is quicker to search using Session A, and then change to AS400, type in the appropriate information and then bring up the digital image to view. Session A also has the index for pre-1855 Old Parish Registers of births/baptisms and marriages. You do not use the mouse, only the keyboard, when the screen is black.

Session A – [24x80] will show on the screen as follows:

WELCOME TO THE INDEX ENQUIRY SYSTEM

Which type of search do you require?

1. Statutory Index (Birth, Death or Marriage)
   (gives access to OPR B & M index)
2. Divorce Index
3. Old Parish Register Index [OPR]
   (gives access to Statutory B & M index)
4. Census Index (1881, 1891 or 1901)

Insert '1', '2', '3', or '4', and then press 'Enter' key.

If your search starts after 1855, and you hope to take it back to include entries in the Old Parish Registers, you should key in '1', when the screen will show:

Which type of search do you require?

1. Birth, Death & Marriage Index
2. Cross check on female deaths using two surnames
3. Cross check on marriages using two surnames.

If you then key in '1' again you should find the following on the screen:

1.	Event type	B for Birth or Christening
		D for Death. M for marriage
2.	Sex	M or F for Male or Female
3.	Year	Year of event
4.	Surname	Surname of subject of enquiry
5.	Forename	Initial, all, or part of forename, or blank
6.	Age range . . .	Death index only. Leave blank if all entries of any
	to . . .	age are wanted

So type in the information fitting your search, and press the 'Enter' key. The screen will then show a selection of names within the confines of the information you have supplied, that is, surname, forename(s) and for deaths, the age. The page on the screen is similar to the paper index page, but it gives more reference information such as the district registration number as well as the name of the parish, but not the county.

As New Register House now works on a self-service system, you must fill in a requisition slip and fetch your microfiche. If on examination this entry does not fit with the information you have concerning the subject, then you must return to the computer and find another entry. It is sometimes more timesaving to make a list of names for about two or three years, but bear in mind *that you are only allowed to take out three microfiches at a time.*

If you are searching for one of the more unusual names, such as Cory, you may find there are no entries for the year you have keyed in, then the screen will show something like:

Indexes to the birth register for male (or female) persons who were born in 1895 surname Cory, Initial J

The record you seek has not been found using the above information. Please select one of the following options:

1. End the enquiry
2. Re-display the search information to allow change
3. Search the year before the period already searched
4. Search the year following the period already searched
5. Display all records with similar sounding names
6. Display all records with the above surname.

The next step is to type in the number you need and press the 'Enter' key. When you are satisfied that you have a possible candidate for your search, then fill in the requisition slip and proceed as before. I would warn you not to trust the programme which promises to display all similar sounding names. It all depends on how you pronounce the name!

To return to 'Which type of search do you require?' press 'F1' until it appears.

Still working from the statutory programme, if you wish to search for the death of a married female, then key in '2' which will lead to the programme:

Cross check on female deaths using two surnames (i.e. married & maiden surnames)
Please enter your enquiry
Year   Any year 1855 to date
1st surname   Surname of subject
2nd surname   Must not be the same as the 1st surname
Forename/Initial

Press 'Enter' key

The computer will search for a woman whose forename starts with the letter or initial you have stipulated, and whose married and maiden surnames agree with the names you have entered. If no entry appears press 'Enter' and change the year; then press 'Enter'. Repeat until you get an entry. It will pick up the first surname you listed.

The finding will be shown as any other death index entry, but with the heading:

Indexes to the death registers for female persons who died in the year . . . (The year will be the one when the entry was found.)

Surname	Forename	Age	Mother's name	Year	RD	Ent	RD name
McKay	Jean	88		1920	282	5	Dundee

Beware! What the index does not show is whether McKay was the maiden or the married surname. Sometimes when you see the entry you find you have the wrong cross, and the maiden surname you needed was, in the entry you found, the deceased's married surname.

The deceased's mother's maiden surname is not shown in the index until 1974.

To return to 'Which type of search do you require?' press 'F1' until it appears.

On the same programme, for 'Cross check on marriages using two surnames', key in '3' for:

Year	Any Year 1855 to date
Bride's name	Forename Initial
Groom's name	Forename Initial
Whose entry?	Enter 'G' for Groom's index entry
	Enter 'B' for Bride's index entry

Press 'Enter' key and the screen will show:

Indexes to the marriage registers for persons who married in year

Surname	Forename	Spouse's name	Year	RD	Ent	RD name
Cory	Paul	Reed	1945	685*	595	St Giles

This deals with what you may find in Statutory Indexes.

Press the 'F1' key to return to the opening menu. No. 2 on this list leads to divorce entries.

Divorce Index Retrieval System

1. Sex   M or F for Male or Female
2. Year   Any year from 1984 to date
3. Surname Surname of subject of enquiry
4. Initial Optional

Enter information and press 'Enter' key for the following:

Indexes to the divorce registers for male persons divorced in the year 1980 Surname Smith Initial B

Surname	Forename	Spouse's name	Date of marriage	Divorce year	Court No	Serial No
Smith	Brian	Black	11/04/70	90	14	04815

If you need to know the full name of the spouse, then press the 'F5' key and read the instructions which will enable you to change the details of your enquiry by entering Black where you had entered Smith and leaving the initial blank. *Do not forget to change the M to F for the sex!*

This entry will be in the same form as before, but with the woman's name in full and the man only shown by his surname.

If you only want to search through records before statutory registration was introduced in 1855, and if you have enough information in detail not to have to use the general index which continues from the statutory programme, then press 'F1' to return to the original menu and for Old Parish Register Index, press '3' for the following programme:

Which type of search do you require?

1. OPR index by county and decade
2. OPR index for all Scotland
(gives access to statutory B & M index)

In choosing No. 1 we find the following explanation:

'This facility allows you to search the index of Old Parish Registers by county and a range of ten years (rather than a single year at a time). As well as grouping the years into decades, several of the smaller counties are also grouped with adjacent counties so that the response to your query will show a wider range of entries than you might expect.

The list of index entries which appears on your screen is unlike the Statutory Index list in that each entry occupies two lines, the second line containing parents' names, frame numbers and other miscellaneous information. The column headed 'S' stands for Sex and you should note that this can be 'U' for Unstated. Where this occurs the entry will be displayed regardless of sex being searched resulting in male names being displayed on a female search [and vice versa; K.C.]. The column headed 'T' is for event type which can be 'B' Birth, 'S' Stillbirth, 'C' Christening or 'M' marriage.

The Old Parochial Records, from which the index has been extracted, can be very difficult to read because of their age and poor condition. It should always be borne in mind that what you are viewing is an interpretation of the original entry made by the compiler of the index, often other interpretations could have been possible.'

When you press 'Enter' there follows:
OPR Retrieval System–By county and decade

1. Event type   B for Birth (incl. christenings)
2. Sex   M or F for Male or Female
3. County Code   Enter 'L' to see list

4. Decade   e.g. 165 for 1650-59
5. Surname   Surname of subject of enquiry
6. Forename   Optional or part name.

Enter 'L' and press 'Enter' key to show the list of counties for you to choose from.

County Name	Code	County Name	Code
Aberdeen	AB	Lanark	LK
Angus [Forfar]	AN	Midlothian	ML
Argyll	AR	Moray	MO
Ayr	AY	Nairn	NN
Banff	BF	Orkney	OR
Berwick	BK	Peebles	PS
Bute	BT	Perth	PH
Caithness	CA	Renfrew	RW
Clackmannan	CL	Ross & Cromarty	RC
Dumfries	DS	Roxburgh	RX
Dunbarton	DN	Selkirk	SK
East Lothian	EL	Shetland [Zetland]	SH
Fife	FF	Stirling	ST
Inverness	IN	Sutherland	SU
Kincardine	KN	West Lothian	WL
Kinross	KR	Wigtown	WG
Kirkcudbright	KK		

Once you have selected the county code you require and pressed the 'Enter' key, you will be returned to the screen showing type of event, sex, name and decade. If all the parameters are correct for your search, then press the 'Enter' key again and proceed as usual.

Some parishes did not record the sex of a child, that is, they did not write 'son of' or 'daughter of', but merely 'child of'. In those instances 'U' for Unstated will be found in the column recording the sex. All birth entries where the sex is not stated have been entered in both male and female indexes. (This is referred to in the introduction on the computer programme.)

An OPR search can be more difficult when the mothers' names were never recorded, but even when this is not shown on the index, if the father's name and the name of the parish fit your requirements, then read the full entry from the microfilm copy of the OPR as you may glean more information from that than can be shown on an index.

A few points to remember when using a computer index

If your fingers go too fast and you inadvertently press the wrong key then the machine will beep at you, and a red cross will appear in the bottom left corner. You will not be able to proceed. To get out of this situation, press the 'Ctrl' key.

Names starting with Mc or Mac are indexed separately; if your search is for McLeod, for example, remember to search under MacLeod as well as McLeod.

Although your ancestor may have always used a middle name, he or she was not necessarily baptised with this middle name, so do not despair if the entry you hope to find is not seen instantly. Look again at the index, this time ignoring the entries with middle names, but bearing in mind the parish of birth if this is known.

If you are not searching in New Register House in Edinburgh, you may be making use of Mormon microfiches held in a local library or hired from Salt Lake City. Whenever you are using a Mormon microfiche index it is most important to search under all spelling variations and also to note that on some IGI microfiches you will find all the spelling variations are together under one agreed spelling.

For example, the surname Caroline and all variations such as Carline, Carolan and so on, are to be found altogether under Carlin. There is more detailed information on names and how to find them in Chapter 5.

If the name you want does not appear on the computer index, it is sometimes a good idea to look at the IGI microfiches to see if there is a spelling variant you had not thought of.

If you cannot get to Edinburgh you may be using the Mormon Church's CD-ROM or internet programme called FamilySearch.

Index with Digital Images

Use the mouse to click on the [AS400 Lookup-Digros] icon on the status bar. This stands for Digital Imaging of the Genealogical Records of Scotland's [DIGROS] people. In this programme you do not get any exercise! There is no need to walk about to fetch microfiches and microfilms.

Note: Carefully read the instructions every time, even if you consider yourself to be a computer whiz-kid.

This programme gives access to the statutory registers index for births, marriages and deaths, and digital images of those certificates to read, as well as for the 1891 and 1901 census returns. You can obtain, at 50p each, a print-off of the digitised page for births 1855–1902, for deaths 1855–1952, and for marriages 1855–1927, as well as the two censuses.

Digitised images of certificates can be viewed for the years 1855–1965, after that year you have to resort to the images on microfiche.

You will be presented with: 'Scottish Record Search – Log In page', where you enter your seat number with the prefix 'E' for East Search Room, 'W' for West Search Room, and 'D' for Dome Search Room, and your surname.

Click the 'Submit' button to continue, and the next screen will show:

General Register Office for Scotland
information about Scotland's people

Census Search | Census Browse | Birth Search | Marriage Search | Death Search | Home Page | Help

The names of the searches are in blue lettering. Once you have clicked on the one of your choice that will turn to black lettering, and the screen changes. At the top of the screen there is a new title bar, a new menu bar, and a new tool bar.

Let us click on 'Death Search', and the screen will show:

Cross check on Female Deaths

Scottish DEATH Search

Year

Surname

Forename

Sex   Male   [if you are searching for a female, then click here,

Age range . . . to . . .   then click again on 'female']

Submit   Clear

Type in your details and click on 'Submit'. The screen will change and inform you: 'Your search found [a number] records', and this sentence is followed by a list.

Surname	Forename	Mother's Maiden Surname	Year Reg	RD No/ Suffix	Entry No	Reg Dist Name

To view a name in the list, click on the surname when the cursor changes to a hand, and you will see the whole page of the register with three entries. If the name you chose is the correct one for your search you can obtain a print-off of the whole page by clicking on the printer icon on the tool bar. You can magnify areas of the entry to assist in reading, by using the left-hand icon on the tool bar.

Beware! The digitised image has been taken from the microfiche image, and a fair proportion are not good images. If this is the case then you will have to get out the microfiche in the normal way.

Beware! You cannot get a print-off of the magnified area.

If the name you chose is *not* the correct one for your search then click on the 'Back' button at the left-hand end of the menu bar. This will return you to the list of names, and you again click on the surname of another entry to view that digitised image. Keep repeating these actions until you have read the whole list, or found the entry you wanted.

If the person you are searching for has not been found in that year, then go to the buttons after the last name of the list.

'Search previous year'

'Search following year'

'Return to Death Search'

Click on 'previous year' or 'following year' and another list of names will appear. Repeat the process.

Once you have found the entry you searched for, and taken down the information or ordered a print-off, click on 'Back' to return to the list of names, and then click on 'Return to Death Search'. This will get you back to the Death Search screen to type in another name and appropriate information to start another death search. If you wish to do a birth or marriage search, then click on the appropriate name, and repeat the process.

Note: All print-offs are collected, and paid for, at the public counter (where you paid for your search pass) *before* 4.15 p.m.

What can I expect to find from a birth certificate from 1855 onwards?

The information found in an 1855 certificate of birth, marriage, or death is the most detailed, as this was the first year of statutory (civil) registration in Scotland.

Unfortunately, the years 1856–60 contain much less information, but thereafter things improve, from the point of view of the genealogist. An 1855 birth certificate contains:

1. Full name of the child and its sex
2. Date and time of birth
3. Address at birth
4. Name, age, place of birth (and if registered there), and occupation of father
5. Name, age, place of birth (and if registered there), and maiden surname of mother
6. Usual address of parents (if this differs from the place of birth)
7. Date and place of parents' marriage
8. Number and sex of children born prior to the registration of the baby in 1855; and if these children were still living or if they had died. No names of siblings were recorded
9. Name of the informant and relationship of the informant to the child (if any)

Birth certificates for 1856–60 inclusive take the form of the 1869 example (see Part II, p. 222) but do *not* show the date and place of the parents' marriage. From 1860 onwards this information *is* shown, which makes the search much easier. Once again, remember that the information, although nearly always accurate, is not unfailingly so. Sometimes, because of illiteracy, 'his X mark' or 'her X mark' was written beside the name of the informant, indicating that the name had been written by the registrar or by a witness, and was not the signature of the informant. Naturally, if the informant could not write his or her name, nor read what had been written, then the information supplied may well be suspect.

As well as the civil registers of births recorded since 1855, there are the following:

Register of adopted children (from 1930)

A record of persons adopted under orders made by Scottish courts; there are no entries relating to anyone born before 1909. There is no general index showing natural parents available to the public. Confidential information about the natural parents is given only to the adopted person concerned if he or she has reached the age of seventeen years.

Because of possible emotional/psychological difficulties, searchers who have been adopted are advised to approach the Birthlink Adoption Counselling Centre, Edinburgh (address in Appendix II: Adoption. See also p. 105, in Chapter 9.

Register of still-births (1939)

Records of still-births which occur in Scotland are compiled by district registrars but are not open for public search. Extracts are issued only in exceptional circumstances, such as for legal purposes. However, some pre-1855 still-birth entries may be found on the computer index of births but the entry will be found in the death register and not the birth register.

The following registers may be useful, but they tend to be patchy, so do not rely on them absolutely. The entries are to be found on the computer index together with the births, marriages and deaths which occurred in Scotland, but the actual entries are only available on microfiche, in the section 'Minor Records'.

Marine register of births (from 1855)

Certified returns received from the Registrar-General for Shipping and Seamen in respect of births on British-registered merchant vessels at sea if the child's father was a Scottish subject.

High Commissioners' returns of births (from 1964)

Returns from certain Commonwealth countries relating to persons of Scottish descent or birth. Some early returns are available for India, Pakistan, Bangladesh, Sri Lanka and Ghana.

Register of births in foreign countries (1860–1965)

A record compiled by the General Register Office until the end of 1965. It relates to the births of children of Scottish parents, and the entries were made on the basis of the information supplied by the parties concerned, after due consideration of the evidence of each event.

Air register of births (from 1948)

A record of births in any part of the world in aircraft registered in the United Kingdom, where it appears that the child's father was usually resident in Scotland. The Civil Aviation (Births, Deaths and Missing Persons) Regulations 1948, state that illegitimate births can be registered in the Air register. In such cases the mother's usual residence should be in Scotland. The question of the mother's usual residence being taken into account would not normally arise if the child were legitimate and the parents were living together.

Service records (from 1881)

These include (1) The Army returns of births of Scottish persons at military stations abroad during the period 1881-1959; (2) The service departments' registers which, since 1 April 1959, have recorded births outside the United Kingdom relating to persons ordinarily resident in Scotland, but who are serving in, or employed by, HM Forces, including the families of members of the Forces.

Consular returns of births (from 1914)

Certified copies of registrations by British consuls relating to persons of Scottish descent or birth.

What can I expect to find from a marriage certificate from 1855 onwards?

An 1855 marriage certificate contains:

1. Date and place of marriage
2. Denominational rites (Church of Scotland, Free Church, Episcopal Church in Scotland, Roman Catholic, etc.)
3. Bridegroom's name, rank and occupation; birthplace; where and when registered; age and marital status (single or widower); whether second or third marriage; living/deceased; relationship of parties (if any); usual residence or residence at time of marriage; name and occupation of father and if he was deceased at the time of the marriage; name and maiden surname (M/S) of mother and if she was deceased at the time of the marriage
4. Bride as for bridegroom
5. Name of officiating minister or priest
6. Names (and sometimes addresses) of witnesses

Marriage certificates from 1856 to 1921 contain the same information as those registered in 1855, except that information concerning previous marriages and birthplace is omitted. From 1922 onwards, the words 'or divorced' are added to marital status.

Note: Very often, on a marriage certificate you will find only the initials, and not the full Christian or forenames for the bride and/or groom. This occurs because the certificate available to the public (which is also the one used when you order an official copy) is a copy of the original marriage schedule. This copy has been produced in different form, and the *signatures* of the bridal couple have been copied; if the groom or the bride signed with initials and not with their full name, then this is what will be found on the certificate. I have sometimes found full names in the index, but only initials on the certificate, indicating that the index was made from the original marriage schedule.

This is a point to bear in mind when comparing signatures. On a birth or a death certificate the signature of the informant is just that, but on a marriage certificate the signature is a copy written by the clerk who was copying out the marriage schedule.

As you will see from the copy of the 1979 marriage certificate of my daughter Alison and Ned Kozowyk, the amount and type of information have not changed much over the years (Illustrations: Fig. 1). Reading the certificate carefully, you will find a great many pointers to direct you to further searching in different countries.

1. The marriage took place in an Episcopal church in Edinburgh.
2. The bride was born in Bermuda. Her date and place of birth (though not her occupation), her parents' names and her usual residence are recorded.
3. The bridegroom is Canadian. His date and place of birth, his occupation, his parents' names and where he was living in Canada are recorded.
4. The bride's father was deceased by 1979, and he had been a Clerk in Holy Orders. This means he had been ordained, and as the marriage took place in an Episcopal church he was likely to have been a priest in either the Episcopal church in Scotland, or in the Church of England. *Crockford*, the register of clergy in the Anglican Church, could be examined and from this could be found where the family had lived.
5. The marriage service was taken by Kenneth Riches, retired Bishop of Lincoln . . . (what was the connection . . . search *Crockford* again?).

As well as civil registers for marriages recorded since 1855, there are the following marriage registers which, like the birth registers, tend to be patchy. They too may be found on the computer index, but the actual entries will be read on microfiche in the 'Minor Records' section.

High Commissioners' returns of marriage (from 1964)

Following the Foreign Marriage Act in 1892, a marriage was allowed to take place in any foreign country, solemnised by or before a designated marriage officer (consul, high commissioner, or army chaplain), as long as one of the parties was a British subject, and a marriage warrant had been given to the marriage officer by the Secretary of State. The marriage warrants are issued and withdrawn according to the circumstances and needs of individual posts, and they were retained after the Foreign Marriage Order 1970 only in those countries where the local facilities were inadequate; for example, because of a restriction on the marriage of divorced persons or the lack of a civil or a monogamous form of marriage.

In the following countries marriage warrants are held by consular marriage officers, as at May 1984, the latest available date:

Afghanistan, Bahrein, Burma, Egypt, Greece, Iran, Iraq, Israel, Jerusalem, Jordan, Morocco, Nepal, Oman, Qatar, Saudi Arabia, Senegal, Somalia, Spain, Sudan, Syrian Arab Republic, United Arab Emirates, Yemen Arab Republic, Yemen People's Republic.

Note: Greece and Spain were due to be removed from this list shortly after its completion.

Register of marriages in foreign countries (1860–1965)

This record was compiled by the General Register Office up until the end of 1965. It related to the marriages of Scottish subjects, and the entries were made on the basis of information supplied by the parties concerned and after due consideration of the evidence of each event.

Service records (from 1881)

These contain (1) The Army returns of marriages of Scottish persons at military stations abroad during the period 1881–1959; (2) The service department registers which, since 1 April 1959, have recorded marriages outside the United Kingdom relating to persons ordinarily resident in Scotland who are serving in, or employed by, HM Forces, including the families of members of the Forces, and certified copies of entries relating to marriages solemnised outside the United Kingdom by army chaplains since 1892, where one of the parties to the marriage is described as Scottish and at least one of the parties is serving in HM Forces.

The Foreign Marriage Act 1947 extended the provision for military personnel to be designated marrying officers, to include the Royal Navy, the Army and the Royal Air Force. As stated above, military marriages by those officers could only be conducted if one party was a member of the Forces.

Consular returns of marriages (from 1917)

Certified copies of registrations by British consuls relating to persons of Scottish descent or birth.

Foreign marriages (from 1947)

These are certified copies of certificates (with translations) relating to marriages of persons from Scotland in certain foreign countries according to the laws of these countries, without the presence of a British consular officer.

Register of divorces (from 1984)

A central register of divorces granted in Scotland has been kept by the Registrar General since May 1984. Extracts from the register show the names of the parties, the date and place of marriage, the date and place of divorce and details of any order made by the court regarding financial provision or custody of children. The index is now on computer. (See page 16 for details.)

Note: From 1855 to 1984 divorces were recorded in Scotland by writing the words 'divorce RCE' (Register of Corrected Entries) against the marriage entry. However, when the index to divorces was introduced in 1984, the practice of stamping divorce (through the RCE) on the Scottish marriage entry was discontinued. If a divorce was granted outwith Scotland, and documentary evidence to that effect was produced to the General Register Office, then the Scottish marriage entry would be annotated. However, this practice was also discontinued in May 1984.

The computer index to divorces only covers the years 1984 to date. The only way to find if a couple obtained a divorce prior to 1984 is to look up the original marriage entry and see if it has been annotated. Entries in the Register of Corrected Entries are to be found on microfiche, but this is not self-service. Fill in a requisition slip and the fiche will be brought to you. If the divorce was granted outside Scotland and the General Register Office had not been notified, then the fact would not be recorded in Scotland.

What can I expect to find in a death certificate from 1855 onwards?

An 1855 death certificate contains:

1. The names of the deceased
2. Date and time of death
3. Address at time of death and usual residence, if not the same
4. Age and occupation
5. Marital status and name of spouse if applicable
6. Names of any issue; their ages at the time of the death, and their ages and when they died, if prior to the death in 1855
7. Name and occupation of the deceased's father, and if he was deceased by this date
8. Name and M/S of the deceased's mother, and if she was deceased by this date
9. Cause of death, and name of medical attendant (if any)
10. Burial place and name of undertaker
11. Signature of the informant, and relationship to the deceased (if any).

An example of an 1855 death certificate, and how best to make full use of the information it contains, may be found in Part II, p. 229.

Death certificates from 1856 to 1860 contain the same information as in 1855 *except* that the marital status (single/widow/widower) of the deceased is shown, although no name of spouse is recorded; and no names of issue are recorded unless the informant happens to be a son or a daughter.

Sometimes the informant was a spouse, which is one of the ways a certificate can be identified as being correct for your search. Another way is if the informant was any other relative, and you can work through their line to prove kinship.

Death certificates from 1861 to 1865 contain the same information as above *except* that the name of the spouse is now recorded; burial place is no longer recorded.

Death certificates from 1866 onwards contain the same information as above *except* that from 1967 the date of birth of the deceased is recorded.

As well as a copy of the 1855 death certificate for Jane Dudgeon (Illustrations: Fig. 19), I have included here a copy of the more modern death certificate of my father in 1947 (Illustrations: Fig. 2). This is an example of having to trace a line back through Army and Navy records. Charles Hubert Reed died aged 54. He was a captain in the Army, and his father, William Reed, had been a naval officer. Searching for the birth entry of Charles Reed *circa* 1893 would therefore put you on the track of William Reed and his naval career. For these service records it will be necessary to go to the Public Record Office at Kew, Surrey, now National Archives, England.

Additional to the civil registers of deaths recorded since 1855 there are the following, but like their birth and marriage counterparts, these registers tend to be patchy and incomplete. They too are now indexed on the computer, but the entries themselves are on microfiche, in the section 'Minor Records'.

Marine register of deaths (from 1855)

Certified returns received from the Registrar General for Shipping and Seamen in respect of deaths on British registered merchant vessels at sea if the deceased person was a Scottish subject.

High commissioners' returns of death (from 1964)

Returns from certain Commonwealth countries relating to persons of Scottish descent or birth. Some earlier returns are available for India, Pakistan, Bangladesh, Sri Lanka and Ghana.

Register of deaths in foreign countries (1860–1965)

A record compiled by the General Register Office until the end of 1965. It related to deaths of Scottish subjects, and the entries were made on the basis of information supplied by the parties concerned after due consideration of the evidence of each event.

Air register of deaths (from 1948)

A record of deaths in any part of the world in aircraft registered in the United Kingdom where it appears that the deceased person usually resided in Scotland.

Service records (from 1881)

These include: (1) The Army returns of deaths of Scottish persons at military stations abroad during the period 1881–1959; (2) The service department registers which, since 1 April 1959, have recorded deaths outside the United Kingdom relating to persons ordinarily resident in Scotland, and who are serving in, or employed by HM Forces, including the families of members of the Forces.

Consular returns of deaths (from 1914)

Certified copies of registrations by British consuls relating to persons of Scottish descent or birth.

War registers (deaths from 1899)

There are three registers:

1. South African War (1899–1902), which records the deaths of Scottish soldiers
2. World War I (1914–18), which records the deaths of Scottish persons serving as warrant officers, non-commissioned officers or men in the Army, or as petty officers or men in the Royal Navy
3. World War II (1939–45), which consists of incomplete returns of the deaths of Scottish members of the armed forces.

These three sets of registers, listed among the Minor Records (Ref. Min.), are arranged in chronological and alphabetical order, and in most cases have been entered on the computer index of deaths, but are only viewed on microfiche.

The computer index gives you the surname/Christian name/year of death/ Reg. Dist. no./entry no./Reg. Dist. name.

Beware! The Reg. Dist. no. (i.e. 129AF) is actually the volume number; the entry no. is actually the page no.; and Reg. Dist. name will be 'Service Returns' or 'Naval Returns' (i.e. Minor Records).

The microfiche titles will be: event/year/vol. no./page no.–page no. The entry gives you the person's regimental number, rank, surname, Christian name, age, country of birth, date of death, where killed, how killed (for the last see below). No genealogical information is given.

Note: For the 1914–18 war, there is no list of officers' deaths held in New Register House except for the *Regimental Rolls of Officers who died in the War* – Part 1: Old and New Armies; Part 2: Territorial Force. These entries are listed alphabetically by regiment or corps, and include all military forces in Scotland, England and Ireland. Each entry contains name, rank, a brief description of how death occurred, and the date. There is no genealogical information to be found; neither the place of death nor the place of birth is recorded. As this book covers English, Welsh and Irish as well as Scottish regiments, and the Scottish names have not been extracted, they are not to be found on the computer index to deaths.

How the death occurred is shown as: K in A = Killed in Action; D of W = Died of Wounds; Killed = Killed other than in action; Died = Died from natural causes etc; MPD = Missing, presumed dead.

World War I Army returns

These include the following regiments for the period 1914 to 1919: Argyll and Sutherland Highlanders; Cameronians; Cameron Highlanders; Gordon Highlanders; Highland Light Infantry; King's Own Scottish Borderers; Black Watch; Royal Scots; Royal Scots Fusiliers; Seaforth Highlanders; 'various regiments'.

Note: Having found a soldier's name and entry in the Minor Records (1914–19) you will have seen his regiment and battalion at the top of the page. You then find 'Soldiers who Died in the Great War 1914–19'. There are eighty-one parts to this – virtually one for each regiment. They are difficult to search without knowing the regiment and battalion.

From the appropriate part no. you will find the additional information of where the soldier was born, where he enlisted, and if he was previously in another regiment.

In New Register House you can view these on microfiche after first referring to the list in the Index to Miscellaneous Records. This publication has been transferred to CD-ROM and can be searched on a surname basis. There is a copy in the National Archives (England), Kew, and the Society of Genealogists, London (see Appendix II: List of useful addresses).

Extracts from Navy returns, including Navy and Marines

In two volumes, surnames A-L and L-Y (1914–20). *Precognitions*: US Transport/*Tuscania*/Islay (February 1918); US Transport/*Otranto*/Islay (February 1918).

World War II returns

Extracts from Army returns (1939–48)
Officers; other ranks.

Extracts from Navy returns (1939–48)
In two volumes, surnames A–Mac and Mac–Y.

Extracts from RAF returns (1939–48)
In three volumes, surnames A–G, G–M and M–Z.

Scotland did not have a regular army until the Union of the Parliaments in 1707. Before that date, only a small standing army existed. Forces were raised when necessary, and disbanded once the wars and skirmishes were over. The National Archives of Scotland hold some army records, the most useful probably being the muster rolls. These date mainly from about 1680, although there are some earlier ones. (See Chapter 4 on 'Other Sources'.)

As time is always an important factor, whether searching in New Register House, where you have to pay a search fee for each day you are there, or working from hired microfilm, you may like to prepare blank mock-up forms of birth, marriage and death certificates from the examples found in Appendix V of this book; it is so much quicker if you only have to fill in details as you find them. Do make sure you *copy all the information* contained on the certificates. I cannot stress this too strongly. People imagine they are saving time by taking notes in brief, and in a shorthand they think they will understand when they get home; but more often than not they misinterpret what they have written and mistakes creep in.

Official copies (extracts) of birth, marriage and death certificates may be purchased from New Register House by post or in person.

CENSUS RETURNS

Census returns are undoubtedly among the most useful records for you to search. They are particularly necessary for bridging the gap between statutory (or civil) registers which start in 1855, and the Old Parish Registers (OPRs) which end in 1854, because they give the place of birth.

Unless you are quite certain that you know the name of the parish or, at least, the name of the county of origin of your family, you will be in deep trouble when it comes to searching through OPRs, as you will have over 900 from which to choose! However, if you have access to the computer index of OPR births, where the names of the parents are recorded, it is not vital to know the name of the parish.

Census returns of the population are taken every ten years. In Scotland such censuses have been taken since 1801, but only statistical reports are preserved for 1801–31. Returns for individual households are available to the public for the years 1841–1901 inclusive and vary greatly in content. Microfilm of census returns is held in New Register House, and can be viewed on payment of the appropriate fee.

Increasingly, local libraries and family history societies are acquiring microfilm copies pertaining to their own parts of the country. It is worthwhile to check this if you are visiting your family's old home, if you do not have time to go to Edinburgh, or if you are conducting your own search by letter. However, do remember that unless your family lived in a small village where there were not many inhabitants, searching through a census return may take several hours. A project is in hand at present to index on computer, by name and age, all the inhabitants of Scotland for the years 1841–1901 inclusive. This project will be of immense value once it has been completed.

In the 'Session A – [24 x 80]' programme the 'Welcome to the Index Enquiry System' screen displays '4. Census Index (1881, 1891 or 1901)' (see page 14). From this, by entering '4' and pressing the 'Enter' key, you move on to:

Census Index Retrieval System

Which Census Index do you require?

1. 1881 Census
2. 1891 Census
3. 1901 Census

Enter the required option number

Type in '1' and press 'Enter' to get:

1881 Census Index Retrieval System

Which type of search do you require?

1. By County
2. All Scotland

Type in '2' and press 'Enter', and you get:

1881 Census Index – All Scotland

1. Surname   press 'TAB' key to go to next line
2. Forename
3. Sex
4. Age Range . . . to . . .

Type in your information and press 'Enter'. For example, you may type: Smith; Cha; M (for Male); and age 18–30 years. On pressing 'Enter' the screen will show:

1881 Census Index for: SMITH   Forename: Ch   Sex: M
living in All Scotland   Age range: 18--30

Surname	Forename	Age	Birth CTY PLACE	RD.No/ Suffix	Enum Dist	Page No

With all Smith, Ch/Charles, of that age range.

Enter 'G' against a record to see household group
Enter 'D' against a record to see the full census entry

After you enter 'G' on the left-hand side, press 'Enter'. The household group will appear with the same headings as before. Against the person enter 'D' and press 'Enter', and the screen will show:

Cnty Code	RD.No.	ED.No.	Page No.
County			
Parish			
Address			

	Surname		Forename	
Sex	Age	Marr. Cond.		Rel. to Head

Occupation
Birth County   Birth Place
Handicap

Press 'Enter' to return to the family group. Enter 'D' for the next person, and press 'Enter'. Repeat for each person in the family group.

Press 'Enter' to return to the family group. Press 'F5' to return to the list of names. Press 'F1' to end enquiry.

When the '1881 Census Index Retrieval System' is back on screen and you enter '1' and press 'Enter', you then put in the information requested with the county name. Again press 'Enter' and you are presented with the option of entering 'G' or 'D'.

Having pressed 'F1' sufficient times to return to the 'Census Index Retrieval System', key in '2' and press 'Enter' to get:

1891 Census Index Retrieval System

Note: There is only the index for this census, there is *no* transcript as for 1881.

You are asked:

Which type of search do you require?

1. By county in the order: Surname, Forename, RD/ED and page number
2. All Scotland in the order: Surname, Forename and Age
3. By Reg. Dist. in order: Surname, RD/ED and page number. (Potential Family Groups.)

Enter the required option number.
Enter '1' and you will find displayed:

1. Surname	Surname of subject of enquiry
2. Forename	Initial, part forename, or blank (part forename must be the first part)
3. Sex	M or F for Male or Female
4. Age range ... to ...	If these fields are left blank all ages will be displayed
5. County code	Enter 'L' to see county list

A copy of the county list is to be found here on page 18.

If the information you have entered is what you want to find, press the 'Enter' key to find the following heading:

1891 CENSUS Index for the Surname . . . Forename . . . Sex . . . living in . . . Age range . . . to . . .

From the list of entries choose whichever entry is appropriate to your search, fill in a yellow requisition slip and fetch your own microfilm copy of the census. You read this on one of the microfilm reading machines in the Dome Search Room. Staff will advise you on how to load the film.

Beware! Rewind the film onto its spool, or the next reader will find it at the end.

If your subject has not been found in the county you chose, and you want to extend the search to the whole of Scotland, then end the enquiry by pressing the 'F1' key as instructed until the original display is obtained.

Enter '2' to search the 1891 Census for All Scotland to find displayed: 1891 Census Index – All Scotland

1.	Surname	Surname of subject of enquiry
2.	Forename	Initial, part forename or blank (part forename must be the first part)
3.	Sex	M or F for Male or Female
4.	Age range	If these fields are left blank all ages will be displayed
	. . . to . . .	

Having typed in the necessary information, once again press the 'Enter' key to find displayed:

1891 CENSUS Index for Surname . . . Forename . . . Sex . . . living in Scotland . . . Age range . . . to . . .

Proceed as before to obtain your entry.

Press the 'F1' key to return to the first display and press '3' for: By Registration District, in order surname RD/ED and page number. (Potential Family Groups).

1.	Surname	Surname of subject of enquiry
2.	County code	Enter 'L' for county list
3.	RD number	Enter 'L' for RD list
4.	RD suffix	Required if one exists
5.	ED	Optional

RD = Registration District
ED = Enumeration District

You then take the following steps:

1. Type in surname
2. Type in 'L' for county code (or take the code from page 18)
3. Type in 'L' for RD list (or take the code from Appendix III)

From the list of county codes, select and type in the one you need for your search and press the 'Enter' key. You will find the screen displays the chosen county code instead of 'L' for 2, but it still displays 'L' for the RD number.

Press 'Enter' key again to find displayed a list of RD names and numbers such as: Auchinleck 577/1. Key in the appropriate number and suffix, press the 'Enter' key and the display will show the chosen surname, county code, RD number and RD suffix. In the above example 577 is the RD number and 1 is the RD suffix for Auchinleck.

Check that you have not made a wrong entry and press the 'Enter' key to find, for example:

1891 Census Index for the surname McDonald RD No.648 living in Lanark

Surname	Forename	Sex	Age	RD No Suffix	ED	Page No	District Name
McDonald	Agness	F	34	648	002	006	Lanark
McDonald	Marion	F	22	648	006	012	Lanark
McDonald	James	M	57	648	008	011	Lanark
McDonald	Janet	F	41	648	008	011	Lanark
McDonald	James	F	46	648	008	032	Lanark
McDonald	Elizabeth	F	56	648	009	005	Lanark

From the above list it can be seen that the names are not in alphabetical order, but have been listed in the order in which they appeared in the books and the pages in the census return.

Remember that you only get what you ask for from a computer, so key in the different spelling of a name like Mc/MacDonald. Under MacDonald the names displayed were not the same as those found for the above example with the spelling McDonald.

Looking at the grouping of the numbers for the enumeration districts, you can pick out possible families.

Returning to the <u>Census Index Retrieval System</u> screen, you press '3' and then 'Enter' to get the:

<u>1901 Census Retrieval System</u>

which you use in the same way as for the 1891 Census.

One point to remember is that the county code leads you to a list of all the parishes in the county, so unless you know the parish where your family had lived, it may take some time to undertake the search. However, if you do not know the names of all the members of the family likely to have been alive in 1891 (or whichever census year you choose), it may well be worth your time to plough through all the parishes in the county.

Census Index with Digital Images

Use the mouse to click on [AS400 Lookup-Digros] (see pp. 13, 19) and click on 'Census Search'. The screen will show:

Census Search Page

Census Browse | Birth Search | Death Search | Marriage Search | Home Page | Help

[The above names will be in black lettering except for Census Browse and Help]

After referring to the list of available census years, please select by clicking on the required year.

The following Census years are available:

<u>1891</u>

<u>1901</u>

Both years are in blue.   Click on 1891 and the screen will show:

1891 Scottish Census Search

Surname	This field is compulsory and must contain the full surname
Forename	Enter initial or all of forename, or leave blank.
Sex	Both
Age	Range from . . . to . . .
County	All Scotland
Registration District	All Districts
	Submit Clear

Let us enter: Smith, Rob   Male   035-042   county Lanark.

Press 'Enter' and you will see:

1891 Census – Record Search Results

To view the Census page – click on the appropriate surname.
Your search found 45 records.

Surname	Forename	Sex	Age	RD. No	Enumeration Dist/Suffix	Registration Dist. Name	Page

Follow the process as you did for the births, marriages and deaths, to read each surname on the list. See page 20.

Click on 'Back' at the top left-hand side to return to: '1891 Scottish Census Search'.

Click on 'Census Search' to get back to: 'Census Search Page'.

Click on '1901' and the same process is repeated.

If you wish to browse the census return, because you have insufficient information for the ancestor you seek, then click on 'Census Browse' on the list along the top of the page. This will get you:

Census Browse Page

After referring to the list of available census years, please select by clicking on the required year.

The following Census years are available

1891

1901

Clicking on '1891' will make the screen change to:

1891 Census Browse

County	Choose a County	
Registration District	Choose a County	only available when you select a county.
Enumeration District		type in Enumeration District number if known, or leave blank. Only available when you select a Registration District.
	Submit	Clear

Click on 'Choose a County' and a drop-down list will appear. Let us choose the county Roxburgh. The 'Registration District' changes to 'All Districts', and when you click on this a drop-down list will appear. Let us choose Kelso. Click on 'Submit' and you will see:

1891 Census Browse Results

Your search found 11 records.

Enumeration Dist/Suffix	RD. No/ Suffix	Registration District Name	Peliminary pages	Individual entries
[list 001–012]	793	Kelso	Preliminary	Data

When you click on 'Preliminary' for one of the Enumeration District numbers you will see and read the first page of the Enumeration book describing the area (usually the street names) covered by the enumerator. Click on 'Back' to return to the Browse Results page and choose another district number if the street you wish to look at was not there. If it was, then click on 'Data' for that Enumeration District and the actual page one will appear. You now read the whole book page by page by using the 'next page' icon on the tool bar at the top of the screen.

Indexes for other census returns are available, but these have no consistent format. They are printed in booklet form or on microfiche. In NRH they are continually being added to the library, as they are produced by local family history societies. Some census years are better represented than others, as are counties. The present list is too long to reproduce here, but it can be found in the Dome Search Room. Local family history societies have them for their own areas.

These indexes are obtained by filling in the green requisition slip and they will be brought to you by a member of staff.

For those parishes which have not yet been indexed on either computer or microfiche, you will have to use the paper indexes which are still available on the open shelves, but these list Registration District No. and film.

The street index, as its name implies, lists all the streets and roads and some large houses in the larger towns and cities; as well as the names of farms and hamlets in rural areas. It gives a reference number to be used to obtain the census you require, and also a reference number to guide you to the correct Enumeration book within the census, for the road of your choice. As the computer index will be by people's name, you may find this street index useful. The 1841–1901 census returns were recorded by district or parish, each district or parish having its own registration number. These were subdivided into Enumeration books, each book having its own number. At the start of each Enumeration book you will find the names of the streets and roads contained within that particular book, and, in a country parish, names of farms in the area covered by the Enumeration book.

Other Census-type lists

Although the first available population census return is for 1841, there are a few parishes where these census returns are extant for 1821 and 1831, or even earlier. However, these are usually lists of people, and, like the 1841 census, do not show kinship. These pre-1841 returns were taken by church ministers and schoolteachers. Some of these lists are to be found in the Old Parish Registers in New Register House, and some in the Kirk Session records in the National Archives of Scotland. Very few have been published, and so they are difficult to locate, but a letter enclosing a stamped addressed envelope or postal coupons to the local archivist or librarian might lead you to your goal. Access would depend on the policy of the local archivist.

A useful list of parishes with communion rolls and census lists, compiled by Mrs A. Rosemary Bigwood, is to be found in the June 1988 edition of the *Scottish Genealogist.*

Other early 'census' sources are lists which were made for military purposes, such as muster rolls, as well as poll and hearth tax lists. These are to be found among various papers which have been deposited in the National Archives of Scotland in Princes Street, Edinburgh, and the National Library on George IV Bridge, Edinburgh (see Chapter 4). To enable a search to be made through these records, it would be necessary to have a fair amount of detail about the family concerned, and where they had lived.

On the whole, these pre-1841 census returns are only useful to establish whether or not the family (often naming only the head of the house) was living in a particular parish at a particular time. They are part of a 'last ditch' search for early information.

Beware! Although census returns are being indexed by occupants' names it is still essential for you to have noted in full all the addresses you may have found in birth, marriage and death entries during the search in statutory (after 1854) records. Without this information as a check, you may take the wrong person from the index. There may be several entries for a John or a Mary McDonald in Glasgow, aged about 60 in 1871, so an address may help to confirm your findings.

Remember, however, that people moved around, so spend a little time reading the names in the nearby streets if you have not found your family through the computer index at the address you noted. To find the reference for the streets, use the paper index books for street indexes where they exist.

If you took the address from a marriage certificate, bear in mind that this address was probably the home address; when the census was taken, your person may have been away working somewhere, and the address given at the time of marriage may have been that of the parents or some other relative. Looking broadly at the census you may find a brother or a sister who had remained near the parents, even if you do not find your immediate ancestor.

If your ancestor was a professional man, or tradesman, you will most likely find his address in a directory. In NRH there are directories for the larger towns/cities.

It is advisable to obtain a map of the place to see where the street is, and, from that, decide how far to extend your search. Again, use the street index for reference numbers.

Make a note of when each census return was taken and bear this in mind when looking for an entry. If great-grandfather George died on 7 April 1861, you cannot expect to find him in the 1861 census which was taken on 8 April. If, however, he died before his wife and the death certificate stated 'married to' and not 'widower of' Mary Brown then you may well find *her* there, or nearby, living with some other members of the family.

Note if the informant on the death certificate was a relation, and if the informant gave an address, as great-grandmother Mary may well have gone there to live.

Similarly, you cannot expect to find a child listed in the census return unless he or she was born before the date on which the census was taken, even if born in a census year, that is, 1841, 1851, 1861, 1871, 1881, 1891 or 1901.

When reading a census return, look at the headings at the top of each page, which indicate the contents of the vertical columns. Be sure to write down, in full, all the information you find there, particularly people's ages. From 1851 to 1901 be sure to note marital status (if the subject was unmarried, married, widow or widower) and the place of birth.

Beware! The enumerator could only record what he thought he had been told. In many instances he was dealing with illiterate people who could not check what was being written on their behalf. Furthermore, he was sometimes unfamiliar with the accent and he was apt to have his own peculiarities of spelling. For example:

1841/651/18/9 at Gardensquer, Airdrie, New Monkland, Co. Lanark.

James	Couk	40	Col. M.	I
Mrs	Couk	35		I
Teen	Couk	16		N
David	Couk	14	Do.	N
Enouch	Couk	12		N
Sarouch	Couk	10		N
Meggey	Couk	7		N
Heney	Couk	4		N
Esebelau	Couk	1		N

Of all these wildly original spellings I think I prefer Esebelau – a wonderful variation on Isabella! This is a good example of an entry where the Irish brogue defeated the enumerator, whose own spelling was slightly suspect, as you can see from the address, and from the occupation. James Couk (Cook) was a coal-miner.

This would be an infuriating entry to find if it involved your own family. The information does not really get you any further in the search, except to tell you the names of the children, the fact that the parents were both born in Ireland, and that none of the children was born in the County of Lanark. Unless you were to find them in the 1851 census, which would tell you their places of birth in Scotland, you would still have a long search on your hands.

The information concerning the subject's place of birth may vary from census to census; it may then be necessary to find more than one census entry before searching the Old Parish Registers for births and marriages prior to 1855. If the subject was born out of Scotland then the precision of the information depends on the accuracy, and/or knowledge of the census enumerator. If the subject was born anywhere else in the UK (England, Wales or Ireland), it was seldom that the enumerator recorded, or even knew of, the actual parish. Those born abroad sometimes fared better, and more detail may be found.

Beware! If you are searching in Shetland (also written Zetland), or Orkney, you may find several people recorded as having been born in Ireland. There is a Bay of Ireland in Stennes, and a Ness of Ireland in Dunrossness, Shetland, and another Bay of Ireland near Stromness in Orkney (Groome's *Gazetteer*). This cautionary note applies to all census reading. Do make a note of the *county* as well as the *parish*.

It is important to realise that a census return included the names and information about *everybody* residing in the place on the night before the census was taken. It is therefore possible that persons born before 1855 who, for one reason or another, had never been recorded in the Old Parish Register, may well be listed in a census return, and their place of birth recorded.

When working on registers after 1854, you should make full use of the census returns to cut down on the time taken to search the index of births, marriages and deaths. If you know that the family lived in a certain place, and you find them there in the 1861 census return, then look for them in the same place in the census returns for 1871, 1881 and 189 1. You may find that during these years either the man or his wife had died leaving a widower or a widow; or that a son or a daughter had married, and grandchildren were living at that address. Using this kind of information you can cut down on the years to be covered when searching for a death, a marriage or a birth in the index to the statutory registers.

When listing a husband and wife and their children, pay attention to the ages of the children, for example:

1871 census (for a fictitious family in Galston, Co. Ayr).

Rich^d	Murray	Head	married	40	Farmer	Born	Kilmarnock, Co. Ayr.
Margt.	Murray	wife	married	39		Born	Irvine, Co. Ayr.
Alex.	Murray	son	unmar	19	Farmer	Born	Galston, Co. Ayr.
Willm	Murray	son	unmar	17	Farmer	Born	Galston, Co. Ayr.
Charles	Murray			11	Scholar	Born	Galston, Co. Ayr.
Sarah	Murray	daur.		9	Scholar	Born	Galston, Co. Ayr.

There you will see William aged 17 (born *circa* 1854), and Charles aged 11 (born *circa* 1860); so it is likely that there was at least one child born between 1854 and 1860. As all the other children were born in Galston, you may well find the missing child or children born, and registered, there too.

These possible other children may have died in infancy (which you can check from the death registers); they may have been staying with relatives; or they may have been working away from home when the census was taken. If the birth of Alexander (aged 19 in 1871) was not found in the Old Parish Register for Galston where he was said to have been born, then try searching in Irvine, as his mother, Margaret, may have gone home to her mother to have the first baby!

You will note from the census return that Margaret Murray was born in Irvine, so their marriage may have taken place either in Kilmarnock, where her husband was born, or Galston, where he was farming, or in Irvine, where she came from. Proclamation of banns for the marriage may have been called in both parishes, and you may find Margaret's family in a census return for Irvine.

A married couple may be found in a census return who had, in fact, had a family, but whose children were never recorded with them. So do not forget about boarding schools, apprentices, and servants. Children sometimes did, and still do, leave home from about the age of seven onwards. Children whose parents had died and who were not to be found living with grandparents or other relatives, may be found sometimes in the census returns for a poorhouse or an orphanage, and occasionally children whose mother had been convicted of some crime may be found in the census return for a prison.

Assuming that your search using records after 1854 has led you to an address or a parish from which to order a census return, then the following are the steps you should now take until the computer index has been completed.

Census Index Reference Books (Dome Search Room)

There are three. One is for reference numbers concerning the 1841 and 1851 returns, one for the 1861 and 1871 returns, and one for the 1881 and 1891 returns. The 1841 and 1851 book contains an alphabetical index to the parishes and districts. Each parish or district is assigned a registration number. For example, Kilmarnock, Co. Ayr, is 597. Having found your parish in the index, note its number, look up this number in the book and you will find a page such as the one illustrated here (Illustrations: Fig. 3).

If you decide to order the 1841 census for Kilmarnock, Co. Ayr, you will need census no. 597, and you will know from the index that there are forty-one Enumeration books to be read through!

The 1861 and 1871 index book has been arranged differently. It contains no separate index but shows parishes and districts in alphabetical order. Each parish or district is assigned a registration number, and there is a column which shows how many enumeration books cover each parish. This applies also to the 1881 and 1891 index book.

Looking at the sample page from the 1861 census index (Illustrations: Fig. 4) you will notice that the Kilmarnock census return has a street index, indicated by an asterisk (597*). At the foot of the page you will note the instruction to 'see Kilmarnock Street Index, Vol. 9'. This street index is usually to be found on the shelf near the main census index books. Look up Kilmarnock in Vol. 9. – some of these street index books contain indexes for more than one town – and there you will find listed all the streets and roads. If you want to find Dundonald Road then turn to 'D', look for Dundonald Road, and you will find:

Name of street or road   Dundonald Road,
No. of Registration District   597
No. of Enumeration District   25

Make a note of this in your own notebook. Before you fetch your microfilm write out a yellow order slip (Illustrations: Fig. 13). Remember to write on the order slip: (1) The year for which you want the census; (2) The Registration District number and the Enumeration book number; (3) Your own name and the number of your desk/seat, *not* the seat you use in the Dome Search Room to read the film. Although the self-service system requires you to fetch your own microfilm, you are not expected to return it to the shelves, but to leave it in a tray for the Repository Assistants' attention.

Having collected the correct film, if you are at all uncertain about how to use a microfilm reader, please ask for assistance from whomever is on duty in the room. If you do not use it correctly, and rewind it correctly, then the next user will be confronted with a film which is upside-down and back-to-front!

Once you have found the entry you want, do take time to write out all the information clearly. Miss nothing out. Leave nothing to memory. Most of all, be sure you have made a note of where you found the entry: write down the full reference numbers and the year.

The entry in your notebook should be headed:

Census 1861/597/25/16 at 2 Dundonald Road, Kilmarnock, Co. Ayr

Now anybody else who may decide to continue the search, or you yourself, if you want to recheck the entry, will know that Dundonald Road in Kilmarnock, Co. Ayr in the 1861 census return is to be found in Registration District No. 597 (which is the number for Kilmarnock), Enumeration Book No. 25, page number 16.

If the name of the place you want for a census return does not feature in the list of places in the index, then probably it is not a parish in its own right, in which case you will have to find a gazetteer. I recommend Groome's *Gazetteer of Scotland,* in six volumes, 1882–5, a copy of which is held in the Dome Search Room in New Register House, and in most main libraries in Scotland. From this you should find the information you need to lead you to a parish. For example, '*Camelon,* a village and quoad sacra parish in Falkirk parish, Stirlingshire'. Therefore, if you were hoping to find your family in Camelon, you would have to search through the Falkirk census return.

Beware! Some parishes have 'look-alike' names such as Kilmarnock, Kilmaronock, and Kilmaronaig, and some have the same name, but are in different counties, such as Ruthven, a village in Aberdeenshire, and Ruthven, a parish in County Angus; also Liberton in Edinburgh and Libberton in

Lanarkshire. County Angus used to be known as County Forfar or Forfarshire, and County Elgin used to be known as County Moray or Morayshire! When you order the census make quite sure you have looked up the correct number, or you could spend several hours searching through the wrong census.

Confusion sometimes arises over which is the name of the parish, and which is the name of the county. I always write the name of the parish, then a comma, followed by the name of the county. For example, Irvine, Co. Ayr. You could, of course, form the habit of writing 'shire' (Ayrshire) instead of 'Co' (Co. Ayr).

Having reached the stage of searching the census returns, we may now summarise what you can expect to find in the various years.

The 1841 Census Return

Taken on 7 June this census return included all the people living in the parish on the previous night. It was the first full census return to be taken, but it does not contain as much information as the later years. Searching in the 1841 census you will find no kinship or marital status recorded; you must therefore be suspicious of any entry which reads, for example:

John Smith (age) 40
Mary Smith (age) 30

John and Mary Smith may well have been brother and sister, and not husband and wife; unless, of course, there were children recorded with them, in which case it is fairly safe to assume they *were* husband and wife, and the children were theirs. I say 'fairly', as it is never absolutely safe to assume anything in genealogy or you may end up being guilty of 'wishful-linking'!

Beware of assuming that the ages are accurate. In 1841 it was the policy after the age of 15 to round down the age to the nearest five years; so for age 20–24, you should read 20; for age 25–29, read 25; for age 30–34, read 30, and so on. This was normal practice, but in *some instances* the enumerator recorded the actual age; so you must read 'your' entry, and read the entries either side of it, to see whether you are dealing with an enumerator who was sticking to the rules or not.

Unlike the census returns for 1851, 1861, 1871, 1881, 1891 and 1901, the returns for 1841 did not record the place of birth of the subject; instead you will find 'Y' or 'N', which stands for Yes or No, and indicates whether or not the subject was born in the county where the census was taken. If the subject was born in England (including Wales) or Ireland then 'E' or 'I' will be found in this column; if abroad, then 'F' for Foreign will appear.

From the 1841 census return for Kilmarnock (Illustrations: Fig. 5), you can see how much information is available.

Headings for the 1841 census return for Kilmarnock, Co. Ayr (597)
1. Parish of Kilmarnock
2. Name of Village, Street, Square, Close etc.

3. Uninhabited building
4. Inhabited building
5. Name and surname of each person who abode in the House on the Night of 6th June
6. Age. (This column is subdivided to show Male & Female)
7. Occupation. Of what Profession, Trade, Employment or whether of Independent Means
8. Where born. This column is subdivided:
>   (a) If born in Scotland, state whether in County or otherwise
>   (b) Whether Foreign, or whether England or Ireland.

From this sample page it is apparent that although the Christian name and surname of the person were recorded, there was no kinship shown.

A double line (//) separated families or households at the same address. A single line (/) dividing the names denoted either (1) Another member of the family living with the head of the house, who was not one of his immediate family; or (2) People living in the house who were not related to the head of the house. They may have been apprentices, lodgers, boarders, and occasionally a baby being wet-nursed. From Figure 5 you can see that a Female Servant (F.S.) was living in the household of John Walker, but divided from the names of the rest of the family by a single /.

Occupations were nearly always, in 1841, written in brief – for example, Female Servant was recorded as F.S., and Hand Loom Weaver as H.L.W. If you are in any doubt about an abbreviation, you should turn back to the introduction to the census return where you will find instructions printed for the use of the enumerator. These instructions include a list of abbreviations to be used for different occupations. In Appendix I at the end of the book I have listed some occupations, their abbreviations and their meanings.

The 1851 Census Return

Taken on 31 March, this was the first census return to show kinship, marital status and the parish or place of birth, if the birth was in Scotland. You may now check that 1841 census entry of John and Mary Smith to see if they really were brother and sister or if they were husband and wife.

Information from the headings for 1851 census return for Kilmarnock, Co. Ayr (597)

Top line:
1. Parish of Kilmarnock
2. Quoad Sacra Parish of [blank]
3. Within the limits of the Parliamentary Burgh of Kilmarnock
4. Within the limits of the Royal Burgh of Town or Village of Kilmarnock

Second line:
1. Name and Surname of each person who abode in the house on the night of 30th March 1851
2. Relation to Head of Family

3. Condition (i.e. married, single, widow or widower)
4. Age (this column is subdivided to show Male & Female)
5. Rank, Profession or Occupation
6. Where born
7. Whether Blind, Deaf or Dumb

Here the information is more detailed than in 1841. Kinship is now given as 'Relation to the Head of Family'. Condition (marital status) was recorded. Place of birth showed parish as well as county. Finally, 'Whether Blind, Deaf of Dumb' was also shown.

The 1861 Census Return

This return was taken on 8 April. It did away with the column relating to being 'Blind, Deaf or Dumb', but now showed the number of children in the household aged between 5 and 15 years, who were attending school, and the number of rooms in the house with one or more windows. If you are interested in parish boundaries, you will notice that the description of the parish was slightly more detailed.

Information from the headings for the 1861 census return for Kilmarnock, Co. Ayr, (597)

Top line:
1. Parish of Kilmarnock
2. Quoad Sacra Parish of [blank]
3. Parish of the Parliamentary Burgh of [blank]
4. Royal Burgh of [blank]
5. Town of Kilmarnock
6. Village of [blank]

Second line:
1. No. of Schedule
2. Road, Street etc. No. or name of house
3. Houses (this column is subdivided to show Inhabited (I), Unin-habited (U), Building (B))
4. Name and surname of each person
5. Relation to Head of Family
6. Condition (i.e. married, single, widow or widower)
7. Age (this column is subdivided to show Male & Female)
8. Rank, Profession or Occupation
9. Where born
10. No. of children aged 5–15 attending school (each family)
11. No. of rooms with one or more windows

The 1871 Census Return

Taken on 3 April, this reverted to stating whether the subject was deaf etc., and added 'Imbecile' or 'Idiot' or 'Lunatic' – a fine distinction! There was a column for the number of children at school – this time between the ages of 6 and 18 years, and it allowed for some children being educated at home.

Information from the headings for the 1871 census return for Kilmarnock, Co. Ayr (597)

Top line:
1. Civil Parish of Kilmarnock
2. Quoad Sacra Parish of [blank]
3. Parliamentary Burgh of [blank]
4. Royal Burgh of [blank]
5. Police Burgh of Kilmarnock
6. Town of Kilmarnock
7. Village or Hamlet of [blank]

Second line:
1. No. of Schedule
2. Road, Street etc. No. or name of house
3. Houses (this column is subdivided to show Inhabited (I), Uninhabited (U), Building (B))
4. Name and surname of each person
5. Relation to Head of Family
6. Condition (i.e. married, single. widow or widower)
7. Age (this column is subdivided to show Male & Female)
8. Rank, Profession or Occupation
9. Where born
10. Whether 1. Deaf and Dumb., 2. Blind; 3. Imbecile or Idiot; 4. Lunatic
11. Number of children aged 6–18 attending school or being educated at home
12. Rooms with one or more windows

The 1881 Census Return

This was taken on 3 April. There was no longer a column for the number of scholars, although of course 'scholar' was recorded in the occupation column. However, the description of the parish was shown in much more detail. It can be seen that in 1881 Kilmarnock was a Civil Parish, with a quoad sacra parish of High Church. It was in the School Board District of Kilmarnock; it was a Parliamentary Burgh, but not a Royal Burgh; it was in the Police Burgh of Kilmarnock; and was in the Town of Kilmarnock!

Information from the headings for the 1881 census return for Kilmarnock, Co. Ayr (597)

Top line:
1. Civil Parish of Kilmarnock
2. Quoad Sacra Parish of High Church (Q.S.)
3. School Board District of Kilmarnock
4. Parliamentary Burgh of Kilmarnock

5.   Royal Burgh of [blank]
6.   Police Burgh of Kilmarnock
7.   Town of Kilmarnock
8.   Village or Hamlet of [blank]

Second line:
1.   No. of Schedule
2.   Road, Street etc. No. or name of House
3.   Houses (this column is subdivided to show Inhabited (I), Uninhabited (U), or Building (B))
4.   Name and surname of each person
5.   Relation to Head of Family
6.   Condition as to Marriage
7.   Age (last birthday) (This column is subdivided to show Male & Female)
8.   Rank, Profession or Occupation
9.   Where born
10. Whether, 1. Deaf; 2. Blind; 3. Imbecile or Idiot; 4. Lunatic
11. Rooms with one or more windows

The 1891 Census Return

This was the most detailed of all, taken on 5 April. As can be seen from Fig. 6, it showed all the details about the parish; it now had a column for Gaelic, or Gaelic and English speakers, as well as a column to show if the subject was an employer or employee or working on his or her own account.

The 1901 Census Return

This census was taken on 31 March and has columns and headings as for 1891, with slight differences. For employment there is one column for 'Employer, Worker, or on Own Account', and another column for 'If Working at Home'. The next to the last column is for:

Whether
1.   Deaf and Dumb.
2.   Blind
3.   Lunatic
4.   Imbecile, feeble-minded

In the column: 'Condition as to Marriage', the enumerator entered 'W' for Widow, 'Widr' for Widower, 'Mar' for Married, and 'S' for Single/Not Married.

When reading a census return, do not be deterred by the fact that the ages have all been crossed out! This only shows that at one point some work was done on the census pertaining to the ages of the inhabitants, and the ages were ticked as the work progressed.

All the information and the photocopy headings are taken from the census returns for Kilmarnock, Co. Ayr., and from these examples you can see there is a great deal to be found out from a census return. Not only the ages and kinship of your family, but how many of their rooms had windows, and what kind of town or village they inhabited.

Beware! Widows often reverted to their maiden surnames on the deaths of their husbands, so do not dismiss such an entry as being wrong for your search. Unnamed babies were sometimes recorded as N (ot) K (nown) in the name column, but the sex may be determined by noticing in which column the age was written. There was one column for males and one for females. Some names are confusing, and it is not always possible to tell whether or not the person was male or female; again, look at the age column to establishthis.

Census Returns for Shipping

As well as the census returns for Scottish parishes, there are some pertaining to shipping, as listed below:

1861 Census, Merchant Navy

This census contains a list of persons on board merchant vessels which were, on the night of Sunday, 7 April 1861, in Scottish ports. These ports are named. It records (1) The name and type of ship (fishing vessel, ketch etc.) and to which port she belonged; (2) Name and surname of each person on board; (3) Age, marital status and place of birth.

1871 Census, Merchant Vavy

This census contains similar information. Taken on 2 April 1871 it records a more detailed list of ports. Scottish merchant ships in English ports are also recorded.

1881 Census, Merchant Navy

This census contains lists of Scottish shipping in English and European ports and shipping at sea. Although these were Scottish ships, the crews were officers and men from all over the world, including Lascar seamen. All names, occupations, places of birth and so on were recorded. There was one entry for the passenger ship *Manitoban* which contained a list of passengers who embarked at Glasgow, including a page of orphan boys aged between 6 and 10 years. There was no indication of the destination of this vessel.

1881 Census, Royal Navy

This census listed drill ships and cutters in Scottish ports, recording the usual information about the crews and vessels.

1891 Census, Merchant Navy

This census contained lists of ships in dock or offshore in ports all round the coast of Scotland, from Shetland to Wigtown. The usual information was recorded about the crews and vessels.

1891 Census, Royal Navy

This census listed drill ships, a cruiser and gunboats in Scottish ports, and recorded the usual information about the crews and vessels.

Note: These shipping census returns are not listed in the index to census returns, and at the moment do not have a reference number, so if you are searching in New Register House, and you would like to see them, you will have to ask specially for them.

Census returns in Scotland have continued to be taken decennially since 1891 except for the year 1941, when the census was omitted because of World War II. However, as the latest date available to the public for searching is 1901, I have not commented on the later returns.

SEARCHING REGISTERS PRIOR TO 1855

The number of registers and records which exist prior to civil registration of births, marriages and deaths in 1855 is enormous, and it is not the purpose of this book to list them all.

I will, however, cover those which you are most likely to need in your search for information to further your quest for knowledge of your family history such as Old Parish Registers in New Register House, and testaments, deeds and so on in the National Archives of Scotland.

Once you have done as much work as you can using civil registers after 1854, and after you have found the members of the family in census returns, then you will be ready to turn to Old Parish Registers.

Old Parish Registers

Old Parish Registers (OPRs) were kept by the session clerk or the minister of the church or parish concerned, and tend to vary in content and accuracy because there was no standard form of recording information. While most parishes have records of births/baptisms and proclamations/marriages, unfortunately not many have registers of deaths or burials. Even if the session clerk or minister has kept death or burial records, they seldom give enough information for you to tie them in accurately with a family.

It is not normally possible to examine the original books owing to the huge number of people who have become interested in looking at them over the years. However, in fairly recent times, the Mormon Church requested permission to microfilm these records for their own religious purposes, and an arrangement was made whereby the Mormons filmed the books and supplied microfilm copies to Register House. If you wish to examine the OPRs you will be provided with a microfilm, for use on a microfilm reader. Usually, the entire OPR has been filmed, but occasionally a page has been omitted, or, more often, repeated several times. Watch the dates and page numbers, and if you find a page missing, report it to the search room supervisor who may be able to check the original book on your behalf. The same applies if the microfilm is in bad order and too faded to read.

If you are not using the records in New Register House for your search, you may be able to obtain the OPR microfilm of your choice from a Mormon library near you, or, if you intend to search in a parish known to you, then the local record office or library, or a local family history society, may have copies of the microfilm which you may be allowed to search. If you decide to work in a local or a Mormon library, then you should write to make prior arrangements. Ask if there is a fee involved, the times when the library is open, and if there are facilities for you to visit and do the search yourself. You should also ask whether you need to book a place or microfilm reader in advance. In Appendix II you will find a list of local record offices and family history societies in Scotland.

If, however, you intend to visit New Register House in Edinburgh to do your searching there, then read on!

The 1553 OPRs for Errol in the County of Perth are the earliest surviving registers. In Appendix III there is a list of OPRs giving the earliest extant date of their entries.

It should be noted that some Presbyterians, such as the Original Seceders of 1733, ceased to be members of the established Church of Scotland and did not always record their births and marriages in the parish register. However, it is worth searching the OPRs as well as the various Free Church records. (See Chapter 3 on 'Searching Records in the General Register House, National Archives of Scotland). Over the years many off-shoots have formed from the established Church of Scotland, and I have included a chart showing these (Illustrations: Fig. 7). If you are interested in reading more I would recommend D. J. Steel's *Sources for Scottish Genealogy and Family History* (Appendix IV: Book list).

In 1783 the Stamp Act (applicable to the whole of Great Britain) was passed, imposing a tax of 3d (three old pence) on every entry of a birth/baptism, marriage and burial. Although this Act was repealed in 1794 it did have the effect of deterring people from registering births, marriages and deaths for about ten years. Ministers who did not agree with the tax refused to keep records and so could not be fined for not having collected the tax! Understandably, people did not always come forward to register a birth, marriage or death if there was a tax to be paid. In addition to the compulsory statutory or civil registration of births, marriages and deaths since 1855, ministers have continued to keep parish registers in respect of their own congregations.

OPRs are essentially registers of the established Church of Scotland,

and only very seldom do they contain entries relating to members of other denominations such as Episcopalians, Roman Catholics, Methodists, Quakers etc. Occasionally such exceptional entries may prove useful. Episcopal, Roman Catholic, Methodist and Quaker registers, as well as the registers of the Free Churches of Scotland, are held in the National Archives of Scotland. (See Chapter 3). For Jewish archives see Chapter 4 on 'Other Sources' and Appendix II for addresses.

In New Register House birth and marriage entries prior to 1855 are now computer-indexed. The index to births/baptisms shows the names of the parents, which is an advantage over the statutory indexes where no parents' names are shown. This computer programme is very user friendly if time is, taken to follow the instructions step by step. You will find details of the computer programme on pages 13–21 with the general introduction to using the computer index. Because this computer index has been compiled from the Mormon microfiche, it contains, as yet, no death entries. For those parishes which have death registers, it is necessary to refer to the paper indexes – that is, the lists of parishes, which give you the Parish Registration No. for the film you will have to read through.

For those of you not conducting your searches using the computer index, I would advise you to use the IGI for the various counties of Scotland. It is a most useful index, but I would warn you that the name of the parish is in the index, and not the name of the place within that parish.

If you have access to the OPR paper index, then you can check under which parish your particular place-name can be found. If not, then you should refer to a gazetteer (see Appendix IV: Book list).

For example, in Shetland, births and marriages in Bressay (Ref. 1/1) and Burra & Quarff (1/2) are all given as *Bressay*. Those in Dunrossness (3/1), Sandwick & Cunningsburgh (3/2) and Fair Isle (3/3) are all given as *Dunrossness*. Those in Tingwall (10/1), Whiteness & Weesdale (10/2) are all given as *Tingwall*. (Weesdale's modern spelling is Weisdale.) Those in Walls (12/1), Sandness (12/2), Papa Stour (12/3) and Foula (12/4) are all given as *Walls*. For instance, if you know your ancestor was born prior to 1855 in Burra & Quarff, you will find the microfiche index records it as Bressay. This principle applies when searching any parishes with joint names, but is not applicable to the computer programme which has used the actual parish for its index.

Beware! Since the main objective of the Mormons in recording entries is for use in their own religious observances, it is worth bearing in mind that if there are two dates shown in an OPR of births (before 1855), then the date chosen by the Mormons for their index may be that of the *baptism* and not that of the birth. Also, not all entries found in the IGI are to be found in the Old Parish Registers. See page 107 of Questions and Answers (Chapter 9) for more details.

To order an OPR you have to work with registration numbers and not the name of the parish, as you discovered when ordering births, marriages, deaths and census returns from 1855 onwards. All parishes prior to 1855 have been assigned a registration number, and while most of these coincide with the numbers with which you have been working up to now, there are some which are different. It is always safer not to assume you know the reference number. Unless you are working with the computer index which will automatically show the required reference, you are advised to look it up in the paper index and make sure. For registration purposes parishes in Scotland have been numbered alphabetically within the county, working from north to south.

In Appendix III you will find a list of parishes, their registration numbers, and the date of the earliest register extant for that parish. This date can be misleading; although the earliest date may be, for example, 1666, there may be gaps in the registers, and after a couple of entries for that year there may be nothing else for twenty or thirty years. Most parish registers were well kept, with the entries made in chronological order. Nevertheless, some were kept in a most haphazard manner, with dates which are jumbled up and easy to miss. Some microfilm boxes are labelled 'RNE', which stands for 'Register of Neglected Entries'. These are entries, nearly always births, which were not registered at the time they occurred, but when statutory registration was introduced in Scotland in 1855 were registered in retrospect. Unless you are using the computer index, it is worth winding on to the end of a reel containing 1820-54 births to see if there are any late entries, even if you have found your family in the correct time span. There may have been a child who had not survived infancy, and so was not known to the family. Even the computer index is not entirely reliable.

If you do not have access to the computer index for OPR births and marriages, and you have to search from 1854 back as far as the register goes, (say, to the early 1700s), then I would advise you always to start with the latest date, 1854, and work backwards; thereby you will get used to seeing the names, which will repeat themselves, and as the handwriting changes you will recognise a name which you may not otherwise have been able to read. I suggest you have the name or names that you want to find written on a piece of paper in front of you, so that you can glance at it from time to time, or keep saying the name to yourself over and over again. It is so easy to become mesmerised by a microfilm.

Most OPRs are lists of people's names, and details of the births and/or baptisms, proclamation of banns/marriages, and occasionally deaths and/or burials. Some are mainly minutes of the Kirk Session and only contain births and/or baptisms, proclamations/marriages, deaths and/or burials inasmuch as a fee was paid and this was entered in the accounts. In these instances the information is brief, and although it takes a long time to read through the OPR to find the information you need, it is often most rewarding as it gives you an insight into the affairs of the parish and its people, not to mention the ways of the session clerk or of the minister. The details of the parish and its people are missed when you work from the computer index straight to the entry.

Births in OPRs (Entries prior to 1855)

In the birth/baptismal registers of a parish you may find: (1) the date on which the entry was made in the register; (2) the date of the birth and/or the baptism; (3) the name of the child and of its parent or parents. Not all registers record more than one date (which may be either birth or baptism), but when you are reading these dates do make sure which of the dates you have noted. Many people, when reading the entry, mistake either the date when the entry was made in the register, or the date of the baptism, for the date of birth.

This point is particularly worth remembering when you are using the computer or the microfiche index, because if the OPR shows both a birth and a baptismal date, then the baptismal date and not the birth date may be the one recorded by the Mormons.

Beware! The computer index has been compiled from the microfiche index, so any errors and omissions found there will have been transferred. However, these are being rectified by the GROs whenever they are reported.

Some OPRs give a wealth of detail, such as those for Dundee, where you will find the names and kinship of the people after whom the child was named. This is most useful when making collateral lines. In other records you may find recorded the occupation of the father, the place of birth (for example the name of the farm), and witnesses or sponsors who were often uncles and aunts or grandparents.

At the other extreme, in some parish records the name of the mother was not recorded, nor was the name or sex of the child. Instead of 'a lawful son called Nicholas' you may read 'a lawful child called Nicholas' and as you will read in the chapter on 'Names', some names were unisex even in those days!

Unless you are using the computer index – in which case the registration reference number will appear on the screen – once you have discovered in which parish you need to search for your family line, you must find the index to OPR registration numbers. There are two such index books, one for parishes from 1–490 and one for parishes from 491–901. Each book is indexed and contains a list of parish names with the registration number applying to each parish.

I must remind you again to search under Mc and Mac, as these may have been listed on separate pages in a book index, separately on a microfiche index, and they are definitely listed separately on the computer index. just occasionally you may find an index where the prefix 'Mac' or 'Mc' has been put after the main name, for example, 'Donald Mac'.

When you have decided on an entry from the computer index, remember to take note of the full reference numbers, including the year of the event, which you will need for the requisition slip. Once again I would remind you that the parish microfilms are filed under their district number, and not by the name of the parish. Also you must remember to fill in your name as well as the number of your desk/seat on the requisition slip. No more than two films are allowed out at once, and you may not write more than one item on each slip. The films are read on the machines in the Dome Search Room. For an example of a completed order slip for an OPR, see Part II: 'Step by Step'.

When you fill in the requisition slip, remember to make a note of the numbers in your own notebook for reference (Fig. 14). Many microfilms cover more than one parish (the numbers are written on the box which holds the film), so make sure that you have wound the film on to the parish that you want to read. Almost every film has its number at the top of every page, so you should have no difficulty. Having wound the microfilm to reach the appropriate year you must start reading the page for the name you require. This will be easier in some registers than others.

When searching for siblings and using OPRs prior to 1841 (after that date census returns are useful), and having found a birth entry, I suggest you next search for the marriage of the parents. Once this date has been established, you have a time-frame within which to work when searching for their children. Do not neglect to start the search for children in the year of the marriage, as it has been known for a couple to marry in the ninth month of pregnancy and still have another child the following year. Or it may be that the child whose birth you found was the last of a long line of children, and the parents were married up to thirty years previously, so don't give up too soon! Having reached this point in your search, it is sometimes difficult to go back much further with any certainty.

For example, when you have a couple marrying in 1816, then it would be reasonable to suppose that the bridegroom had been born between 1800 and 1776, that is, aged between 16 and 40 at the time of marriage. If this man lived until 1855 then his death certificate should show the names of his parents, and the search for his birth entry can be undertaken in the knowledge that it could be recognised if it had been registered. If, however, this man had died prior to 1855, then the names of his parents are pure conjecture unless you can find them by some other means such as a known sibling who did live until 1855, or presumably a monumental inscription.

In some cases a search for a birth will get back to a point where two or more possible candidates present themselves, and the parents' names are unknown. There was one such case where a search led me to two possible birth entries:

1. *1791 William Sutherland s/o Alex. Sutherland & Katherine Ross*
2. *1794 William Sutherland s/o Robt. Sutherland & Isobel Munro*

The William Sutherland I was searching for died in 1850 in Perth, and had been a sergeant in the army. His army records gave his place of birth as Alness, County Ross, and his age on enlistment in 1811 was 18. So he was born *circa* 1793. Unfortunately his army records did not state parentage.

The 1841 census return for Perth showed a William Sutherland aged 46, army P. (Pensioner) not born in county, and his wife Ann who was born in Ireland.

I searched Monumental Inscriptions for Perth (tombstones from which genealogical information has been noted), where I found an entry which showed William and his brothers. The ages were not accurate, but this was probably due to the condition of the lettering on the tombstone:

William Sutherland, late colour sergeant, aged 42, died 1850 w. (wife) Ann Mckeone, aged 43 died 1845 bro. (brother) John late of the 42nd aged 43 died 1813 (?1833?) Spain. bro. Hector late serjeant maj. died 1840 Montreal.

Now knowing that William Sutherland had brothers named John and Hector, I searched the birth records for County Ross, where I found John born 1791 and Hector born 1799, both sons of Robert Sutherland and Isobel Munro.

This not only proved that the 1794 birth entry of William Sutherland was correct for the search, but added colourful and interesting information about his brothers whose deaths I would never otherwise have found.

So you see, if you dig around, it is sometimes possible to find the birth, and even more information, about a person who died prior to 1855 and whose parentage was unknown to you.

Marriages in OPRs (Entries prior to 1855)

In the marriage registers of a parish the date you find is more likely to have been the date of the proclamation of banns or the date when the marriage was contracted than the date of the actual marriage, though in some registers both dates are recorded. As in birth/baptismal entries, the form varies from parish to parish, but in marriage entries you will nearly always find recorded the name of the parish of the groom and the name of the parish of the bride. This is essential to note. If, for example, an entry found in an OPR for Dunfermline read 'James Murray of this parish and Katherine Henderson of the parish of Kinghorn', it would be worthwhile examining the OPR for the parish of Kinghorn for the marriage entry. Kinghorn having been the bride's parish they may well have been married in the church there, and that record may therefore contain information in greater detail, such as the name of her father.

OPRs for larger parishes usually show marriage entries as a straightforward record of the facts. You should find the date of the proclamation of banns and/or of the marriage, names of the bride and groom, sometimes the name of the father of the bride, often the occupation of the groom but seldom the name of his father. However, in smaller parishes it is common to find the session clerk has merely kept an account of the monies paid in (as already stated for births), and so the marriage entry would consist of only the names of both parties, or in some cases, the name of the groom only, and a note of the fee paid.

Beware! The computer index for OPR births/baptisms and marriages has been copied from the Mormon Church's IGI. Not every entry in its index has been verified. It is essential that you read *every* entry in the OPR. I once found parents named in the index of births had married two and a half generations later! And the mother of the children was *not* named in the OPR entry.

Where you find a couple were 'irregularly married' – an irregular marriage is one which is perfectly valid but for which no banns were called, rendering the marriage clandestine – the couple were often severely reprimanded by the Kirk Session, who tended to fine and forgive!

The whole subject of marriage in Scotland is an interesting one and for further reading I would recommend D.J. Steel's *Sources for Scottish Genealogy and Family History* as well as *Irregular Border Marriages* by 'Claverhouse' (see Appendix IV: Book list). The latter is, I believe, out of print, but well worth reading from a library or searching out from a secondhand bookshop, as I did.

For more information on irregular marriages see page 86 in Chapter 4: Other Sources.

Deaths in OPRs (Entries prior to 1855) (not indexed)

Here we come across problems, as not many parishes recorded deaths, and of those which did, only a few recorded them in enough detail to enable the entry to be verified as belonging to the search in hand. There are a few death registers which, in recording the deaths of people in the parish, give cause of death, age, and even address, as well as some degree of kinship, but as with some births and marriages, most deaths were only recorded by the session clerk if a fee was involved – for the hire of a mortcloth or pall.

The *Lists of Old Parish Registers* in the Dome Search Room will show if there are death/burial registers for the parish of your search. There are no personal indexes for deaths in the OPRs as there are for births/baptisms and marriages.

Monumental Inscriptions

Luckily, over the past years people have been collecting information from tombstones all over Scotland, and now it is a race against time before the stones deteriorate. This work is of great assistance to the field of genealogy, through recording the inscriptions which otherwise might have been lost, and collating this information with references to early testaments and hearth and poll tax lists. Printed lists of tombstone inscriptions are usually referred to as Monumental Inscriptions (MIs.) As well as MIs there are war memorials and church monuments to be considered.

I have shown previously how it is possible to pinpoint a birth entry through a tombstone; so do not neglect this valuable source of information. These MIs are held in their entirety by the Scottish Genealogy Society, Edinburgh, and copies of most of them are in the South Search Room and Library, New Register House, in the National Library of Scotland, and in some local libraries. Copies of monumental inscriptions are on sale from the Scottish Genealogy Society, and members may write and ask for an entry to be forwarded in a stamped addressed envelope; if you are not a member then there is a fee involved (see Appendix II: List of useful addresses).

The booklets are continually being produced, so keep in regular contact with the Scottish Genealogy Society and local family history societies.

BURIAL RECORDS (CEMETERIES)

Since 1855 it has been compulsory for parishes and other bodies maintaining cemeteries to keep a register of all burials. Most of these records have been kept by the local authorities which took over responsibility for the upkeep of most graveyards in 1925. Some of them have been transferred to New Register House, but most were held by the District and Islands Councils which replaced the Town and County Councils in 1974 and which were replaced in 1996 by the new local authorities. Similar records are kept of cremations, which were introduced at the end of the nineteenth century and now outnumber burials in some areas.

All these records are normally open to public inspection, sometimes for a fee, and some local authorities are willing to answer inquiries about them; but in general these records are unlikely to yield any information beyond what is on the death certificate, apart from the location of the grave, and possibly other family members buried there.

A few cemeteries are or have been maintained by Roman Catholic or other churches or by private companies. Most of their burial records for recent years are available for public inspection, while some of the earlier records are held by the National Archives of Scotland in West Register House.

Material available in the South Search Room
(first floor of New Register House)

The South Search Room is also the main library room. There is a library catalogue of all reference books – including those in the Dome Search Room.

Available in this room there are copies of *Fasti Ecclesiae Scoticanae*, and other church denomination histories, some family histories, Commissariot records published by the Scottish Record Society, and an ever-increasing collection of monumental inscriptions.

Laid out on the tables there are the 1890s Ordnance Survey maps covering the whole of Scotland (one inch to one mile), and on the shelves some miscellaneous maps and plans.

There are some computer terminals dedicated for reading the CD-ROMS, which are: the Mormon Church's *FamilySearch* for the British Isles; 1881 British Census Index; UK Info Disk 2000; the Mormon Church's Vital Events Index for the British Isles; National Burial Index: 1538–2000 (incomplete – continually being added to); North America Vital Events Index; USA Social Security Death Index; Irish Wills: 1484–1858; and Miscellaneous 1841 and 1851 Census Indexes.

On microfiche there are the following: IGI 1981-edition: all Scotland by surname; IGI 1988-edition: all Scotland by county; OPR County Index

(Scotland): births/baptisms and marriages; 1881 Census Index (Scotland) – five categories and colour coded: pink/ Surname Index, green/Birthplace Index, orange/Census Place (Parish) Index, yellow/Census Record as Enumerated Index, and brown/Miscellaneous Notes and Institutions; 1881 Census Index (England & Wales); Statutory Index to Births, Marriages and Deaths: 1837–2000 (England & Wales); Statutory Index to Overseas Events: 1761–1994 (British Subjects); Edinburgh and Glasgow Post Office Directories; Some Monumental Inscriptions.

This material is continually being added to – so do not be afraid to ask the librarian.

3
Searching Records in
General Register House
(National Archives of Scotland)

The National Archives of Scotland (NAS) are based at General Register House, Princes Street, Edinburgh, and often referred to as 'The Old House', to distinguish it from New Register House which is usually known as 'The New House'.

The Historical Search Room in HM General Register House, Princes Street, and the West Search Room in West Register House, Charlotte Square, are open from 9.00 a.m. to 4.45 p.m. from Mondays to Fridays. As with New Register House, these search rooms are closed for some local and public holidays, so you are advised to write or telephone in advance to check this. There is an experiment at present (August 2003) to see if demand warrants an evening opening on Thursdays.

There is no fee for searching the records held in the Historical Search Room, or in the West Search Room, for literary and historical purposes (including ancestry research), but you will have to obtain a reader's ticket to enable you to have access to the records. You have to apply personally (not by post), and produce some evidence of identity. Tickets issued in the Historical Search Room are valid in the West Search Room and *vice versa*. Access is difficult for wheelchairs, but facilities can be made there, by prior arrangement. It is about a ten- to fifteen-minute walk from the NAS to the West House, and there are buses which run along George Street and Princes Street (see street plan of Central Edinburgh).

Information concerning the holdings in both buildings is contained in the NAS's leaflet No. 7. This is an impressive list of documents, but only a few of them will be used by the searcher of family history.

The system in the NAS is similar to that in New Register House, except that you may choose any desk which happens to be free when you enter the search room. Each seat has a number on the back and each desk has the same number, and this number is the one you write on the order slip. Waiting time is longer than in the New Register House because not only is the building larger, but more records are now being housed in other parts of Edinburgh. As the delay may be a day or so, I would advise you to order your records in advance when possible; however, you do have the advantage of nearly always working with an original document. To conserve these original documents, more are being copied onto microfilm, and slowly into digital images. In the NAS it is even more important to use a *lead pencil* at all times. As most of these documents, being originals, are invaluable and irreplaceable it is vital not to lean on them when writing. There are strict rules too, about no smoking and no eating in the search room, and no mobile phones.

There are many avenues of search available to you here, and to start with I shall deal with the Church records which are grouped under the reference CH. (NAS).

CH1 = Church of Scotland General Assembly Papers

These papers are very varied and deal mostly with internal matters within the Church, ministers writing about moving from one parish to another, and various complaints. For example:

CH 1 /2/38/78–102. *Case of John Dunlop, Minister of Mousewald, deposed by Synod of Dumfreis in 1715 for not administering Sacrament, clandestine proclamation of his daughter's marriage, travelling on Sunday, neglecting family worship, assaulting parishioners.*

CHI/2182/289/300. *Irregular marriage, John Buchanan, baker in Glasgow, and Mary Robertson, widow of Peter Barlinnie, fencing master there. 29 Sept. 1742.*

This information is to be found in the index, so you need only order the volumes containing details pertaining to your search.

At one time, ministers of each parish were directed to list all Roman Catholics residing there. These lists are to be found for 1704, 1710 and 1713, but not all parish lists have survived. Look for *Lists of Priests and Papists* (CH.1/2/22–82).

CH2 = Church of Scotland Synods, Presbyteries and Kirk Sessions

Of these records, the most useful to the genealogist are the Kirk Session records. Searching through the OPRs in New Register House, you may have found birth, marriage, and death entries recorded within the Kirk Session Minutes for some parishes, but this is not so in the majority of cases. Most Kirk Session Records are held in the NAS, and are not part of the OPRs. Records of births/baptisms, marriages, deaths and burials, and lists of heads of families to be found in the different parishes' Kirk Session records have been listed by Mrs Diane Baptie (see Appendix IV: Book list).

The Kirk Session is composed of elders of the congregation, with the minister as moderator. They are responsible for the general organisation of the affairs of the congregation, and concern themselves with discipline over members. Kirk Session Minutes give an interesting insight into the workings of a parish, and into the lives of its parishioners. There you may find details about an illegitimate birth, reporting the name of the alleged father. Some Kirk Session records contain lists of male heads of families who were communicants, which is useful pre-census information.

These Kirk Session Minutes are not indexed, but principals' names are often written in the margin.

Sometimes parishioners were issued with certificates when they moved from one district to another. These were known as 'testificates' or 'testimonials', and were the attestation given by the minister, or by the Kirk Session, of the moral character of a church member, who was about to leave one parish for another. Finding these testificates for your family can often help you to follow their journeyings from place to place.

As the parish was responsible for looking after its poor people, it obviously did not want to have more of them on the books than necessary! Lists of monies paid out to the poor and needy form a large part of the accounts of any parish.

Presbyterian Churches in England

Some records are held in the NAS, and they are noted in the CH2 index. Otherwise, apply to the Church of Scotland Office at 121 George Street, Edinburgh, EH2 4YN.

CH3 and CH13 = Free Church Records

These include the records of the United Free, and United Presbyterian, and other smaller churches. Because many United Free Churches agreed to union with the Established Church of Scotland in 1929, and consequently altered their designations, it is essential that these two repertories (CH2 and CH3) should be consulted in conjunction with each other since pre-1929 and post-1929 records of a particular church may be split. Where a direct cross-reference is possible, for example, Longforgan Free Church and Invergowrie East Church of Scotland, this is inserted in the appropriate entry in each repertory.

Records of Presbyterian churches which were not within the established Church of Scotland are also housed in the NAS, and will be found under Ref. CH3 and CH13. These records are all indexed by parish and church or chapel, and you will be shown where on the shelves to find these index books, and how to look them up and order the ones you need. CH3 contains mainly Session Minutes, but sometimes there are lists of members and seat rent books which can be a useful source.

Records of baptisms, marriages and deaths, and lists of members in the Scottish Secession Churches have also been collated by Mrs Diane Baptie (see Appendix IV: Book list).

CH9 = Ministers' Widows' Funds Records

These records were transmitted to the NAS by the trustees of the fund in 1968, following an agreement between the trustees and the Keeper of the Records, Scotland. They are made up of two different schemes; firstly, the records of the original Ministers' Widows' Fund of the Church of Scotland with records dating from 1743, and secondly, the records of the Free Churches' Ministers' Widows' Fund dating from 1844. The two funds were united following the union of the Churches in 1929. Some of the material is indexed. For example, CH9/14 contains an alphabetical list of widows from 1752 to 1801.

CH10 = The Religious Society of Friends (Quaker) Records

CH10/1   Relates to the South East Scotland Monthly Meeting 1569–1959
CH10/2   Relates to the Aberdeen Two-Monthly Meeting (19 Items) 1931–65
CH10/3   Relates to the Aberdeen Religious Society of Friends 1664–1983.

Not all this material is of genealogical interest, but there are some entries concerning births and marriages. These are indexed by subject and not by name. Quaker records are also to be found in New Register House among the Miscellaneous Records: Births, Marriages and Deaths 1622–1890 (Ref. MP5/2 NRH).

CH11 = Methodist Records

These records are arranged in alphabetical order of place, and contain lists of members and seat holders. The dates vary greatly from place to place. The records are closed for sixty years, unless written permission has been given by the Superintendent Minister of the Circuit.

CH12 = The Episcopal Church in Scotland

This series comprises records deposited by congregations, dioceses, and others of the Episcopal Church in Scotland, and records deposited in 1983 by the trustees of the Episcopal Theological College, Edinburgh (Ref. CH12/10–24, 26, 28–9, 33–5). The arrangement of the papers in the 'Episcopal Chest' by the Revd J. B. Craven, and others, has been retained (Ref. CH 12/12). The papers comprising the (Bishop) 'Jolly Kist' have been grouped as CH 12/10–11, 26, 28–9, 33–5. Most of these records relate to Church matters, and letters from one clergyman to another, but there are some instances where early births, marriages and deaths were recorded. A detailed list of Episcopal Church records *not* deposited in the NAS has recently been produced. The staff will allow access for inspection of this large binder giving information on the records of the individual Episcopal congregations. They may also be found in the surveys of the National Register of Archives for Scotland (NRA(S)) (see Other Sources, Chapter 4).

These Episcopal records of baptisms sometimes show dates of birth, but not the mother's maiden surname; of marriages give the groom's Christian and surname and title, the bride's Christian and maiden surname, her father's name, and the place of marriage; of burials give name, dates of death, burial and age.

CH13 = Records of the United Free Church of Scotland

These records were deposited in the NAS in 1976, under an agreement similar to that with the Church of Scotland. These records are of congregations which did not join in the union of 1929 between the Church of Scotland and the United Free Church. They should be consulted in conjunction with the records listed as CH3, which include the former United Free Churches, which joined in the 1929 union.

RH21 = THE ROMAN CATHOLIC CHURCH IN SCOTLAND (NAS)

This comprises a list of holdings in the NAS with an index to parishes and dioceses. The records consist of baptismal and marriage registers, together with lists of Easter communicants, which have been copied as negatives (white writing on black page), and some of them are difficult to read.

The information given in Church records varies from church to church or chapel and so does the time-span covered. Many of the registers are held locally, so it would be worthwhile to visit the local parish and church or chapel should your family not be members of the established Church of Scotland.

Again, I advise you to write in advance of your journey, as it is wise to establish what records are held locally. A letter to 'The Minister or Session Clerk', or to 'Priest-in-Charge', or to 'The Incumbent', and then the name of the church or chapel, and the parish, should find them if you do not have a name and address. Or you could write either to the local public library or the local Record Office and they would probably help you, although they are not obliged to do so (see Appendix II: List of useful addresses).

See also Church of Scotland General Assembly Papers (CH1).

Testaments and Wills

If you are lucky and find a will left by a member of your family, this may help a great deal and give names not otherwise known to you. When a person dies, he or she may or may not have left a will, but in either case an executor will have been appointed. Records of the confirmation of executors are known as testaments. In Scotland there are two kinds of testaments: a testament testamentar which applies when a person dies testate, i.e., leaves a will and names the executor or executors; a testament dative which applies when a person dies intestate, i.e., does not leave a will and the executor is appointed by the court. The executor so appointed was (and is) usually a near relative such as a spouse or a son or creditor. In either case (testament testamentar or testament dative) an inventory was usually made of the deceased's 'goods, gear, debts and sums of money', or, as you may see in the testament, which was often written in Scots, 'guidis, geir, debtis and somnes of monie'.

Prior to 1868 testaments were only concerned with moveable property and not with land (which descended according to the law of heritage). It is therefore worthwhile to look for a testament or will of somebody of fairly humble origin. For example, a man may leave the tools of his trade to his son or son-in-law, and a woman may leave a brooch or some other favourite piece of jewellery to a daughter or a granddaughter; and of course, there was always the linen and furniture to be divided up between the remaining members of the family.

When a widow and children survived, the moveable estate would be divided into three parts. One third would go to the widow, one third to the children (known as the 'bairns' pairt') and the remaining third would be left to whomever the deceased wished (the 'dead's pairt'). When the husband or wife was already deceased, then one half of the property would go to the children, and the other half to whomever the testator wished. If there were no children, then the estate would be divided in two, with one part going to the beneficiaries named and the other to nearest kin.

Testaments up to 1823 are kept with the records of the Commissary Courts (reference NAS 'CC'). These took over the jurisdiction of the Bishops' Courts after the Reformation. The commissariots correspond roughly to the old dioceses – not to the counties.

For more detailed information on Scottish testaments I would recommend the books by Gerald Hamilton-Edwards, D. J. Steel, and The National Archives of Scotland (see Appendix IV: Book list).

Testaments may be recorded in the Commissary or in the Sheriff Court of the parish where the person died, or in Edinburgh. It is particularly important to search the Edinburgh Commissary Court or Sheriff Court records in cases of persons who may have died abroad or outside Scotland. If you do not find the testament listed in the year of the death, then you should continue to search, as testaments were sometimes recorded several years later when the need to prove something arose. Or they may never have been recorded at all, as happened in the more remote parts of the country when the goods and gear were disposed of within the family without recourse to law.

Until 1800 there are printed indexes to testaments for each commissariot, and from 1801 to 1823 there is a typescript index for all commissariots, except for those of Edinburgh, Glasgow and St Andrews, which are covered by separate indexes. After 1823 the boundaries of the commissariots and sheriffdoms were aligned and testaments with indexes are kept with the records of the Sheriff Courts (Ref. NAS 'SC'). I have included here a copy of an index to Sheriff Court Commissary Records to be found in the NAS (Illustrations: Fig. 8).

All testaments/wills up to 1901 have now been digitised, and even now many are available on the internet, through the Scottish Archive Network. The website is www.scottishdocuments.com where one views a comprehensive index. For a standard fee of £5 a digitised image can be downloaded.

Beware! Make sure you carefully read the instructions for downloading to your imaging programme.

Searchers in the Historical Search Room can now no longer view original testaments, inventories and Wills/Trust settlements dated *before* 1901. The adjacent Robertson Wing has now been refurbished and there are a sufficient number of computer terminals for searchers to find these documents and view digitised images. Soon there will be facilities to enable one to obtain copies of these images.

Index to Inventories of Personal Estates of Defuncts

This covers all commissariots from 1846 to 1867 and shows in which Sheriff Court the inventory was recorded, the year it was recorded and the date of the deceased's death. At the beginning of each volume there is a key to the abbreviations used throughout. You will be able to order the records you require by using the numbers found in the index books marked 'CC' and 'SC', and you will be shown how to do this by a member of the staff. In each case you will need three numbers on your order slip, e.g., CC1/5/2 or SC5/2/3.

From 1876 all testaments are fully indexed. On the spine of the books you will see the year and *Calendar of Confirmations and Inventories*. Inside, the book is arranged alphabetically by surname followed by first name. There is an abridged extract of the contents of the testament, so it is easy to spot the one you want. It is possible to buy copies of any of the testaments or inventories which you may have found, and it is advisable to do so, as you can then enjoy reading them again once you have arrived home, and you will not have had to spend time writing down the contents. Inventories hold so much information other than family names. You can often tell how your family lived and how much money they had. Even though it seems little by our standards they were probably more comfortably off than it appears.

In Appendix III you will find a list of parishes showing the commissariot and date of the earliest testament for each parish.

Just occasionally you will find a splendid entry in the index to one of the commissariots, such as this one in the index to the Commissariot of Lanark (1595–1800):

Campbell, John, servant to John Stewart, younger, in Moat, son to the deceased George C., in Lows, par. of New Cumnock, who was brother-german to umquhile Euphame C., who was spouse to John Arthur of Borland Smithy, par. of Lesmahago. 22 June 1733.

In the Commissariot of Dumfries index there is this entry which takes the family back a couple of generations:

Hay, Margaret, widow of William Carruthers, physician in Dumfries, thereafter in Quarrellwood, the only lawful daughter to umquhile Mr John Hay, apothecary, who was son of mr Alexander Hay, his Majesty's apothecary, and Mary Blackburn, spouses. 11 June 1775.

Register of Deeds

This is another valuable source for the genealogist. The NAS has produced a leaflet (No. 19) of indexes in the Historical Search Room to deeds, sasines and testamentary records. There is a Register of Deeds, kept by the Court of

Session, extant from 1554 until the present time, and it is in three series.

1. The first series is 1554–1657, with calendars (partly indexed) for 1554–95. Between 1596 and 1660 there are no calendars and no indexes, and so you have to use the five series of Minute Books.
2. The second series is 1661–1811. It is in three sections containing registrations by the three principal clerks whose names were Dalrymple, Durie and MacKenzie. The abbreviations 'Dal', 'Dur' and 'Mack' are used when ordering records for the years 1661–1811. There are printed annual indexes, except for 1711–49, 1753–65 and 1766–70.
3. The third series is 1812 to the present time and is growing at a great pace each year.

Various kinds of deeds were registered, but for the purposes of family history, some of the more useful are marriage contracts. These marriages may not have been found in Old Parish Registers; sometimes the record was incomplete, and sometimes pages have been damaged or lost. Marriage contracts were normally registered as deeds *after* the death of one or both spouses, and so can be awkward to find. You will also find wills, trust dispositions and settlements in which mention is made of children, and people nominated as their guardians, who also may have been relatives.

If you are working in the NAS in Edinburgh, you will find these references are used for the different series of deeds: Register of Deeds: General RD/ . . . (etc.); Sheriff Court . . . SC/ . . . (etc.); Burgh . . . B/ . . . (etc.).

D. J. Steel in his book *Sources of Scottish Genealogy & Family History*, gives a detailed list of Registers of Deeds. See also National Archives of Scotland's *Tracing Your Scottish Ancestors* (see Appendix IV: Book list).

Register of Sasines

After an heir proves right to land, or when it is transferred to a grantee rather than to an heir, the act of taking possession, known as 'sasine' or 'seisin', (pronounced 'saysin') is recorded. A notary recorded the action in an Instrument of Sasine, and this constituted title to the property. Sasine is a mode of investiture in lands. In giving sasine of lands, the symbols were 'earth and stone of the lands'; of an annual rent out of lands, 'earth and stone, with a penny money'; of fishings, 'net and coble'; of mills, 'clap and happer'; of houses within burgh, 'hasp and staple'; of patronage teinds, 'a sheaf of corn', of patronage, 'a psalm-book and the keys of the church'; of jurisdiction, 'the book of court'.

Delivery is the test of the transfer of property, whether heritable or moveable. As the actual delivery of heritage is impracticable, the law of Scotland recognised a symbolical delivery which was indispensable in the transference of such property.

However, by the Infeftment Act, 1845 (8 & 9 Vict. cap. 35), the ceremony of giving sasine on the lands was dispensed with, and a simpler means of infeftment was provided.

A sasine can be of use to the genealogist because it often narrates earlier transactions concerning the land which may have belonged to the family for some time; it may also refer to persons who rented property, and to occasions where property was used as security to raise money. In all these instances, mention of kinship may be found.

From 1781 onwards you have the advantage of being able to use the printed abridgements. These will probably give you all the information you require without consulting the original document, and will certainly give you the reference number to enable you to order the Register of Sasines, and to read the whole document for yourself if you so wish. It is recommended that you read the actual sasine, despite its length, because abridgements can miss out valuable family relationships. These abridgements are arranged by county and each county is indexed by 'Places' and 'Persons'. So first, look along the shelves until you find the county in which you are interested, then find the index marked 'Places' (that is, if you know the name of your family's residence), and the index marked 'Persons', and see if your family is there. You will find a number written against each 'Place' entry and against each 'Person' entry, and if any of these numbers coincides, then turn to the Sasine Register abridgement which contains the numbers and read the abridgement. You will become familiar with the different abbreviations used in these abridgements (e.g. 'Disp.' = Disposition; 'Pr.Cl. Con.' = Precept of Clare Constat; 'Assig.' = Assignation = Assignment).

If you do not know the name of a place, but only that the family came from a certain county, then you will have to search through the 'Persons' index in that county and note all the numbers against the name you are searching, and look them up in the abridgements. These abridgements are kept at the bottom of the staircase to the Historical Search Room. You order the actual Sasine Register in the Historical Search Room.

Beware! Some users do not replace the volumes of abridgements in their correct place, so you may have to hunt in that county section.

Beware! There is a gap in the index for 'Places' from 1830 to 1872.

Searching sasines prior to the indexed abridgements in 1781 is, naturally, a more difficult task. There exists: the Secretaries Register, 1599–1609 (some indexes); the General Register of Sasines, 1617–1868 (some indexes); the Particular Register of Sasines, which runs parallel with the General Register.

The Secretaries Register (a register begun in 1599 under the superintendence of the Secretary of State) was discontinued in 1609. However, in 1617, by Act of Parliament, a new register was begun, consisting of particular registers (each for a district, which was not necessarily a county), and a general register for sasines of lands in more than one jurisdiction.

There was a new Land Registration Act in 1868, but it did not have any effect on Burgh Registers of Sasines which were eventually abolished under the 1926 Burgh Registers (Scotland) Act. This laid down procedures for discontinuing the registers, which took effect at different dates for each royal burgh; the last register (Dingwall) was not discontinued until 1963. The Land

Registration Act (Scotland) 1979, established a new land register which is a map-based system. For a registration of title search you are advised to contact Registers of Scotland, Meadowbank House, 153 London Road, Edinburgh EH8 7AU, Tel. 0131 659 6111, or preferably Land Registers, Erskine House, 68 Queen Street, Edinburgh, EH2 4NF.

More details about sasines are given in George J. Bell's *A Dictionary and Digest of the Law of Scotland*, Robert Bell's *A Dictionary of the Law of Scotland* and the National Archives of Scotland's *Tracing Your Scottish Ancestors*, Ch. 8 (see Appendix IV: Book list).

Services of Heirs or Retours

When lands were inherited by an heir and not given to a grantee, a 'brieve' was issued from Chancery. This instructed the Sheriff of the county concerned to empanel a jury whose responsibility it was to discover what lands the deceased possessed at the time of his death, and to obtain proof from the heir as to his right to inherit. This jury was made up of local trades/professional men who knew the families of the locality. The jury returned or 'retoured' their verdict to Chancery who then issued the heir with his 'retour' and the heir could then take possession of his inheritance.

As with sasines, services of heirs are worth searching as they give information on the kinship of the heir to the previous holder, together with places and a date of death. It is worth remembering that sometimes heirs were not served heir to the property for several years after the death of the owner, particularly if they had emigrated. Do not give up the search too soon!

Services of heirs up to 1699 have been indexed and published under the title *Inquisitionum ad Capellam Domini Regis Retornatarum Abbreviatio*, known simply as 'Retours', and are mostly in Latin.

From 1700 onwards, there are decennial indexes, which give kinship and most of the information in the original document, albeit in a shortened form. These ten-yearly abridgements continued from 1700 to 1860, after which time they were produced annually. More detail about these records is contained in Gerald Hamilton-Edwards's *In Search of Scottish Ancestry*, D. J. Steel's *Sources of Scottish Genealogy and Family History*, and the National Archives of Scotland's *Tracing Your Scottish Ancestors* (see Appendix IV: Book list).

Note: The Scottish Genealogy Society have these Retours published (and for sale) on two CD-ROMs (1544–1699, and 1700–1859).

Register of the Great Seal and Signatures

If your ancestor was fortunate to own land, then another source, other than Sasines, is the *Register of the Great Seal*. This was both a record of grants by the Sovereign, and recognition of ownership by the Sovereign.

The Charters issued under the Great Seal date from 1314 and are published up to 1668 in eleven volumes of the *Register of the Great Seal of Scotland* (or *Registrum Magni Sigilli Regnum Scotorum*), found on the open shelves in the

Historical Search Room. They will also be found in most large libraries. Each volume is indexed, and they are in Latin until 1651.

From 1668 to 1919 there is a 4-volume index in both the NAS and West Register House. Order up with the call number C2 and volume number. The actual registers, handwritten in Latin, can only be read at West Register House.

These charters often refer back to earlier charters and immediate past ancestors.

'Signatures' are warrants, or drafts written in English of those charters in the Great Seal Register, which are in Latin. They date from 1607 to 1847, and there is a 2-volume index. SIG.1 are bundles of papers in boxes, whilst SIG.2 are in volumes. These Signature documents are out-housed on the west edge of Edinburgh and it takes twenty-four hours for them to be made available for reading.

Beware! Not all Great Seal Charters have Signature documents.

Register of Tailzies

In the services of heirs, and the sasines, you may have found that an inheritance was as 'heir of taillie'. This is the Scots form of 'entail', spelt 'tailzie' but pronounced 'taillie'.

An Act of the Scottish Parliament in 1685 allowed a landowner to decide who would succeed to his heritable estate for future generations, by a deed of tailzie which had to be recorded in the Register of Tailzies (NAS, RT.1).

The naming of a series of substitutes, in the event of one generation failing through lack of male heirs, can include much detailed family information, the normal stipulation being that the males who married the succeeding female had to take her maiden surname and designation, to continue the patrinominal name.

There is an index for 1688 (when the register starts) to 1833. For more detailed information refer to the National Archives of Scotland's book *Tracing Your Scottish Ancestors* (Appendix IV: Book list).

Beware! Some Deeds of Tailzie are not registered until long after they were made. For example, Sir Alexander Gilmour, Baronet of Craigmillar, died in 1732 but had drawn up a Deed of Tailzie in 1683 which was not registered until eighty-seven years later, in 1770!

4
Other Sources

Details of the various taxes which have been imposed over the years may be found among the Exchequer Records (Reference E) in the National Archives of Scotland.

Hearth Tax Records (Ref. E69 NAS)

In 1690 Parliament imposed a tax of 14s. on every hearth in each dwelling within the kingdom for one year, the proceeds to be applied towards paying off the sums advanced by the shires and burghs and the arrears of the army. The tax was payable by Candlemas (2 February) 1691 by the inhabitants of all houses having hearths; hospitals and poor persons living on the charity of the parish were exempted. The records, arranged by shires, comprise:

1. lists of hearths on which tax was collected, with lists of deficients (hearth books)
2. accounts of hearth money collected, which are in the same form but record the actual sum paid
3. reports of the new surveys made in 1692 (Aberdeenshire only)
4. general accounts, depositions of surveyors, and miscellaneous papers.

Poll Tax Records (Ref. E70 NAS)

Poll Tax (poll money) was first imposed by Parliament in 1693, for paying debts due to the country, and the arrears of the army from 1 November 1689 to 1 February 1691. It was to be levied at the rate of 6s. per capita and upwards according to a scale based on rank and means, poor persons living on charity and children being exempt. The Commissioners of Assessment for the shires and the magistrates of burghs were to make up lists of pollable persons, and payment was to be made at or before Martinmas (11 November) 1694. In 1695, a second Poll Tax was imposed for providing ships of war and maintaining seamen. Two Poll Taxes were imposed in 1698 for clearing the arrears due to land and sea officers, and seamen.

These poll books and lists are arranged by shires or counties. The information they contain varies greatly from parish to parish within a county, but the best of them give a record of everybody liable to be taxed over the age of 16, and in some cases, of children under the age of 16. They do not, however, contain the names of the poor as these are shown in separate lists, and, as you know, may also be listed in OPRs and Kirk Session Records.

Note: A number of poll tax records have been published for individual parishes, by local history groups and local family history societies. At present Aberdeenshire is well served in this respect.

Assessed Taxes (Ref. E326 SRO)

By the Act 20 Geo. II, cap. 3 (1747) under which assessed taxes were first levied in Scotland, duplicates of all assessments (otherwise called surveys) were ordered to be transmitted to the Office of the King's Remembrancer. These duplicate schedules furnished the necessary checks and charges upon the Receivers- General of the respective duties, as well as upon the collectors in the several counties and burghs. It was also upon them that all prosecutions on account of the duties were founded. On receiving the schedules the King's Remembrancer was required to examine them to see that the assessments or charges were made in strict conformity with the Acts of Parliament imposing the duties. The extant schedules for the various taxes are arranged in the following sections:

1. Window Tax (duties on houses and windows), 1748–98
2. Commutation Tax (additional duties on houses and windows), 1784–98
3. Inhabited House Tax, 1778–98
4. Shop Tax (duties on retail shops), 1785–9
5. Servants Tax (duties on male servants), 1777–98
6. Female Servants Tax, 1785–92
7. Cart Tax (duties on carts and waggons), 1785–92
8. Wheel Carriage Tax (duties on carriages with two wheels and four wheels), 1785–98
9. Horse Tax (duties on carriage and saddle horses), 1797–8
10. Farm Horse Tax (duties on workhorses and mules), 1797–8
11. Dog Tax, 1797–8
12. Clock and Watch Tax, 1797–8
13. Aid and Contribution Tax, 1798–9
14. Income Tax 1799–1802.

Following the Consolidating Acts (38 Geo. Ill, cap. 40 and 41), the duties on windows, inhabited houses, male servants, carts, carriages and dogs were incorporated in comprehensive assessed taxes schedules. Income tax, and later property tax, remained on separate schedules. No property tax schedules have been preserved, and there are comprehensive assessed taxes schedules for 1798–9 only. There are, however, assessed taxes and property tax schedules for Midlothian, 1799–1812 (E327 NAS).

The following records are to be found in the NAS in Princes Street, or West Register House in Charlotte Square, Edinburgh:

Valuation Rolls (Ref. VR NAS)

These rolls are available for every year since 1855 to 31 March 1989, and cover every piece of property in Scotland. They show name, and the value of the property, the name of the owner, and the name of the tenant and occupier (only the head of the household is named). From 1 April 1989 Valuation Rolls contain only non-domestic properties. It is necessary to know the name of the county or the burgh, and as some of the earlier rolls are not indexed, a search may take some time.

On 1 April 1989 a Community Charge (Poll Tax) was introduced in Scotland, but it proved to be unpopular and impossible to impose. It was followed on 1 April 1994 by a Council Tax for which there is a list of properties and their valuation bands (A–H) but with no mention of people by name. This loss of more detailed information in the registers is a sorry state of affairs.

Electoral Registers (Voters Rolls) (Ref. NLS, ECL & NAS)

Copies of these registers are held in the National Library of Scotland (NLS) and in the Edinburgh Central Library (ECL), both situated on George IV Bridge, Edinburgh. The NLS holdings are from 1946/7 to date, and also for Edinburgh 1856–1914/15 (incomplete). The ECL holdings (only concerning Edinburgh) are: 1832–1914 (incomplete), and 1924 to date (wanting 1933–55.)

By statute, the Electoral Registration Officer is obliged to preserve the Voters Rolls for a period of two years only. All copies sent to the NLS and EPL are kept indefinitely.

From 1918, under the Representation of the Peoples Act, only men who had attained the age of 21 years, and women who had attained the age of 30 years were allowed to vote in national elections. In 1928 the voting age for women was lowered to 21 years. The latest Representation of the Peoples Act, in 1969, allowed both men and women to vote in local and national elections once they had attained the age of 18 years. Prior to 1918, only men who were proprietors or tenants of lands, houses and so on had the right to vote. Women who were either married but were not living with their husbands, or were unmarried (provided they too were proprietors or tenants and so on), had the right to vote, but only for burgh and county councillors. Such records may be found in the NAS among Burgh Records (Ref NAS B) and Sheriff Court Records (Ref. NAS SC).

If you are searching the current Voters Rolls in the NLS you must know the name of the place and its ward number. Having found the ward number from the street index, find the box file containing this number. The street index and the box files are kept on the open shelves to which you will be directed.

Electoral Registers are pages stapled together recording the name of the road or street in alphabetical order. Under each street name is the surname, first name and initials of the voter, followed by the house number. By looking at the house number you can ascertain how many people aged 18 years and over were living in that household on the specified qualifying date. For example my own entry shows:

Register of Electors
Qualifying Date: 10 October 1993
In Force: 16 February 1994 to 15 February 1995
Parliamentary Constituency: Edinburgh East
Regional Electoral Division: No. 29 Portobello/Milton
City of Edinburgh District Ward: No. 45 Portobello

Brunstane Road
CORY   Kathleen B.   4

Also in Brunstane Road is the Conkerton family.
CORKERTON   David J. P.   11
CORKERTON   Selina J.   11
CORKERTON   18/5/94 Torquil A.G.   11

From these entries you can see that there is only one person over the age of 18 living at No. 4, but at No. 11 there are two people over the age of 18, and one who would attain the age of 18 on 18 May 1994.

Beware! There may be other residents: who had not attained the age of 18 years; who had not registered their right to vote or; who were visitors not legally entitled to vote. Also as no kinship is given, do not jump to conclusions or you may find that you have acted like a cuckoo and put someone in the wrong nest!

Customs and Excise (Ref. E. WRH)

The NAS holds a list of excise officers taken from the salary books 1707–1830. These contain name, the various appointments throughout his career, name of wife (or widow), names of children, and dates of births, marriages and deaths. This list of excise officers is a modern compilation and is available only on microfilm (2 reels)(Ref: RH.4/6).

Records of the Board of Customs & Excise (Ref. CE 1–61 NAS)

Deposited in the NAS in 1958, the records contained in this inventory should be ordered by entering on a production slip the class reference and piece number only. The class references are shown at the top left-hand corner of each page. The piece numbers are shown in the left-hand margin.

The Scottish Board of Customs Minute Book (closed for seventy-five years) was established following on the Act of Union of 1707. In 1722 a statute (9 Geo. I C. 21) authorised the creation of a single Board of Customs for Great Britain, and in the following year a unified board was established by patent. However, certain of the commissioners named in this unified board were deputed to reside in Edinburgh for the transaction of business. In 1742 an independent

Scottish Board of Customs was again appointed in terms of a new patent and was continued until the year 1823, when a unified board for the United Kingdom was established by statute (4 Geo. IV C. 23). Certain powers were delegated to a subordinate board in Scotland. This subordinate board ceased to operate with effect from 5 July 1829 and was formally abolished in 1833 (3 & 4 Will. IV C. 511). Until 1 May 1798 the Commissioners of Customs also controlled the collection of salt duties.

Muster Rolls (Ref. E 100 NAS) and Militia

Before the Union of the Parliaments of Scotland and England in 1707, Scotland had only a very small standing army, and landowners were compelled to provide forces according to their financial means. The best source of information containing names is to be found in the Muster Rolls for 1641–1707. These Muster Rolls are arranged by regiment, and list all the officers and men at a certain place and date. Unless you know which regiment your ancestor was in, you are in for a hard time.

Some Muster Rolls are to be found in GD (Gifts and Deposits) collections where a member of that family had been granted a commission to be a colonel. See C. Dalton's *The Scots Army: 1661–88* (republished 1989, Greenhill Books).

Militia records name the young men who were balloted to serve in the militia. The records which survive are usually to be found in the Sheriff Court (SC) or County Council (CO) records and will be catalogued under 'Lieutenancy' and/or 'Militia' or 'Miscellaneous'. See also Jeremy Gibson in Appendix IV: Book list.

For more detailed information concerning Scottish army records, I suggest you read the late Gerald Hamilton-Edwards' book *In Search of Army Ancestry*, and Dr Diana M. Henderson's book *The Scottish Regiments* (see Appendix IV: Book list).

Chelsea Pensioners (National Archives (England) Kew)

You may find in a census return, in the column for occupation, the words Chelsea P, or Chelsea Out P. This stands for Chelsea pensioner or Chelsea out-pensioner. Chelsea Hospital in London was founded by King Charles II in 1682, and still gives shelter (in-pensioners) and pensions to certain ex-service men. Those pensioners who continue to live at home are known as out-pensioners.

The records for Chelsea pensioners are held in the National Archives (E), at Kew, Surrey, and if a member of your family was a pensioner it is well worth a visit to search these records. If you do not know the name of the regiment, then it is a long search, but there are some short cuts if you know where the pensioner died, and where he was likely to have been paid his pension.

For example, I was searching for a John Williamson, found in the 1851 census for Stromness, County Orkney, aged 70, a widower, 'Chelsea Out-

P.' and born in Antrim, Ireland. He had died prior to statutory registration in 1855.

In the NA(E) at Kew, I searched WO 22, noted all the Pension Returns Offices in Scotland, and chose the two most likely to have handled the returns for Orkney. These were Aberdeen and Thurso. I knew John Williamson was alive in 1851, and probably deceased by 1855, so I started searching the records in 1851, and found his name in the Thurso Pension Returns for 1851.

WO 22/139. Thurso Pension Returns. (including Kirkwall & Lerwick)

Returns of Charges	Pension ceased by death
Regt	9th Veterans
Rate of Pension	-/9d
Date of Admission to Out-Pension	30th Aug 1814
Rank	Drumr (Drummer)
Name	John Williamson
	Permanent Pension
Date of Decease	20th August 1851
Age at Decease	70

Knowing now that John Williamson had been a drummer in the 9th Veterans, I turned to WO97/1135: 9th Battalion, Veterans 1760–1854, Soldiers' Documents, and found out more about him. Without knowing with which regiment he had served, the search for the Soldiers' Documents would have taken days!

Pension returns also include transfers from one place to another, so if a pensioner moved around it should be possible to follow his tracks. The Payment Offices listed for Scotland are: Aberdeen, Ayr, Dundee, Edinburgh, Glasgow, Inverness, Paisley, Perth, Stirling and Thurso.

Burgh Records (Ref. B. NAS)

The records of the burghs and the royal burghs of Scotland are another useful source for genealogists. These include Council Minutes, Craft Records, Burgess Rolls, Apprentice Rolls, and the royal burghs have their own Land Registers from the seventeenth century. Extracts from the early records have been printed by the Scottish Burgh Record Society, and some indexes have been printed by the Scottish Record Society.

Copies of printed Burgh Records and indexes are also held by the Scottish section of the Edinburgh Central Library on George IV Bridge, and the Mitchell Library in Glasgow, as well as other large libraries.

Burgess and Guild Records (NRH and NAS)

A burgess was originally an inhabitant of a burgh who held a piece of land there from the Crown, or other superior. In later years, however, a burgess was a merchant or a craftsman who was influential in burgh affairs. The

Scottish Record Society has published a number of Burgess and Guild Rolls which are available in most large libraries. As a man could become a burgess or a guild brother through marriage or through his own family, these lists are of great value and interest.

Lists of burgesses and guild-brethren have been published for Glasgow (1573–1750; 1751–1846), Edinburgh (1406–1700; 1701–60; 1761–1841), Dumbarton (1600–1846), Canongate (1622–1733), Inveraray (1665–1963).

There are also privately published lists for Aberdeen (1600–1700), Banff (1549–1892), St Andrews (1700–55), Stirling (1600–1902). Contact the Scottish Genealogy Society for lists continually being produced.

Recently published is that for Ayr (1647–1846) by the Ayrshire Archaeological and Natural History Society.

Burgess Tickets from 1584 (Ref. RH10 NAS)

These records are arranged alphabetically by place, and then chronologically; they contain useful genealogical material, for example, RH10/501: *John Lamb, (in right of spouse Elspeth Thomesoune, daughter of John T. Merchant). 1 July 1646.*

Apprentice Records (NAS, NA(E) and The Society of Genealogists)

The Scottish Record Society has published lists of apprentices, and some Apprentice Rolls are to be found in burgh records. Other sources are The Society of Genealogists (London) and the National Archives (England), Kew, where you will find an index of masters' and apprentices' names. These include Scottish masters and apprentices (see Appendix II for list of addresses).

The Scottish Record Society lists are for Edinburgh (1583–1666; 1666–1700; 1701–55; 1756–1800). Other lists privately printed are for Aberdeen (1622–99; 1700–50) and Fife. Contact the Scottish Genealogy Society for lists continually being produced.

Gifts and Deposits (Ref, GD NAS)

'GDs' are the deposited collections of private papers; they are mostly family muniments, but also include papers from business firms and lawyers' offices. Where the collection belongs to an important landed family it will contain documents such as land titles, legal writs, marriage contracts and wills, correspondence and estate papers. Estate papers are of particular importance to the genealogist, for, while it may be possible to find the owner of lands in the Register of Sasines, tenants are more difficult to trace.

The two invaluable sources here are leases and rent rolls (tacks), whereby the owner granted certain parts of his lands to the tenant for a specified rent over a certain time, often a period of nineteen years. If you are searching here it is necessary to know in which part of the country your ancestor lived, or, at least, at county level to whom the lands belonged, and where the family papers are. See also Loretta R. Timperly's *A Dictionary of Landownership in Scotland, circa 1770* (1976), Scottish Record Society).

To guide you through the maze of papers, the NAS has produced a list of topics, mainly for GDs, and a summary catalogue which, in turn, will lead you to the papers concerned. I have listed only those topics which I think will be of some use to a genealogist; when you see the entire list you may find other topics of interest: Africa, South and South-East Asia, Australia, Brewing and Distilling, Business Archives, Canada, Emigration, France, Germany, Highlands and Islands, Jacobites, Mexico, Military Affairs, Naval Mercantile, Netherlands, New Zealand, Orkney and Shetland, Russia, Schools, Skye, South America, Sweden, USA, West Indies. Much of the above material consists of letters which will give you background information, but, of course, you will find names as well. There is an index to the summary catalogue, but the list is only the tip of the iceberg, so do allow yourself plenty of time to search. The NAS is in the process of indexing GDs on computer. This index is very detailed and not difficult to use.

The Register of the Privy Council (NAS)

The Council was the chief administrative body of Scotland before the Union of 1707, and dealt with every topic. The Register, 1554–1691, is printed and indexed, and to be found on the open shelves in the Historical Search Room. The volumes are written in Old Scots, and require time and study if they are to be understood. But the reward is well worth the effort to gain an interesting insight into the lives of Scots at that period. It is also a source of names and relationships. (See 'The Plantation of Ulster' on page 84).

Also found in NLS, ECL (Scottish Room), the Mitchell Library, Glasgow, and other major libraries.

County Records (Ref. CO NAS)

There is a list of all the county records in the NAS, but many of these are now held only by the local authority. The poor relief records are mainly those of parochial boards and parish councils which are classed as county records. These records contain a great deal of personal information on families applying for relief, some of it extremely lurid! The NAS now holds only parish records for East Lothian, Midlothian and Wigtownshire, and these do not include many registers of the poor.

The Mitchell Library, Glasgow holds excellent poor records for Glasgow and Lanarkshire.

Forfeited Estates (Ref. E NAS)

The Forfeited Estate Papers are those papers which concerned the estates forfeited by Jacobites involved in the risings of 1715 and 1745. As a class they are part of the Exchequer records, that is, the records of financial administration, because the estates were in the charge of commissioners of the Exchequer.

Justiciary Court Records (Ref. JC WRH)

Details of criminal court cases are to be found in these records, including cases of transportation, and some of them make fascinating reading.

Court of Session Records (Ref. CS WRH)

The Court of Session is Scotland's supreme civil court, and the records of the civil cases which have come before the court over about four hundred years are massive – both volumes of acts and decrees and bundles of processes.

There is now a searcher's guide, *Court of Session Processes after 1660*, which is available on request from the supervisor in West Register House. This guide contains General Minute Books, Unextracted Processes (UPs) and Extracted Processes (EPs). A 'process' is the papers lodged in the course of an action which remain at the time of the transmission to the NAS. The difference between a UP and an EP is simply Extracted Processes are those where a decree of the Lords of Council and Session has had to be copied from the records of the action to act as a warrant to implement the terms of that decree. It does not mean that UPs are those where the actions were dropped or otherwise left unconcluded.

The Court of Session had sole jurisdiction in divorce actions in Scotland 1830–1984. Prior to 1830 the responsible court in such actions was the Commissary Court of Edinburgh, whose records are held in the NAS in Princes Street. However, between 1831 and 1835 some actions were still heard in the Commissary Court. Since May 1984 Sheriff Courts also have jurisdiction in divorce actions; their records will also come to the NAS, but usually not until twenty-five years have elapsed.

For actions from 1830 onwards you should consult the appropriate UP card index. All cards are filed alphabetically by *pursuer* only, *not the defender* and they show the names of the pursuer and the defender, the type of action (e.g. divorce) and the date of the summons. If you are uncertain about the date of divorce, there is a special series, *Register of Decrees in Consistorial Causes*, on an annual basis from 1971 (Ref. CS17/3). These registers are in the form of an index, being arranged alphabetically with full names and address of the parties, and one column contains the date when the decree of divorce was pronounced. Before 1971 you would have to check the General Minute Books (CS 17/1) for the date of decree.

From 1 May 1984 the General Register Office for Scotland receives all divorce decrees and maintains a centralised register which is indexed on computer of all divorces granted in Scotland (see Chapter 2).

The various civil jurisdictions exercised by the ecclesiastical courts prior to the Reformation included causes or actions relating to marriage, legitimacy and divorce, as well as executory. The Commissary Court of Edinburgh, instituted in 1563–4, acted as a general court for the whole country for such matters. Local commissary courts retained a more limited jurisdiction. In 1830 almost the whole of the old commissary jurisdiction was transferred to the Court of Session.

Chapter 5 of Professor Gordon Donaldson's *Scottish Church History*, published in 1985 by Scottish Academic Press, deals with church courts. The Scottish Record Society has published a useful index: *Consistorial Processes and Decrees, 1658–1800*, for the Commissariot of Edinburgh (1909). The following extracts are examples of the kind of information you could expect to find there:

1663. Process of Divorce – Jean Reid, now residenter in Edinburgh against William Paul, now keeper of the store in the Citydeal of Leith, her husband, married June 1650, within the Old Kirk of New Aberdeen.

1677. Process of Divorce – Catherine Sutherland, lawful daughter of Robert Sutherland, residing in Elgin, against Andrew Dunbar, son to Robert Dunbar, sometime in Peterhead, her spouse, married in December 1667 in the parish kirk of St Geull's Elgin.

1704. Process of Declarator of Illegitimacy, etc. – George Dundas of that ilk, against William Dundas, merchant in Edinburgh pretending to be son to Ralph Dundas, eldest son to Walter Dundas of that ilk, and his wife Elizabeth Sharp, sister to Houston Sharp, and claiming heir-male of the family of Dundas, complainer alleging said Ralph Dundas was impotent.

1751. Conjoined Processes of Declarator of Marriage – Thomas Gray, merchant in Edinburgh, against Mrs Jacobina Moir, daughter and only lawful child to the deceased Mr James Moir of Earnlaw, and her tutors and curators, et e contra alleged marriage 3 May 1751. Defender assoilzied from declarator of marriage and decree in her favour against said Thomas Gray, 6 May 1752. On 24 July the said Thomas Gray, Christina Duncan, mantua maker in Paterson's Court, Lawnmarket, James Syme, merchant Edinburgh, and Thomas Brown, alias William Jamieson, were convicted by the High Court of justiciary of the abduction of the said Jacobina Moir, and banished to His Majesty's plantation in America.

As you can see, the index itself gives a great deal of genealogical information.

Home and Health Records (Ref. HH WRH)

A detailed repertory (catalogue), and the HH records are held in West Register House, Charlotte Square, Edinburgh. These records contain, among other things, prison and police registers, criminal records and hospital registers; some dating from 1794. A copy of the summary catalogue is held in the NAS in Princes St, Edinburgh.

Doctors and Surgeons

Medical professionals practised after either being apprenticed or attending courses at a university. See under Apprentice Records and Universities. Many

Scots medical practioners in the seventeenth century attended universities on the Continent – such as Leyden and Paris, and also practised in London.

There are records at the Royal College of Physicians of Edinburgh, the Royal College of Surgeons of Edinburgh, the Royal College of Physicians and Surgeons of Glasgow, as well as the records of graduates of universities. See Appendix IV: Book list: Medical; and Appendix II: List of useful addresses.

General Medical Council: Scottish Branch Records (Ref. GMC WRH)

The Scottish branch office of the General Medical Council was established in 1858. It has been responsible for the registration of doctors qualifying at Scottish universities and at the Royal Colleges of Surgeons and Physicians, and it has maintained up-to-date records of doctors registered in Scotland, whether practising or not. The branch office was closed in January 1982, and its functions were transferred to the London office of the Council. These records, which are open to public access, are held in West Register House, Charlotte Square, Edinburgh.

Maps and Plans (NAS and WRH)

Thousands of plans and maps are held in the NAS and WRH. Some of these relate to the colonies, and show the early divisions of the country.

Universities (NRH and NAS and National Library of Scotland)

Lists of graduates have been printed for the older universities of St Andrews, Aberdeen, Glasgow, Edinburgh, Oxford and Cambridge. These books are available in most large libraries, in New Register House and the NAS, and in the universities' libraries.

Schools (NRH and NAS)

Most schools' records or lists of pupils, if they have survived the passage of time, are to be found in local archives. However, there are printed books for many of the fee-paying schools which contain names of pupils. They are to be found in most large libraries in Scotland, as well as in New Register House and in the NAS.

For schoolmasters you will have to search Burgh Council records, or heritors' (i.e. landowners') records in the different parishes (NAS: HR). Also, Presbytery Minute Books record confirmation of the appointment of schoolmasters.

The Society in Scotland for Propagating Christian Knowledge (SSPCK) was set up in 1709 and organised schools and masters in remote areas. After the 1872 Education (Scotland) Act there was no need to continue. See NAS reference GD.95. Also, for a collated list see A. S. Cowper's *SSPCK Schoolmasters: 1709–1872* (Scottish Record Society, N.S.20: 1997).

After 1872 records for school teachers will be found in County Council records.

Fasti Ecclesiae Scoticanae

If you have an ancestor who was a minister in the established Church of Scotland, you will find *Fasti Ecclesiae Scoticanae* an invaluable source of information. This book is usually known simply as *Fasti*. With additional addenda and corrigenda, it gives not only the succession of ministers from the middle sixteenth century to 1975, but records details of each minister's family, parentage and education. *Fasti* is indexed by the name of the congregation as well as by the name of the minister (see Appendix IV: Book list).

For Presbyterian ministers not in the established Church of Scotland there are the following printed sources which are also found in the book list:

History of the Congregations of the United Presbyterian Church 1733–1900 is a history of the congregations. It contains a certain amount of genealogical information about ministers, but it does not give names of wives or parents. It is indexed by the name of the congregation and the name of the minister.

The Fasti of the United Free Church of Scotland 1900–29 is set out in the same fashion as *Fasti Ecclesiae Scoticanae,* and contains similar information.

Jewish Records

Searching for births, marriages and deaths from 1855, of course, presents no problems. However, searching records earlier than that date may be more difficult. The early Jewish community in Scotland consisted mainly of immigrants from Eastern Europe who only came in any number in the middle 1800s; consequently, census returns are invaluable in helping to discover places of birth.

The National Archives (England) in Kew, Surrey, holds naturalisation papers and records for change of name for the whole of Great Britain, and there you may find your family. The information contained in these records should tell you the place of birth of your ancestor and family details at the time of his or her naturalisation.

The Scottish Jewish Archives Centre in Glasgow (see Appendix II for address) has collected material of use to the genealogist. The two main newspapers are the *Jewish Echo* which has been the paper of Scottish Jewry since 1928, and the *Jewish Chronicle,* which is the national Jewish newspaper, published in London since 1841. The *Jewish Chronicle* has always covered Scotland, and is useful for providing information prior to 1928. These newspapers record events such as births, bar mitzvahs, engagements, marriages and deaths, as well as advertisements and social comment.

Miscellaneous Manuscript Records (Ref. NRH. MS)

These records consist mainly of duplicate or scroll copies of Old Parochial Registers, fragments of other Kirk Session records and private records of births, and so on, kept by individual ministers. Also included are a few Registers of Secession, and other churches, placed in the Registrar General's custody for preservation. An index of places covered is given at the end of the inventory. I have listed here a few items which would be of use to a genealogist:

'Blotter Marriages': Affidavits that parties desiring proclamation have no legal impediment to marriage. The prospective bridegroom is usually one of the signatories. ('Blotter': a term applied in counting houses to a wastebook. A rough draft of a letter. *Oxford English Dictionary).*

Glasgow 'Blotter' Marriage Registers (Ref. MR2/17–25 NRH): These registers cover the years 1815–54.

Barony Parish 'Blotter' Marriage Registers (Ref. MR3/1–100 NRH): These registers cover the years 1829–54.

Edinburgh 'Blotter' Notebooks of Births/Baptisms and Affidavits prior to Proclamation of Marriage. The entries are transcribed into two separate series of scroll registers of baptisms and marriages as seen here:

Edinburgh Scroll Registers of Births/Baptisms (Ref. MR4/23–42 NRH): These registers cover the years 1724–1850, and include marriages for the years 1724-26.

Edinburgh 'Blotter' Marriages (Ref. MR4/43–69 NRH): This series apparently runs parallel with volumes MR4/1 to MR4/22. These registers cover the years 1780–1854.

St Cuthbert's Parish, Edinburgh (Ref. MR5/1–11 NRH): Scroll registers of births/baptisms. These registers cover the years 1743-1855, and include marriages for the years 1744-55 and 1768-72.

St Cuthbert's Scroll Proclamations of Marriage (Ref. MR5/12–18 NRH): These registers cover the years 1818-55.

Canongate Parish, Edinburgh (Ref. MR6/1–6 NRH): Kirk Session Treasurer's Accounts 1689–93. Including baptisms, marriage and mortcloth dues (Ref. MR6/2 NRH): A private register of marriage kept by the Revd William Dun, minister of New Street Chapel-of-Ease, Canongate, 1814–22 (Ref. MR6/4).

Jenat Thomson's Midwife Register of Births (Ref. MT/1–4 NRH): Kilmarnock 1777–1829.

Lamberton Toll Marriages 1833–49 (Ref. MR/101).

W.S. (Writers to the Signet)

Writers to the Signet are solicitors. Not all solicitors are Writers to the Signet. *The Register of the Society of Writers to the Signet* (1983) has superseded previous lists and provides details of all members from the fifteenth century to the 1980s. This list is arranged alphabetically. It records the member's date of birth, father's name, date of marriage and name of spouse; also to whom the member was apprenticed. A copy of this register is available in the Historical Search Room in the NAS, in NRH and in most large libraries.

Members of the Society of Advocates in Aberdeen are also solicitors, not barristers. A list of members, 1549–1911, giving the same sort of information, is found in *History of the Society of Advocates in Aberdeen* by John H. Henderson (New Spalding Club, 1912). A supplement, 1912–38, was published in 1939. This should be available in NLS, and other large libraries.

The Faculty of Advocates

In Scotland, an advocate is the equivalent of a barrister, and the Faculty of Advocates is the Scottish Bar. The Lord Advocate is the principal law officer of the Crown in Scotland. A very useful book was edited by Sir Francis J. Grant which contains names, with genealogical notes (see *The Faculty of Advocates in Scotland: 1532–1943* (Scottish Record Society, 1944) in Appendix IV: Book list).

Chartered Accountants

Dr Stephen P. Walker has written *The Society of Accountants in Edinburgh 1854–1914.* This book contains information of genealogical interest, and Dr Walker has donated a copy to the Scottish Genealogy Society's library (see Appendix IV: book list).

In NRH there is a *List of Deceased Accountants* by Richard Brown (1905)which covers Edinburgh, Glasgow and the rest of Scotland.

Company Records

If you want to find out about business records, then a visit to the Registrar of Companies, Companies House Public Search & Incorporation, 37 Castle Terrace, Edinburgh EH 1 2EB will be necessary. This office is open from 9.00 a.m. till 5.00 p.m., Monday–Friday and you will be able to inspect company records in the search rooms. For £3 you can buy a microfiche copy of the records you need, and there you can read the records and make photocopies for 10p per page. There is a postal service for £5.50 with an additional cost for a search. I suggest that you check this when you write (see Appendix II for address).

Companies House holds the records of over 50,000 companies with a registered address in Scotland. The range of documents includes annual returns, accounts, memoranda of association, articles of association, charges registers, liquidators/receivers statements of account and appointments of liquidators. You will find that most annual returns contain a list of shareholders. Companies House also holds some dissolved companies' papers.

West Register House, Charlotte Square, Edinburgh also holds some records of dissolved companies and railway companies in Scotland. Extensive shipbuilding and engineering records are held by the Glasgow City Archives in Glasgow (see Appendix II for address).

Newspapers

I have never found as much information in newspapers as I had hoped for. If the person was well-known in the locality, then most probably there will be an obituary, but if not, then it is unlikely that their death entry will appear in the earlier papers. However, as years went by it became the practice of families to insert death notices listing all the names of those who mourned the loss – often in verse, or worse! It may be worth searching through newspapers if you know the date and place of a death, to see if a member of the family, unknown to you, was mentioned. In local papers you may find articles about families who emigrated, or on occasion, news from such a family.

Newspapers provide interesting information on contemporary life and conditions.

Alice Mackenzie has compiled a list of Scottish newspapers with dates and places of availability (see Appendix IV: Book list).

Shipping Lists (GDs. NAS)

Recently there have been several books published giving lists of names of persons who emigrated to America and Canada (see book list in Appendix IV), though, naturally, they cannot contain the names of everybody who left Scotland. See 'Emigrants to North America' on page 85.

One of the great drawbacks to searching in this area is the lack of shipping lists. These lists were usually kept at the port of arrival, so very little survived in Scotland. There are no lists of emigrants or shipping lists held in the NAS; in fact, a comprehensive record of shipping lists is not extant until the very end of the nineteenth century, when the Board of Trade in London began to keep them.

However, there are other avenues of approach which can be tried. For those who wished to emigrate but did not have the means to purchase a passage, there was the indenture, whereby the emigrant bound himself to service in return for a passage. It is difficult to search in this area unless it is known by whom the servant was employed. These papers may be found in GDs which are in process of being computer indexed. If you have the time to search diligently through the GDs, you should find enough information in the index to enable you to choose which papers to order. For example:

GD 17013339. Inventory of Campbell of Barcaldine Muniments (3 Vols)
1737. Indenture between John McLeod, indweller in Edinburgh, and William Campbell, son of deceased Hugh Campbell, tenant in Argyllshire, for 4 years from said William's arrival in Carolina.

The actual document recorded that William had no parents alive and was aged 16.

EMIGRANTS

It is well known that many of the Scottish emigrants to America came by way of Ireland, which is not surprising, considering how close the south-west of Scotland and the east coast of Ireland are. However, in the late fifteenth and early sixteenth centuries, the kind of people who went to Ireland were unlikely to figure prominently in the records. In many cases they were disaffected to the central government, particularly in the border region of Scotland; others were mercenary soldiers, also unlikely to appear in the records.

Information concerning Scots who emigrated from Ireland is often found in unexpected places, for example, in a petition to the General Assembly of the Church of Scotland (Ref. CH1) where Irish people of Scots descent living in Pennsylvania wrote to the General Assembly, in 1706, requesting a minister (Illustrations: Fig. 9).

It is not at all easy to trace names of people who left Scotland for Ireland; it is perhaps easier to try to trace from Irish records the names of Scots who arrived there. (See Appendix IV for book list and II for addresses.)

The Plantation of Ulster

In the introduction to volumes VIII (pp. lxxii–xciv) and IX (p.lxxix) of the printed Register of the Privy Council there is a wealth of interesting information concerning King James VI's scheme for the Plantation of Ulster.

After the suppression of the O'Dogherty Rebellion in 1608, came King James's scheme for the Plantation of Ulster in 1609. There was a great deal of forfeited Ulster land at the King's disposal, so it was decided that 'there was to be no general dispossession of the native occupants of the Ulster lands; but there was to be introduced among them a sufficient number of Protestant colonists from the main island to temper and overawe the native Irish material and constitute a Protestant core of the Ulster population for the future'.

There follows a summary of the scheme, describing the location and size of the estates to be parcelled out to the first seventy-seven applicants. These are listed alphabetically with their designations, the names of their sureties and the quantities of land for which they had applied. However, too many people applied for too small parcels of land for the scheme to be workable, so proceedings were halted until the autumn of 1610, by which time the original list had been superseded by careful selection and new competition. This left only a proportion of the seventy-seven who had first applied. A new survey of the forfeited lands was found to be necessary, and in 1610 the Scottish part of the business of the Ulster Plantation was withdrawn from the Scottish Privy Council altogether, and taken into the hands of King James himself and his English Council in London. Thereafter the allotments of Scottish shares as well as English shares and shares reserved for the native Irish, were made under the Great Seal of England.

While the 1609 probationary list consisted of seventy-seven persons, the 1611 list consisted of only fifty-nine persons, in which only eighteen of the original list appear. These lists, to be found in volume IX (pp. lxxx and lxxxi), are arranged with names and designations and show to which county in Ireland each person went.

The Plantation of Ulster Papers (Ref. NAS RH15/91/33)

These are papers relating to the Plantation of Ulster (1611–17), and are listed as miscellaneous papers, but contain the names of only six people.

If you are trying to find an early ancestor who may have been part of the Plantation of Ulster, you have a great deal of research to undertake! It is important to remember that not all applicants of the first list (1609) were accepted, and that for later information (after 1610) you may have to search in England. But before you do, I suggest you read the introduction to volumes VIII and IX of the *Register of the Privy Council* in the NAS in Edinburgh, and other large libraries.

The Highland Emigration Society and the Board of Relief of 'Highland Destitution' (WRH)

These are important files in connection with emigration, and are held in West Register House, Charlotte Square, Edinburgh.

Lists of Emigrants to Australia from the Highlands of Scotland (NAS and WRH)

These records of persons who were assisted by the Highland and Island Emigration Society (1852–7), are held in the NAS in Princes Street, Edinburgh as well as in West Register House in Charlotte Square, Edinburgh. They give names of people, and the ships on which they sailed (Ref HD21/53). Although this HD record is held in the NAS, all the other records with this reference, as well as HH and BT references, are held in West Register House, Charlotte Square.

The Board of Relief of Highland Destitution dealt with emigration to America, Upper Canada and Australia (Ref. HD WRH). Similar types of records are those of the Board of Trade, wherein are recorded limited companies formed to carry out mining and other activities in the colonies (Ref. BT WRH).

American Loyalists (Ref. T50, T79, held in NA(E) Kew)

In the NA(E) Treasury Papers there are documents (1780–1835) relating to American Loyalists who were eligible for pensions, and minute books of the American Loyalists' Claim Commission (1777–1812), including an index of claimants.

Among the Treasury Papers in the NA(E) at Kew are four volumes (T 47/9–12) which give details of emigrants going from England, Wales and Scotland (Illustrations: Fig. 10). Details of these sources are to be found in A. Bevan's *Searching your Ancestors in the PRO* (see Appendix IV: Book list).

Finally, one last place to try is the Bureau of Emigration at Merseyside Maritime Museum, Liverpool, England. So many Scots sailed from Liverpool.

Emigrants to North America

There are now many books of lists of emigrants to America and Canada. These are too numerous to list here, but they should be found in large libraries. Most of them are held in the NAS, the NLS, the Scottish Library (Edinburgh Central Library) and the Mitchell Library, Glasgow.

The Genealogical Publishing Co., Baltimore, has published books by David Dobson, Michael Tepper, Peter Wilson Coldham and Robert Barnes. Carl Boyer 3rd has published a series of four books of *Ship Passenger Lists*. Filby and Meyer published in three volumes in 1981 *Passenger and Immigration Lists Index*. These were followed by four Supplements 1982–85, and then annual Supplements 1986–93. P.W. Filby compiled *American & British Genealogy & Heraldry: a selected list of books*. (New England Historic and Genealogical Society, Boston 1983). From this you can compile your own list of sources for Loyalists who went to Canada from the American Colonies immediately after 1783.

All these books list names and places of origin, ports of arrival, sometimes final destination, and dates. They also give sources of where the information was originally found.

Beware! As with all family history searching, those original sources should be read if possible. I once found someone's supposed ancestor in one of the lists of those transported to one of the American colonies. On searching the original sources referred to, I found the sentence for him to be so transported, but reading following entries I found that he had been reprieved and *not* transported – only being forbidden to return to his home parish.

Another useful source, probably now difficult to access, is *Lists of American Documents* (1976). This incorporates all known documents accessioned and catalogued up to 31 December 1975 by the then Scottish Record Office. The list is a calendar divided into four sections, that is: Gifts and Deposits; Maps, Plans and Charts; Various Classes; and Photocopies and Microfilms. The first section is the largest, and there is also an Appendix for archives surveyed by the National Register of Archives (Scotland).

National Register of Archives (Scotland) (NRA(S))

This, started in 1946, is a survey describing the papers held by private individuals and families, landed estates, clubs and societies, businesses and law firms. Around 3,500 surveys have been placed on the Register.

The Register is available in the Historic Search Room, NAS, the NLS, and the National Archives in England (formerly the Historic Manuscripts Commission).

Enquiries about individual collections are made to the Secretary, NRA(S), West Register House, Charlotte Square, Edinburgh. It can take up to three months for permission to come through to view these private archives. Owners may not grant such permission.

Irregular Marriages

These marriages were 'irregular' in that the Established Church disapproved of them. A valid marriage in Scotland was effected by a simple verbal declaration by each of the two parties before witnesses. Many of these occurred in the eighteenth and nineteenth centuries.

Various places on the Scottish–English border became 'centres' for irregular marriages. Most such marriages were usually of non-local couples, and some were even supervised by parish ministers, much to the dismay of the Presbytery. The most 'notorious' centre was Gretna, just within Scotland, in Dumfriesshire.

Arthur Brack has compiled three lists, each with a valuable Introduction. These are: *Irregular Border Marriages: volume I; The Registers of Henry Collins: Marriages at Lamberton Toll; 1833–49* (1995, Northumberland & Durham FHS). The original registers are in New Register House – see page 81 of this book; *Irregular Marriages: Annan, Dumfriesshire: 1797–1854* (1997, Dumfries & Galloway FHS); and *Irregular Marriages: Portpatrick, Wigtownshire: 1759–1826* (1997, Dumfries & Galloway FHS). The Gretna Green for Ireland.

The Scottish Record Society has also published two volumes for irregular marriages: *Marriages at Gretna Hall: 1829–April 30, 1855*. Edited by E.W.J. M'Connel (1949); and *Calendar of Irregular Marriages in the South Leith Kirk Session Records: 1697–1818*. Edited by J.S. Marshall (1968).

India (NLS)

Many Scots went to India and served with the Honourable East India Company (HEIC Service) as administrators, civil servants, or in a military capacity (army and navy, and medical), or served with trading companies. The sphere of activity extended to Penang, Singapore and Malacca.

The HEI Company ruled the subcontinent of India until 1858 when its powers were transferred to the British Crown. Administratively it was divided into the three Presidencies of Bengal, Madras and Bombay.

The records of service, of births, marriages and deaths, pensions and wills, and much more, up to 1947 (when India gained independence) are housed at the British Library, Oriental and India Office Collections. See Appendix II; Addresses; England.

A very useful publication for sources is that by Ian A. Baxter: *A Brief Guide to Biographical Sources*. See Appendix IV: Booklist; India.

In the National Library of Scotland, Edinburgh, there is a very good run of directories, which include births, marriages and deaths, and appointments and promotions. These are: *The East India Register and Directory*; two editions per year 1805–41. There is a gap 1814–21; continued as *The East India Register and Army List*; annually 1844–60; continued as *The Indian Army and Civil Service List*; annually 1861–76; continued as *The India List, Civil and Military*; annually 1877–95.

There are also volumes of *Indian Monumental Inscriptions*, which are indexed: *volume I: Bengal*. Editor C.R. Wilson (1896); *volume II: Punjab, North West Frontier Province, Kashmir and Afghanistan*. Part I: Inscriptions, compiled by M. Irving (1910), Part II: Biographical Notices (including genealogical information), compiled by G.W. De Rhe-Philipe (1912); *volume III: Madras,* compiled by J.J. Cotton (1905). (Includes biographical/genealogical note with entries of the inscriptions). Another compilation of monumental inscriptions is: *List of Burials at Madras: 1680–1900 (from the Register of S. Mary's Church, Fort St George)*, by Revd C.H. Malden, MA (4 vols: 1903–5).

Also in the NLS (and the Scottish Genealogy Society Library) there are lists of army and medical officers. See Appendix IV: Book list; India.

5
Names

SURNAMES

If you are interested in the origin of your surname, and if it is Scottish, I suggest you consult *The Surnames of Scotland* by Dr George F. Black (see Appendix IV: Book list). This is one of the 'bibles' for the genealogist; it is a most interesting, informative book, and is to be found in most large libraries. There, not only will you find the origin of the surname, but mention of some of the famous people who have borne the name. For example, the entry for the name Pinkerton starts by explaining that it originates from the name of the old barony near Dunbar, East Lothian; it refers to several people of the name between 1296 and 1826, and concludes by mentioning Allan Pinkerton (1819–84), the famous American detective, who was born in Glasgow. The entry also gives the various spellings of the name Pinkerton.

There are several names which change their form, and one on which it is worth commenting is the name Dalziel. It may be found as Dayell, Deyell or even as Yell. The letters 'z' and 'y' are used interchangeably in some cases. (See Appendix IV Book list for Grant Simpson's book on *Scottish Handwriting*.)

Names which are derived from occupations may be found in different versions. The name Dyer may be found as Litster and Baker as Baxter; particularly in the earlier Old Parish Registers – so, if your name is an occupational one, bear such variations in mind and do not pass them by as not being your name!

If you are searching for a name which has the prefix 'Mc' or 'Mac' note that these are indexed separately in the index for births, marriages and deaths; you may find the same family indexed under either spelling, so do not say that you *know* your family was always 'Mac' and not 'Mc' or *vice versa*. You may know now, but the registrar or your ancestor may not have been so positive.

Names like McLaughlin take a long time to search, as all the variations must be examined in the index if the name is not immediately found. For example, McLauchlin, McLauchline, McLaughlin, McLaughline, McLachlan, McLachlane, McLaghlan, McLaghlane, and of course, all those variations under 'Mac' as well as 'Mc'. And I am sure that somebody reading this paragraph has heard of yet another spelling of the name!

You most probably know that 'Mac' or 'Mc' means 'son of, but you may not have come across 'Nic' which is a shortened form of 'nighean mhic' and means 'daughter of Mac'. This is not in common usage but you may meet it in Old Parish Registers in Gaelic-speaking parts of Scotland. Black's

Surnames of Scotland gives a great deal of interesting information under 'Mac' and 'Nic'.

Irish names sometimes start with 'O' which is the Irish equivalent of 'Mac' or 'Mc', and I had one search where the family had come from Ireland to Scotland with the name O'Fie. This they changed to Mac 'O' Fie which eventually became MacFie. And while you search Mac/McFie, do not forget all the variations of Mac/McPhie!

Another Irish name which changes its spelling and form is Murphy: I have found this written as Murchie or Murckie in some records.

Old handwritten registers – both the written index, and the actual registers – may be difficult to read, which in turn may lead to names being missed when searching the index. Here are a few names which I found only after re-searching, and which may help you to overcome the problem: Boyd/Boyce/Bryce; Stratton/ Stratten/Straiton/Strachan; Stewart/Stuart; Thompson/Thomson; Robertson/Robinson/Robson etc.; Chalmers/Chambers; Jameson/Jamieson; and Rae, which having searched under Rae and Rea I finally found under the spelling Raw. But once I saw the death certificate, and the handwriting of the registrar, I had every sympathy with the indexer! Remember that 'Qu' = 'W', so in some Old Parish Registers you will find names such as White written as Quhytt.

In 1864 the most frequently occurring Scottish surnames were (first) Smith, (second) Macdonald, (third) Brown, (fourth) Robertson, (fifth) Thomson, (sixth) Stewart (from *Sixth Detailed Annual Report of the Registrar General of Births, Deaths and Marriages in Scotland* (1864)). There is no reason to doubt that this situation would remain constant for a long period of time.

Two surnames have more romance and infamy in their history than any others in Scotland: Ruthven (often pronounced Riven) comes from the old barony of that name in Angus. Because of the family's involvement against the young King James VI, the surname in 1600 was extinguished and abolished, and those with it had to take another surname (Acts of Parliament vol. IV, p. 213); this was rescinded in 1641. MacGregor is the most famous surname, for its bearers' lawless acts and depredations to be proscribed and abolished – by Act of Parliament in 1603. These bearers were obliged to take and use such surnames as Stewart, Campbell, Grant, Ramsay. This Act was finally rescinded in 1784 – about five generations later.

Patronymics

A patronymic is a surname formed by using the father's Christian name, and this you will find mainly when using Shetland records. For example, a John Donaldson's son would have Johnson as his surname, and if his Christian name were Peter, then in turn his son would have Peterson as his surname. Manson is an example of a surname derived from a Christian name, being a contraction of Magnusson, son of Magnus.

Beware! Donald and Daniel are interchangeable, so John Donaldson may have been the son of a Daniel!

Daughters' surnames tended to end with 'dr', not 'son', and were frequently contracted. For instance, you may find Ann Williamsdaughter written as Ann Wmsdr or WmDr.

Working on Shetland records I once came across a family similar to the following example:

Robert Laurenceson	Widower		aged	58
Mary Laurencedr	daur	unmar	aged	30
Ann Laurencedr	daur	unmar	aged	28
Laurence Laurenceson	son	unmar	aged	25

In due course the son, Laurence Laurenceson, married, and left home after which time he was known as Laurence Robertson. His children bore the surname of Robertson until they, in turn, left home, after which time they were known as Laurenceson. His unmarried sisters kept the surname of Laurencedr, and sometimes Laurenceson, until their father died, after which time they were known as Mary and Ann Robertson. I did not find them recorded as Robertsdr.

The problems with Highland and Island names are graphically presented by the late Professor Gordon Donaldson in his foreword to this book.

These difficulties are reinforced by Bill Lawson in his article 'Name-change and Patronymics' in the *Journal of the Highland Family History Society/ Comunn Sloinntearachd Na Gaidhealtachd* (vol.10, no. 4, August 1992).

To-Names

In the close-knit fishing communities of the north-east coast of Scotland there are not many different surnames, consequently the name of the fishing boat is tacked onto the surname and becomes an accepted part of the family's name. This is known as a to-name or a t-name. Even in the index to births, marriages, and deaths well after 1855, this practice is to be found. An entry, for example, 'Bain, David, Mackenzie', is also indexed as 'Mackenzie, Bain, David.' The name of the boat was printed in italics in the paper index and the practice continued in the computer index, however with many omissions. This usage of boats' names was to distinguish which David Bain was meant, although details on the certificate should leave the reader in no doubt. Female members of the family are also indexed under both the name of the family, and the name of the boat. Once I had to write to tell a man that his name was not MacKenzie but Smith, and that MacKenzie had been the name of his great-grandfather's fishing boat!

Note: Mrs Cory was working on checking the indexes, to correct and amplify the computer index, at the time of her death.

Another very interesting article is 'Tee-names and Surnames Associated with the Coastline of North-east Scotland' (*Aberdeen and North East Scotland Family History Society Journal*, no. 70, February 1999).

One last word of warning – some names starting with 'Mac' are not as Scottish as they may seem. Some time ago I was talking to an American who told me that her son had married a Vietnamese girl: understandably the couple decided to name the baby after both sets of grandparents. The two grandfathers' names were Karl and Vinh, which with a little imagination made up 'Calvin'. The two grandmothers' maiden surnames were Rea, and a name which phonetically sounded like 'Mac', so they named the baby Calvin MacRea. Fortunately the grandmother is a genealogist, so I expect that not only the names, but the interesting reason for their existence will be handed down in the family history. Otherwise future genealogists may spend fruitless hours searching Scottish records in vain!

Beware! Since the indexes for both statutory and OPR records have been put on computer, you will find only the name you have typed in, so remember to try the various spellings. It is worthwhile looking at the IGI where all name variations may be found.

CHRISTIAN NAMES AND FORENAMES

When it comes to Christian or forenames, people in most, if not all countries tend to use names which are, or have been in the family. Scotland not only does this but has a naming pattern which is still used, although not to the same extent nowadays, since filmstars and TV programmes have left their mark. The following naming pattern is useful to know, but it is not always used: the eldest son named after the paternal grandfather; the second son named after the maternal grandfather; the third son named after the father. The eldest daughter named after the maternal grandmother; the second daughter named after the paternal grandmother; the third daughter named after the mother. There are variations on this pattern, and the late Gerald Hamilton-Edwards gives details of these in his book *In Search of Scottish Ancestry* (see Appendix IV: Book list).

There is a well-known story of a family where all the sons were named John through following the naming pattern, because the two grandfathers as well as the father were named John, and the mother had a brother named John too. The youngest son was always known as Baby in spite of having grown into a large and tough fisherman!

In the course of one search, I found a family where twin boys were both named William. It must have saved a lot of bother when mother wanted to call them in for tea, but it certainly made it impossible for me to be sure which man married which wife. Only local knowledge could sort out that kind of problem.

Sometimes you will find a second, or even a third child called by the same name. This was not always a case of using the grandparents' and other family names, but indicated that the previous children of the name had died.

If you find a name which does not fit in with the family list of names, there is always a chance that the child was named after the minister, particularly if the child was the first one to have been baptised by the new minister. This habit applied to girls as well as to boys. For example:

OPR Dumfries Co. Dumfries (821/3) Births and Baptisms 1806
Scot, lawful daughter to Alexander Grier, Shoemaker, born Aug 1. bapt. Aug 2.

Note: The parents at first intended the child's name to have been Jenny but afterwards agreed to the present name because she was the first baptised by the Revd Alexander Scot DD after his translation from New to Old St Michael's Church, Dumfries, and this appropriation of a name is an honour generally shown ministers.

This is all very well, but, if when the minister was not listening they continued to call the baby Jenny, and she grew up and married calling herself Jenny, then her marriage and death entries will be difficult to find if anybody is researching her family line today! Such a habit of naming children still goes on, as does naming the child after the doctor or the midwife.

In the north of Scotland, some names which are generally thought of as male are used for girls, so if you are searching through the index for a female whose name is Nicholas or Bruce or John, and you do not find it there, it is always worthwhile checking the male index. For instance, a Lord Provost of Edinburgh, Charles Lawson, married a lady named Graham Stoddart.

Girls' names are often made by adding 'ina' to the boys' names, for instance, Jamesina, Andrewina, Hughina, and are sometimes indexed under Ina (pronounced Eye-na).

As with male names being used for girls, there are some names which are generally thought of as feminine, but are used for boys, such as Ann and Primrose (the latter being a surname used as a Christian name). If you do not find the name in the male index, it may have been included wrongly in the female index. This also applies in cases where the subject bears a surname as a Christian name, and where consequently the sex is not obvious.

There are some Christian names which are generally considered to have a separate identity, but were, and are, used with a fine impartiality even by their owners, such as Peter for Patrick, and Donald for Daniel. While these are distinctly different to some of us, even today I know a Patrick who answers to Peter when he returns to the north of Scotland!

The Gaelic influence is still to be found. Ian/Iain is the same as John; Hamish is the same as James; and Callum is the same as Malcolm. Among girls' names, Ishbel is, of course, Isobel, but a more unusual alternative is Morag for Sarah. Finally, Ninian can be Ringan, and this is to be found in the place-name St Ninians or St Ringans.

Diminutives, contractions and variations

Diminutives can cause problems. When you are searching for an Elizabeth do not forget that she may have been indexed as Eliza, Liz, Betty, Beth or

Bess. A few names for which diminutives are commonplace are: Bella or Isa for Isabella/lsobel; Euphan for Euphemia; Ina for any girl's name that has been made from a boy's name (see above); Maggy/Maggie/Meg/Peggy for Margaret; Polly for Mary; Jack/Jock for John; Jamie/Jim for James. Ned/Ted for Edward; Olla for Oliver; Rob/Rab/Rabbie/Bob for Robert; Sandy/Ecky for Alexander; Tod/Dod for George, and Tom/Tam for Thomas. The boys' names are more obvious than the girls'.

As contractions are often used in an index, and in the OPRs, I have listed a few which you may miss although they look obvious: Barb. = Barbara; Eliz. = Elizabeth; Isa. = Isabella; Margt. = Margaret; Alex/Axr. = Alexander; Chas. = Charles; Jas. = James; Jo (e). = Joseph (but Jo. or Jno. could be John); Patk. = Patrick; Robt. /Rob. = Robert (Robtson or Rtson = the surname Robertson); Rodk. = Roderick; Thos. = Thomas; Willi/Wm. = William.

Several Christian names are interchangeable in Scottish registers. Jean, Jane, Jessie or Janet tend to be interchangeable and I have on rare occasions found Janet written as Chunnet or Channet, which if you say it aloud to yourself makes an odd kind of sense, particularly when you realise that in Caithness the letter 'J' is sometimes pronounced 'Ch' as in 'chair'. Professor Donaldson told me that this habit is also to be found in Orkney and Shetland.

Elizabeth, may of course, be spelt with an 's' as Elisabeth, and the name can be interchangeable with Elspet/Elspeth, although these are usually names in their own right. Elizabeth is sometimes interchangeable with Isobel/Isabella, but not often.

Catherine may be written as Catharine, and both names are to be found starting with the letter 'K' and not 'C', so all spellings should be thought of when searching the index. Kathleen and Katheryn are not usual variations, but should be borne in mind.

In more modern records, and usually in Glasgow, you may find the girl's name Senga. If you do, then do not be surprised to find that the grandmother was Agnes, as Senga is Agnes written backwards! Christina is often Christian, and in some Mormon microfiche indexes is indexed under 'X', as in rare cases the session clerk has written 'Xtian' in the Old Parish Register – like writing Xmas for Christmas! Christian is rarely used as a boy's name in Scotland. Finally, Grace and Grizel are the same name.

It is particularly important to remember these contractions if you are using the computer index because this index has been compiled from the Mormon microfiche, and with a computer you will only get what you ask for. If the Christian or forename does not appear on the computer index, try using just the initial. I found the name Donald, in the index as Don^d, but only after typing in the initial D. This is another instance of the snags of using the computer instead of the paper index!

6
Heraldry

Heraldry, although allied to genealogy, is a subject in its own right, and too important to be summarily dismissed by a short paragraph. It is a fascinating study, and one which, once you have started, I am sure you will wish to continue. Just look around and you will find coats of arms on public buildings and in many other places. A coat of arms is usually termed 'arms'.

In Scotland the Lord Lyon King of Arms is the final arbiter of all things heraldic, and the Court of the Lord Lyon is in New Register House, Princes Street, Edinburgh. The Court of the Lord Lyon issues a leaflet giving general information concerning armorial bearings and so on, and the Lord Lyon has kindly allowed me to quote parts of it here:

> The Chief's coat of arms fulfils within the clan or family the same purpose as the Royal Arms do in a Kingdom. There is no such thing as a 'family crest' or 'family coat of arms' which anyone can assume, or a whole family can use.
>
> Armorial bearings, being for distinguishing persons of, and within, a family, cannot descend to, or be used by, persons who are not members of the family.
>
> It is not only *illegal,* but a *social crime* and error of the most grave character, to assume and purport to use your Chief's arms without due and congruent difference. Anyone who does so merely publishes their own ignorance and lapse into bad manners, and the use of such on seal or notepaper will close the doors of all the best families against the presumptuous upstart.
>
> There is so such thing as a 'Clan coat of arms'. The arms are those of the Chief, and clansmen have only the privilege of wearing the strap-and-buckle crested badge to show that they are such a Chief's clansmen.
>
> You cannot have a crest without first having a shield or arms, because a crest was a later addition. Misuse of crests arises from misunderstanding of the badge rule under which junior members of the family may wear in specified manner their Chief's crest as a *badge.*
>
> The Crest of the Chief is worn by all members of the Clan and of approved Septs and followers of the Clan, within a strap-and-buckle surround bearing the Chief's motto. This is for *personal wear* only, to indicate that the wearer is a member of the Clan whose Chief's crest-badge is being worn. The badge or crest is not depicted on personal or business stationery, signet rings or plate, because such use would legally imply that the tea-pot etc. was the Chief's property!

Those who wish to use arms in any personal sense must petition for a 'Grant of Arms' or – if they can trace their ancestry back to a direct or, in some cases, a collateral ancestor – a 'cadet-matriculation', showing their place within the family. Forms of Petition and sample proof-sheets relative to such applications can be supplied if required.

When a grant, or a matriculation of arms is successfully obtained, an illuminated parchment, narrating the pedigree as proved, is supplied to the Petitioner, and a duplicate is recorded in the *Public Register of all Arms and Bearings in Scotland*.

Application for such a Confirmation, by Letters Patent or Matriculation, from the Lord Lyon King of Arms is *the only way to obtain a genuine coat of arms,* and use of bogus heraldry only leads sooner or later to social humiliation.

British Commonwealth. Anyone domiciled in Her Majesty's overseas realms or in the Commonwealth (except those of English, Welsh or Irish ancestry, who should approach the Garter King of Arms in London or The Chief Herald of Ireland in Dublin) can apply to the Lord Lyon King of Arms of Scotland, HM New Register House, Edinburgh EH1 3YT, for a grant or matriculation of arms.

Canada. In June 1988 a separate Heraldic Administration was set up in Canada under the control of The Chief Herald of Canada, Mr Robert D. Watt, at The Chancellery, 1 Sussex Drive, Ottowa, K1A OA1, Canada.

Foreign Countries. Arms are not granted to non-British citizens (though those of Scottish ancestry can apply to the Lord Lyon King of Arms for cadet-matriculation). However, even if not of direct armigerous descent, foreigners of Scottish descent can often arrange for a cousin in Scotland, or in one of Her Majesty's overseas realms, to get arms established by the Lord Lyon King of Arms, and thereafter themselves obtain a cadet-matriculation. Each party is in such cases supplied with an illuminated parchment.

The Heraldry Society of Scotland exists for people with an interest in heraldry. You do not have to be knowledgeable to be a member – just interested! *The Double Tressure,* a journal with coloured illustrations, is issued annually (see Appendix II for the address). www.heraldry-scotland.co.uk

7
Clans and Tartans

So much has been written about clans and tartans that I do not intend to go into detail here. I have listed some books for your pleasure and interest, where you will find names, and their clans and tartans (see Appendix IV).

Wearing of Tartan (according to the Court of the Lord Lyon)

A lady of Scottish family married to someone not entitled to a clan, family or district tartan, shall continue to wear her own tartan in skirt and so on, but wear her sash over the right shoulder and tied in a bow over the left hip.

Unless her child or children, or one of the children, takes the mother's name, these children have no right to wear their mother's tartan at all. They are not members of their mother's clan.

Those not entitled to wear a clan, family or district tartan have no right to wear any royal tartan, and particularly not the so-called 'Royal Stuart Tartan', which is the tartan of the Royal House, and accorded to the pipers of the Sovereign's royal regiments.

Those of Scottish descent with no clan, family or district tartan wear one of the following:

1 . The now so-called 'Hunting Stewart', which was originally a general Scottish hunting tartan, and only named 'Stewart' about 1888.

2. Caledonia tartan.

3. Jacobite tartan – for those with ancestors of Jacobite proclivities.

4. Black Watch or 'Government' tartan in its exact regimental form, or one of the modified forms for those of Hanoverian or Whig ancestral proclivities.

There are a number of district tartans which are worn, or wearable, by persons belonging to, or descended from ancestors belonging to, these districts. The districts, however, only cover certain small areas of Scotland.

The wearing of the kilt was proscribed in Scotland from 1747 to 1783 as part of the Government campaign to break up the unity of the Highlanders, and to merge them with the Lowlanders. It was thought by some that the Highland costume enabled the wearers to endure exposure in the field, and so make them more difficult to conquer, but I doubt if that was the reason for the Government's actions!

If you are interested in finding out more about your family tartan, I suggest you write to the Scottish Tartans Authority, and/or join that body (see Appendix II: Societies, for the address). The research department of the Authority answers questions on the origin of Scottish names, their connection with clans and families and their associated tartans. There is a charge for an enquiry.

8
Searching for Present-day Relations

A great many people whose grandparents or great-grandparents left Scotland decide to try to find a present-day relation with whom they might make contact. The ease of searching depends on when your ancestor left Scotland, and if any member of the family remained behind. Assume your ancestor – let us call him Paul Barnard – left Scotland about 1865, when he was aged three, with a sister Kate (age unknown) and with his parents, whose names were James and Elizabeth Barnard. You do not know the maiden surname of Elizabeth Barnard and you do not know the names of the parents of James Barnard.

1. You would look for the birth of Paul Barnard in 1862. This would tell you the maiden surname of his mother, and the date and place of his parents' marriage.
2. You would look for the marriage of his parents, and this would tell you the names of Paul Barnard's grandparents, and possibly an address which you would use for a census search.
3. You would search the census return for 1861 or 1851 using the addresses in the birth certificate and in the marriage certificate.
4. If you have found the family, you should know the names of some brothers and sisters of Paul's parents, and the ages of his grandparents if they were still alive.
5. If you have not found the family in the census return, then examine the marriage certificate, and (a) if Paul Barnard's grandparents were still alive, then search for their death entries. (Remember to search for the death of the woman first, as her married and maiden surnames should be cross-indexed.); or (b) see if one of the witnesses at the marriage was a brother or a sister whose line could be followed.
6. From the death entries note the names of the informants.
7. If they were sons or daughters or grandchildren, then use this information to further the search.
8. Search for the deaths, and/or marriages of the informants.
9. Search for their children.
10. Use this information, i.e., the children's names, to search for a later generation through marriages and deaths, and carry on working like this until you come to the present day, when you can look up the telephone directory or search the voters' rolls.

In some cases the names of parents are not known, but it is known where the family had lived, and it is known that the persons who left Scotland – say again Paul Barnard and his sister Kate – used to write to their cousins Alexander, William and Charles Murray. From this information it should be possible to search without knowing the names of the parents.

You would first search the index of births for the two Barnard children, Paul and Kate (this means searching all the entries for Kate, Catherine, Katherine etc.); and when you find a Barnard family with those two children, you will know the names of their parents. You would next search the index of births for the three Murray children, Alexander, William and Charles, and when you have found a Murray family with those three children, you will know the names of their parents. Now, you know they were cousins, so the kinship should be obvious from the surnames of the fathers and mothers. Once you have made this link with Scotland, you can go ahead, as suggested above, until you come down to the present day.

Once you have reached 1929, searching for a birth entry is easier. From that date, as the mother's maiden surname is shown in the index, the required entries are easily noted. Once you have reached 1929, searching for a marriage is easier. From that date the spouse's surname is shown in the index. Once you have reached 1974, searching for a death is easier. From that date the maiden surname of the mother is shown in the index.

Searching for a present-day relative without using the records held in New Register House, Edinburgh is also possible. However, unless you have specific details it may be difficult.

1. You could visit the place where you know your ancestor originated and try to find people of the same surname still living there. As you can imagine, this approach is not very feasible if you plan to visit one of the larger cities like Edinburgh or Glasgow, and the time gap is long.

2. You could search for a will if you know when your ancestor died in Scotland. This may lead to hitherto unknown names and addresses.

3. You could search through newspapers for the district where your ancestor died. Although it is not common to find obituaries unless the person is well known, you may find a death intimation, and this may mention members of the family.

4. Unless the surname is extremely unusual, I do not recommend trying to find somebody through calling all the names in a telephone directory!

5. The Department for Work and Pensions (DWP) deals with people who are drawing retirement pensions. You should contact your local DWP to see if it can help. It will not give you any information, but may forward a letter on your behalf. The recipient hopefully will wish to respond.

6. The Office for National Statistics (ONS) offer a service called Traceline (see Appendix II: List of useful addresses: England) for which a fee is charged. They will attempt to trace the whereabouts of a person, and if successful will ask permission to forward a letter from an enquirer. Normally Traceline will only deal with same sex enquiries.

However, all this is applicable only if your ancestor left Scotland after the introduction of statutory (civil) registration in 1855. If he or she left earlier than that, particularly in the eighteenth century, then, unless you have specific information about a member of the family who remained in Scotland, it is almost impossible to bring the search down to the present day.

Perhaps in future things will be easier. I have a young friend, Ruaridh, who was born in Scotland, and his date and place of birth are reflected in his National Insurance number. The first three digits are the district number, the second two digits are the year (77) and the last three digits are the entry number in the birth book. After a certain date, provided you know somebody's National Insurance number, it should be possible to find their name and parentage!

Can you remember when . . .?

Asking questions about earlier generations in your family may not be as simple as it sounds. You may have a list of useful things you want to know, and the only reply, as I know from experience, is, 'Oh, I can't remember', or, 'What do you want to know all that rubbish for?'. Memories not only play people false, but some of them may be painful, so ca' canny along the way.

Unless you have a keen and co-operative person to ask, I suggest you try to record a conversation, having previously decided the direction which you want the conversation to take. Most people enjoy talking about themselves, and I found my mother was fascinated to hear her own voice when I played back the tape-recording. I had previously tried to elicit the information by giving her a list of questions which had only a 'yes' or 'no' answer, but she steadfastly refused to read it. So I borrowed a tape-recorder. I found the best line of approach was to ask my mother about her wedding. From what she wore, we went on to who was there. That led back to her pre-marriage days; where the family lived; where my mother, her brother and sisters went to school; and finally, if her grandparents were alive either when she was at school or when she was married. Bit by bit I winkled out enough names, and approximate dates, to enable me to make a chart. Unfortunately, my father died long before I was interested in genealogy; my mother never kept up with her own family, and knew very little about my father's relations.

Let that be a lesson to all. You are never too young to start – in fact, the younger the better. You stand a much better chance of gathering information from parents or grandparents while they are in their sixties than in their nineties!

9
Questions, Answers and Notes

Q. If I were to employ a professional genealogist or record searcher to work on my family tree, how much would it cost me?

A. Most professional genealogists or record searchers charge by the hour, and it would depend largely on the name being searched and the locality. Surnames like Lumsden or Denholm have fewer entries in the index each year than names like Wilson or Macdonald. Families who lived in rural areas or in Orkney or Shetland are easier to find in census returns than people who lived in big cities such as Glasgow or Edinburgh. For a search starting about 1870 you should allow at least six hours initially. For a search starting before 1855 you could also allow six hours initially, but you may not receive as much information, as the searching in most cases takes longer, owing to the sparsity of information in each entry. For example, marriage entries prior to 1855 do not give the surnames of the parents or ages of the bride and groom, and they seldom give addresses.

Note: Always stipulate for exactly how many hours you want to pay initially. Do not allow yourself to be liable for a large bill. Unless you only require a specific entry, it is not practical to stipulate less than three hours.

Q. How much information will I get for a six-hour search?

A. Depending on the surname and the area, starting around 1870 you should get back between two and three generations; remember that each generation brings in more surnames. You should stipulate which surnames you would like to take priority in the search. You may want your father's line to take priority over your mother's line or the other way round; or you may prefer to have the stipulated time divided between them both.

Note: Make sure you have contacted an accredited genealogist or record searcher to undertake the work for you. So many people have 'jumped on the band-waggon' over the past few years, and although they advertise in reputable magazines, in some cases their work can be expensive and unreliable. You may have been recommended to a searcher by a friend who can vouch for the standard of work, but if you are in any doubt you should write to the Scottish Genealogy Society, and they will send you a list of genealogists and record searchers whose work is of a recognised standard (see Appendix II for address). Read this list carefully and choose someone whose description of work undertaken agrees with what you want done. Some specialise in certain areas, and not all the people whose names are on the list undertake to carry out a full genealogical search involving wills, deeds etc. Also, you will find a variation in the fee charged, so write to more than one and find out.

Q. What is the minimum amount of information needed to start a search in Scottish records?

A. *If your ancestor left Scotland after 1854,* you must give the *full names* of your ancestor (many people write 'my father' or 'my grandmother' without supplying a name for either the father or the grandmother!), approximately when he or she was born and some piece of information to make identification possible. For instance, John Wilson born about 1890, in Scotland, place unknown, parents' names unknown, is an impossible search. There were ninety-nine John Wilsons born in 1890 in Scotland and unless you know the names of his parents or some of his brothers or sisters, it would not be possible to identify the correct entry. If, however, John Wilson married and had children before he left Scotland, then the search should be possible.

If your ancestor left Scotland before 1855, a search could be made through the OPR computer index, which, unlike the computer index for statutory records, shows the names of the parents of the child. If you know the names of any siblings, then you should be able to complete a family search. It would help to know the name of the county in Scotland whence they came.

Q. Is there any way out of the difficulty if I do not know even the name of a county of origin?

A. Yes. Sometimes the subject is to be found in either David Dobson's or Donald Whyte's directories of settlers or emigrants. Either of these sources should show a place of origin (see Appendix IV: Book list).

Note: Just occasionally it is worth looking at the early names of farms and houses of your own family. People coming from 'the old country' liked to bring with them the name of their old home or farm even when they had to leave behind everything else.

Q. Can the name of the ship be found?

A. This is more easily done from your end as not many shipping lists exist in Scotland; there are few lists to be found in the Scottish Record Office.

Note: Bear in mind that your ancestor may have disembarked at a port and travelled some distance from there before settling. The shipping list is most likely to be found at the first port of call.

Q. Can I undertake the search myself although I live overseas?

A. Yes. More and more libraries and family history societies are buying microfilm copies of the Old Parish Registers and census returns, and the IGI is a useful tool as long as you remember that it is not a complete list of all the births, marriages and deaths recorded in the parish. Remember, the IGI is only an index, if you are in any doubt you can write to New

Register House and they will send you a full official copy of the entry, for a small charge.

More and more indexes and digital images of records are being made available on the internet.

Note on records: In English records B may stand for Burial as well as Birth, and a Baptism is usually called a Christening, so when you read 'C 1890', the contraction could mean either 'C(hristened) 1890' or 'C(irca) 1890', whereas in Scottish records B stands for Birth, Baptism is generally contracted to 'Bapt', and D stands for Death. 'Burials' is usually written in full. Therefore in the Scottish records there is less chance of confusion. The Mormon microfiche index uses 'C' for Christening and not 'B' for Baptism. Of course, 'M' stands for Marriage whichever record you read!

'Stayed' in Scotland implies a permanent place of abode, whereas in England this suggests a temporary place of abode and 'lived' implies a permanency. To a Scot, 'I stayed in Brunstane Road, in Edinburgh' means that was his permanent address, but to an English person this means that he was merely there with friends or as a lodger.

Q. What if I cannot find the Christian name or names I need in the index?

A. Read Chapter 5 on 'Names' and see if the Christian name you want may have a shortened form or a diminutive which was used in the index, such as Elizabeth being indexed as Eliz, Liz, Lizzie, Beth, or Betty.

Q. I know my grandfather was George William King, because he signed his name when he was married, but I cannot find his birth in the General Register of Births Index *circa* 1858.

A. Often the order of Christian names was changed or a name was added in later life. Search under William George, George William, just William or just George, and do not forget that William may be entered as Wm – so look for that too.

Q. I have searched for a birth using every possible spelling variation and over a wide time-span after 1855, but cannot find it at all. It is a Scottish birth.

A. The child may have been born before the parents married, in which case it may have been registered under the mother's surname. An illegitimate child is registered under both the father's and the mother's surname only if paternity is admitted. Even if the parents were married in Scotland and all the siblings were born in Scotland, there is just the chance that one child was born in England, Wales or Ireland. Try to find a census entry for the family.

Q. I have found an entry in an OPR of an illegitimate child; is there any chance of finding the name of the father?

A. Yes, search the Kirk Session records for this parish because the father may have appeared before the Kirk Session (see Chapter 3). Sometimes the mother's allegations are not accepted and are disputed.

Q. My mother was adopted. How can I start a search?

A. This may be difficult if your mother is no longer alive because such information is usually only given to the adoptee.

A useful guide for counsellors on where to find adoption records has been compiled by Georgina Stafford (see Appendix IV: Book list). This guide lists voluntary agencies in Scotland, England, Wales and Ireland. There are the following homes in Scotland: Aberdeen (2), Balerno (1), Bishopton (1), Dundee (2), Edinburgh (15), Galashiels (1), Glasgow (10), Kilmarnock (1), Leith (1), Musselburgh (2), Perth (2), and Rutherglen (1). Your local authority Social Works Department may be willing to help locate records from the above homes. A list of these offices can be obtained from Birthlink, Edinburgh (see Appendix II).

The guide also has a section suggesting ways of searching: how adoptees can use their birth certificates, both the original birth certificate and the birth certificate after adoption. A copy of the guide is to be found in the Reference Room of the City Library, George IV Bridge, Edinburgh (their ref. HV1875).

See Adopted Children on page 22 in Chapter 2.

Q. The census return states that my great-grandfather was born in a certain parish, but I can find no trace of him there although I did find entries for his siblings.

A. Try searching the surrounding parishes, or the parish where the mother was born, or where the parents were married. Census returns are sometimes inaccurate. Your great-grandfather may have wrongly supposed he was born in the same place as his brothers and sisters, or his birth may not have been registered; it was not compulsory before 1855. If you know the names of the parents, search the computer index for births for Scotland which shows parents' names for births prior to 1855.

Q. I found a great-*grandfather* whose Christian names were Ann Primrose. Was this a mistake made by the registrar or session clerk?

A. No. There are some Christian names which, although we attribute them to girls, are sometimes given to boys. Ann is one of these, and Primrose is a surname used as a Christian name (see Chapter 5).

Q. Are there any boys' names given to girls?

A. Yes, the most common are Nicholas, Bruce and John (see Chapter 5).

Q. In an OPR I found a birth entry where the child's Christian names were Gibson Kennedy, and the entry only stated 'lawful child', not 'lawful son' or 'lawful daughter'. How can I tell whether this child was a boy or a girl?

A. In Scotland, surnames, usually the name of a grandmother, were, and still are, often used as Christian names. Unless this child grew up and married, or died in Scotland after 1855, or was found in a census return, I am afraid you may never know!

Sometimes the name Frances is given without the sex of the child being indicated. Later research will find out which sex the child was.

Q. My grandmother's name is sometimes Jean, sometimes Janet or Jessie. Which is the correct form?

A. The name used in the birth (after 1854) or birth/baptism (prior to 1855) register is the correct form, but these names tend to be interchangeable. (See Chapter 5.)

Q. When my grandfather died the name of his mother given on the death certificate was not the same as that given when my grandfather was married.

A. There are several possible explanations: (1) Are you sure you found the correct death entry? For instance, was the spouse's name correct? Were the age, address and/or informant known to be correct? (2) Who was the informant? A son-in-law, daughter-in-law, grandchild or neighbour may not have known the Christian name and/or the maiden surname of your great-grandmother, especially if your grandfather was an old man when he died. (3) Did the informant sign his or her name or was it 'His/Her X Mark'? On a death certificate the subject is hardly in a position to rectify any wrong information! The information on the marriage certificate is therefore more likely be correct.

Q What does 'Her X Mark' or 'His X Mark' mean?

A. This means that the person testifying to the information, as an informant or as a witness, could not write, so the name was written by somebody else and the informant wrote 'X' in the presence of a witness. If a person could not write then it was more than likely that he or she could not read either; any information from such a source may therefore be inaccurate, and is at least suspect.

Q. When I searched in England I found the information on a death certificate to be rather scant. Is it worth searching for deaths in Scotland?

A. Yes. In Scotland death records after 1854 are of great importance and a great deal of information is to be gained from them (see Chapter 2).

Q. I found my family in a census return and know the village where they were born, but I cannot find it in the list of parishes for Old Parish Registers.

A. This is probably because it is not a parish in its own right, but a village or a hamlet within a parish of another name. Consult a gazetteer; look up the name of the place you know and this should tell you the name of the parish you need (see Chapter 2).

Q. I was told that our family came from 'The Mearns'. What or where is that?

A. The Mearns is another name for Kincardineshire. It is not to be confused with Mearns, which is the name of a parish in Renfrewshire.

Note: Other such places are (1) Badenoch, a district in south-eastern Inverness-shire, which comprises the parishes of Alvie and Rothiemurchus;

(2) Cunninghame, a district in Ayrshire, which comprises the parishes of Ardrossan, Beith, Dalry, Dreghorn, Dundonald, Dunlop, Galston, Irvine, Kilbirnie, W. Kilbride, Kilmarnock, Kilwinning, Loudon, Stevenston, Stewarton and Symington.

Q. My ancestor was a minister in the Church of Scotland; are there any printed records I could search?

A. Yes. Look at *Fasti Ecclesiae Scoticanae* which is a list of biographies of all the ministers in the Church of Scotland since the Reformation, *circa* 1560. It is usually known as *Fasti* and is found in most libraries (see Chapter 4 and the book list in Appendix IV).

Note: For ministers of other – Free, etc. – churches in Scotland, see Chapter 4, and book list in Appendix IV.

Q. I found a marriage in 1820 where the groom was of the parish of Edinburgh and the bride was of the parish of Bathgate. I found birth entries of their children in Edinburgh from 1825 onwards, but none for the years 1820–4 in Edinburgh. Where else should I search?

A. Remember that Edinburgh is in three different districts for OPRs: Edinburgh (685[1]), St Cuthberts (685[2]) and Canongate (685[3]). If you have searched all these Edinburgh parishes, I suggest you try Bathgate, where the mother came from. She may have gone home to her mother to have the first child. Check there is no gap in the records. Lastly, if you do not find any other children, unless you know to the contrary, perhaps there was none born alive any earlier than the one you found.

Q. What is the difference between the IGI and the OPR index?

A. The Mormons (The Church of Jesus Christ of Latter-day Saints), have produced four sets of microfiche indexes – in 1981, 1984, 1988 and 1991. These are known as the IGI (International Genealogical Index) and contain baptism/birth and marriage information. The 1988 index was compiled by the Mormons from a variety of sources. Old Parish Records can be found in the index as well as information submitted by individuals, for instance from family bibles. Also contained on the index are most of the first twenty years of statutory records of births and marriages 1855–75, and some entries from the decennial census 1841–91. The index is alphabetical by surname within each county and can be useful when only a limited amount of information is known. The source of material can be identified by noting the 'batch number' shown on the fiche and consulting the Search Room Supervisor.

As this information was not collected solely from original sources, for example from OPRs, there is some hearsay to be found, and I would strongly advise you to use the IGI only as a useful guide. Bear in mind, too, that the main reason for collecting these records was for the Mormons' own religious purposes and rites. Consequently the date recorded was usually that of a baptism and not that of a birth, and death entries were not recorded.

The Registrar General arranged to allow the Mormons to index the Old Parish Registers (OPRs) of births and marriages, and this index is to be found on computer in New Register House.

The IGI is now available on CD-ROM (known as *FamilySearch*), and also on-line via the internet www.familysearch.org.

Remember to go and read the original OPR entry as soon as possible.

Q. How can I tell from the microfiche index which records were submitted by Mormon individuals and are not necessarily in the OPR?

A. A letter from their correspondence unit states: 'Entries from original or printed sources, such as vital records of births and marriages have batch numbers that begin with C, E, F, J, K, M, (except M17 and M18), P, 694, 725, 744, 754, and 766. Entries submitted by individuals have all-digit batch numbers, with the third digit being smaller than 4, such as 7108514–67.'

Note: Many entries in the OPRs were not recorded in chronological order. You may find an entry in a given year in the index, but the entry is not recorded in that year in the OPR. To help you to find such entries note the frame number on the computer index, or in the miscellaneous column on the microfiche index, e.g., FR246. This number will be found at the top of each page/frame of the microfilm of the OPR. Although in some cases it is almost illegible, it should help you to find the entry if you persevere.

Q. My family came from Shetland and I find it difficult to search as the surname tends to change with each generation.

A. Read Chapter 5 on 'Surnames' which explains about patronymics. There is also a microfiche index to births and marriages under Christian names, which may help when searching for a patronymic. The following counties, in addition to Glasgow (incomplete) and Dundee, are so indexed: Aberdeen, Banff, Caithness, Inverness, Kincardine, Moray, Nairn, Orkney, Ross and Cromarty, Shetland, Sutherland.

Q. I should like to visit the church where my great-grandparents were married in 1890. How can I find it?

A. If your great-grandparents were married in Scotland and you have a copy of the marriage certificate, this should give you the name of the church and the name of the minister or priest. In a country area there will not be many churches so you should find it easily. In a city or a town it may be more difficult, but from reference books held in the library of the parish, you should be able to find where that church was. Unfortunately, owing to building developments in cities or towns, there is always the chance that the church is no longer there.

Note: Not all Scottish marriages took place in church. It was not uncommon for the ceremony to have been held in a hotel, in a house, or in the manse.

Q. On a marriage certificate I found the words 'cousin german'. What does that mean?

A. The word 'german' placed after brother, sister or cousin means they are in the fullest sense of relationship. Cousins german are first cousins. A brother or a sister german have the same parents. German is pronounced 'germane'.

Q. What is a second cousin, and what is a second cousin once removed?

A. A first cousin (or german) is the child of one's uncle or aunt; a second cousin is the child of one's parent's first cousin. A first cousin once, or twice, etc. removed is (1) The child of one's first cousin (grandchild etc.); (2) The cousin of one's parents, grandparents, etc.

Q. Why do some OPR birth/baptism indexes only record the names of sons and not of daughters?

A. When you come across such an index, showing only male names, these will be the names of the fathers, and not the names of the children.

Q. What does 'HEICS' after a name mean?

A. This means that the person was in the Honourable East India Company Service.

Q. What do the letters 'LAC' after the name of my grandfather, and 'LACW' after the name of my grandmother, on the marriage certificate dated 1944 mean?

A. This means that they were both serving in the Royal Air Force during World War II. 'LAC' stands for Leading Aircraftsman, and 'LACW' stands for Leading Aircraftswoman. You may find other service titles – there are too many to list concerning men, but for women the main ones are variations of the above LACW for women serving with the RAF: ATS (Auxiliary Territorial Service) for women serving in the Army, and WRNS (Women's Royal Naval Service) for women serving with the Royal Navy.

Q. I found the words 'Baptised Do.' in an OPR birth entry. What does 'Do.' mean?

A. 'Do.' stands for 'Ditto' meaning the 'same as before'. So if a child was born on 18 January and baptised 24th Do. that means that the child was baptised on 24 January.

Note: 'inst.' stands for instant and means 'this month'; 'ult.' stands for ultimo and means 'last month'.

Q. What does 'RCE' at the side of an entry mean?

A. This means 'Register of Corrected Entries': for a birth or a marriage entry, generally recording an alteration of name or date, or a subsequent marriage making a child legitimate; for a death entry, generally recording the result of a precognition if the death was sudden or the result of an accident. It is possible to view the register and copy down the information.

Note: One final thought. When you are noting the father's occupation from a birth certificate, do not confuse this with the name of the father. I overheard the following conversation between a searcher and Mr Alex Cunningham, Senior Repository Assistant, now retired:

Searcher   'Why has this child got two fathers?'

A.C.   'The entry states "Father: James Brown, Bill Poster". There is only one father.'

Searcher   'Then who was Bill Poster?'

Illustrations

Figures 1–6, 11–16, 17 and 19 are reproduced by kind permission of the Registrar General for Scotland and the Controller of Her Majesty's Stationery Office and Queen's Printer for Scotland.

Extract of an entry in a REGISTER of MARRIAGES

Registration of Births, Deaths and Marriages (Scotland) Act 1965

MARRIAGE	District No. *742*	Year *1979*	Entry No. *56*

IN THE DISTRICT OF *Canongate and Portobello*

1. When and where married
19.*79* *March Twentyfourth*
St. Mark's Episcopal Church, Edinburgh

	BRIDEGROOM	**BRIDE**
2. Surname	*Kozowyk*	*Cory*
Name(s)	*Ned John*	*Alison Catherine Barnard*
(Signed)	*Ned John Kozowyk*	*Alison Catherine Barnard Cory*
3. Occupation	*Professional Engineer*	——

4. Marital states	*Single*	**5. Date of birth** Year *1904* Month *5* Day *4*	**4.** *Single*	**5.** Year *1955* Month *10* Day *26*

6. Birthplace	*Canada*	*Bermuda*
7. Usual residence	*6 Weybridge Court Islington, Ontario, Canada*	*4 Brunstane Road Edinburgh*
8. Father's name(s) surname and occupation	*Alex Kozowyk Sprinkler Fitter (retired)*	*Paul Alexander Barnard Cory Clerk in Holy Orders (deceased)*
Mother's name(s), surname(s), and maiden surname	*Betty Kozowyk ms. Panagapko*	*Kathleen Beatrice Cory ms. Reed*

9. Person solemnizing the marriage
(Signed) *Kenneth Riches* Designation *Bishop of Lincoln (retired)*

Witnesses with addresses
(Signed) *Vern Lennox* Witness
Rural Route No. 1, Mar, Ontario, Canada
(Signed) *Eleanor A. Logan* Witness
16 Lorne Crescent, Monifieth, Dundee

10. When registered	Year 19*77*	Month *3*	Day *26*	**11.** *Gwyneth C. Forbes* Asst. Registrar

12.

Given under the Seal of the General Register Office, New Register House, Edinburgh on *2nd February 2004*

The above particulars incorporate any subsequent corrections or amendments to the original entry made with the authority of the Registrar General.

This extract is valid only if it has been authenticated by the seal of the General Register Office. If the particulars in the relevant entry in the statutory register have been reproduced by photography, xerography or some other similar process the seal must have been impressed after the reproduction has been made. The General Register Office will authenticate only those reproductions which have been produced by that office.

Warning

It is an offence under section 53(3) of the Registration of Births, Deaths and Marriages (Scotland) Act 1965 for any person to pass as genuine any copy or reproduction of this extract which has not been made by the General Register Office and authenticated by the Seal of that Office.

Any person who falsifies or forges any of the particulars on this extract or knowingly uses, gives or sends as genuine any false or forged extract is liable to prosecution under section 53(1) of the said Act.

This extract is evidence of an event recorded in a Register of Marriages. It is NOT evidence of the identity of the person(s) presenting it.

RXM8(M)
2/2003

Fig. 1 1979 Marriage Certificate

Extract of an entry in a REGISTER of DEATHS

Registration of Births, Deaths and Marriages (Scotland) Act 1965

No.	1 Name and surname Rank or profession and whether single, married or widowed	2 When and where died	3 Sex	4 Age	5 Name, surname and rank or profession of father Name and maiden surname of mother	6 Cause of death, duration of disease and medical attendant by whom certified	7 Signature and qualification of informant and residence, if out of the house in which the death occurred	8 When and where registered and signature of registrar
338	Charles Hubert Reed. Captain Royal Scot, retired. married to Beatrice King	1947 May twelfth St. Ann. Gun. 45 Belgrave Crescent Edinburgh. usual residence: 232 Joylichan Row Edinburgh	M.	51	William Reed, Naval Officer (deceased) Alicia Reed, m.s. Cooke (deceased)	Cardio vascular degeneration. Bronchitis so Cert. by J. Carmichael M.B	Beatrice Reed widow. Crown Hotel. 232 Joylichan Club Edinburgh. Present	1947 May 12t At Edinburgh Geo. Donald Registrar.

The above particulars are extracted from a Register of Deaths for the .... District .... of ...... St. Andrew

in the .... City .... of .... Edinburgh

Given under the Seal of the General Register Office, New Register House, Edinburgh, on .... 2nd February 2004

The above particulars incorporate any subsequent corrections or amendments to the original entry made with the authority of the Registrar General.

This extract is valid only if it it has been authenticated by the seal of the General Register Office. If the particulars in the relevant entry in the statutory register have been reproduced by photography, xerography or some other similar process the seal must have been impressed after the reproduction has been made. The General Register Office will authenticate only those reproductions which have been produced by that office.

Warning
It is an offence under section 53(3) of the Registration of Births, Deaths and Marriages (Scotland) Act 1965 for any person to pass as genuine any copy or reproduction of this extract which has not been made by the General Register Office and authenticated by the seal of that office.

Any person who falsifies or forges any of the particulars on this extract or knowingly uses, gives or sends any false or forged extract is liable to prosecution under section 53(1) of the said Act.

RXD4(C)
1/2004

Fig. 2 1947 Death Certificate

NO	PARISHES	1841 CENSUS		1851 CENSUS	
		Reference	Remarks	Reference	Remarks
		CEN 1841	Enumeration Books	CEN 1851	
	AYR - contd.				
587	Dalry	587	15 "	529-530	
588	Dalrymple	588	4 "	489	
589	Dreghorn	589	5 "	510	
590	Dundonald	590	12 "	509 522	
591	Dunlop	591	6 "	450 526	
592	Fenwick	592	11 "	519	
593	Galston	593	10 "	507	
594	Girvan	594	18 "	480-482	
595	Irvine	595	7 for Irvine Harbour see Dundonald Book 12	521-2	
596	Kilbirnie	596	11 "	533	
597	Kilmarnock	597	41 "	512-517	
598	Kilmaurs	598	7 "	511	
599	Kilwinning	599	11 "	525-6	
600	Kirkmichael	600	8 "	485	
601	Kirkoswald	601	18 "	486	
602	Largs	602	7 "	532	
603	Loudoun	603	12 "	518	
604	Mauchline	604	11 "	504	
605	Maybole	605	19 "	487-8	

Fig. 3 Page from Index to Parish/Registration District Nos: 1841 and 1851 Census

REGISTRATION DISTRICT	1861 CENSUS			1871 CENSUS		
	Reference	No of Enum. Books	No of Vols containing foregoing Enum. Books	Reference	No of Enum. Books	No of Vols containing foregoing Enum. Books
	CEN 1861			CEN 1871		
Kilbirnie	596	8	2	596	8	1
Kilbrandon and Kilchattan	515	6	1	515	6	1
Kilbride	553	9	1	553[2]	6	1
Kilbucho	763	1	1			
Kilbucho, Broughton and Glenholm				763	5	1
Kilcamonell	516[1]	2	1	516[1]	2	1
Kilchoman	540	7	1	540	7	1
Kilchrenan	517[1]	3	1	517[1]	3	1
Kilconquhar	436	9	1	436	8	1
Kildalton	541	7	1	541	7	1
Kildonan	52	8	1	52	8	1
Kildrummy	208	4	1	208	4	1
Kilfinan	518	4	1	518	4	1
Kilfinichen and Kilvickeon	542	7	1	542	7	1
Killean and Kilchenzie	519	5	1	519	5	1
Killearn	482	5	1	482	5	1
Killearnan	68	4	1	68	4	1
Killin	361	9	1	361	9	1
Kilmacolm	569	6	1	569	6	1
Kilmadock	362	8	1	362	8	1
Kilmallie	520	16	2	520	16	2
Kilmany (Fife)	437	2	1	437	2	1
Kilmarnock	597*	30	6	597*	33	5
Kilmaronock	497	4	1	497	4	1
	*See Kilmarnock Street Index (Vol 9)			*See Kilmarnock Street Index (Vol 14)		

Fig. 4 Page from Index to Registration District Nos: 1861 and 1871 Census

Parish of _Kilmarnock_

1			2			3	4	
PLACE	HOUSES		NAME and SURNAME, SEX and AGE, of each Person who abode in each House on the Night of 6th June.			OCCUPATION	WHERE BORN	
Here insert Name of Village, Street, Square, Close, Court, &c.	Uninhabited or Building	Inhabited	NAME and SURNAME	AGE		Of what Profession, Trade, Employment, or whether of Independent Means.	If Born in Scotland, state whether in County or otherwise.	Whether Foreign-er, or whether Born in England or Ireland.
				Male	Female			
Portland Street			James D°	2			Y	
			Thomas D°	3	months		Y	
			Sarah Waugh		65			E
			Margret Williamson		15	F. S.	Y	
		1	James Gilmer	15		H. L. W.	Y	
			Janet D°		15	Shaw Thd. W.	Y	
			Jean D°		15		Y	
		1	Elizabth Fife		25		Y	
		1	John Wood	30		Cabinet M.	Y	
			Elizabth D°		25		Y	
			Archabld D°	10			Y	
			John D°	8			Y	
			Ann D°		4		Y	
			David D°	2			Y	
		1	Peter Clark	20		Journeyman Slater	Y	
			Mary D°		20		Y	
	the		Elizabth D°		5 months		Y	
		1	Robert Roxburgh	20		H. L. W.	Y	
			Elizabth D°		20		Y	
		1	James Mear	75		Shoe maker	Y	
			James D°	6			Y	
		1	John Walker	40		Sho	Y	I
			Mary D°		25		Y	I
			Robert D°	7			Y	
			Sarhart Hutton		15	F. S.	Y	
TOTAL in Page 5	12	7		13	12	50		

Fig. 5 1841 Census Heading

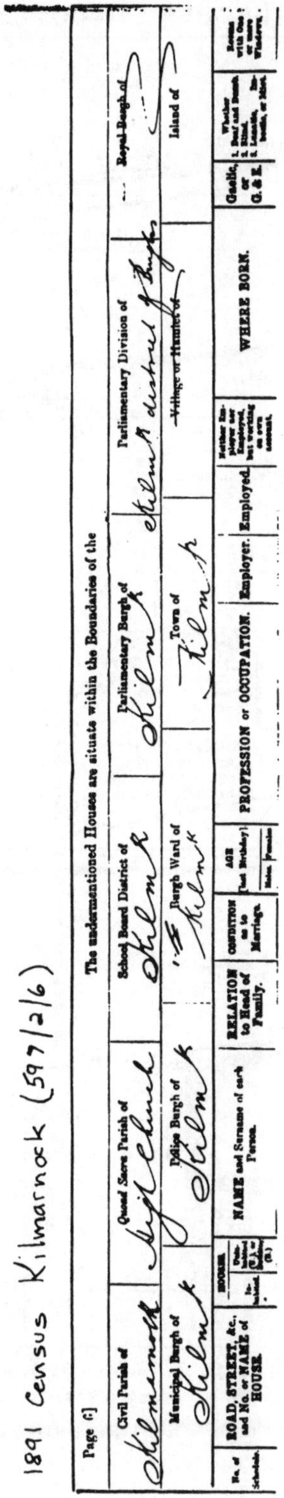
1891 Census Kilmarnock (597/2/6)

Page [ ]

The undermentioned Houses are situate within the Boundaries of the

Civil Parish of	Quoad Sacra Parish of	School Board District of	Parliamentary Burgh of	Parliamentary Division of	Royal Burgh of
Kilmarnock	High Church	Kilmk	Kilmk	Kilmk district of Burghs	
Municipal Burgh of	**Police Burgh of**	**Burgh Ward of**	**Town of**	**Village or Hamlet of**	**Island of**
Kilmk	Kilmk	1st Kilmk	Kilmk		

No. of Schedule.	ROAD, STREET, &c., and No. or NAME of HOUSE.	HOUSES: Inhabited.	HOUSES: Uninhabited (U.), or Building (B.)	NAME and Surname of each Person.	RELATION to Head of Family.	CONDITION as to Marriage.	AGE [last Birthday] of Males	AGE [last Birthday] of Females	PROFESSION or OCCUPATION.	Employer.	Employed.	Neither Employer nor Employed, but working on own account.	WHERE BORN.	Gaelic, or G. & E.	Whether 1. Deaf and Dumb. 2. Blind. 3. Lunatic, Imbecile, or Idiot.	Rooms with One or more Windows.

Fig. 6 1891 Census Heading

CHURCHES IN SCOTLAND

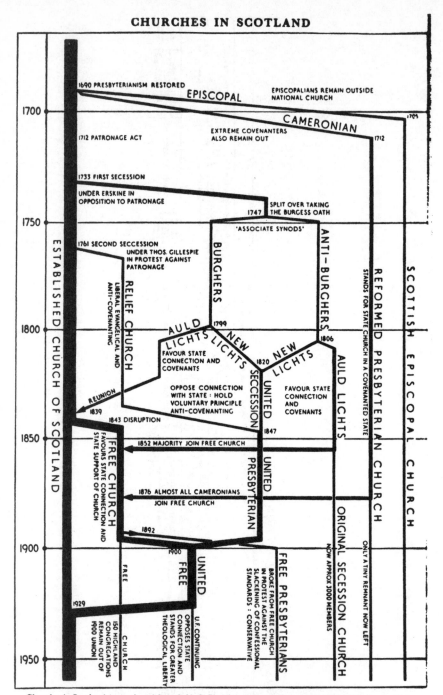

Churches in Scotland (reproduced from J. H. S. Burleigh *A Church History of Scotland*, 1960, by permission of J. K. Burleigh, Mrs Anne Macrae and the Hope Trust)

Fig. 7 Burleigh's Chart of Scottish Churches

Aberdeenshire	1824–1900	SC.1	Aberdeen	
Angus	1824–1900	SC.47	Forfar	County of Angus (Forfarshire)
	1832–1900	SC.45	Dundee	Dundee only
Argyllshire	1815–1900	SC.51	Dunoon	(typed index 1815–1900)
Ayrshire	1824–1900	SC.6	Ayr	
Banffshire	1824–1900	SC.2	Banff	
Berwickshire	1823–1900	SC.60	Duns	
Buteshire	1824–1900	SC.8	Rothesay	
Caithness	1824–1900	SC.14	Wick	
Clackmannan	1824–1900	SC.64	Alloa	Includes Kinross-shire 1824–46
Cromarty	1824–1900	SC.25	Dingwall	(typed index 1824–1900)
Dumbartonshire	1824–1900	SC.65	Dunbarton	
Dumfriesshire	1806–1900	SC.15	Dumfries	See also CC.5 Dumfries up to 1827
East Lothian	1830–1900	SC.40	Haddington	Prior to 1830 included with Midlothian
Fife	1824–1900	SC.20	Cupar	(typed index 1823–92)
Inverness	1823–1900	SC.29	Inverness	
Kincardineshire	1824–1900	SC.5	Stonehaven	
Kinross-shire	1847–1900	SC.22	Kinross	Prior to 1847 included with Clackmannan
Kirkcudbright	1824–1900	SC.16	Kirkcudbright	
Lanarkshire	1824–1900	SC.36	Glasgow	
	1888–1900	SC.37	Hamilton	(typed index 1888–99)
	1888–1900	SC.38	Lanark	
Midlothian	1808–1900	SC.70	Edinburgh	Includes East & West Lothian up to 1830 Printed indexes 1824–67
Morayshire	1823–1900	SC.26	Elgin	Includes Nairnshire 1824–39 and 1861–76
Nairnshire	1839–1900	SC.31	Nairn	1824–39,1861–76 included with Morayshire
Orkney	1824–1900	SC.11	Kirkwall	Records held at Orkney Library, Kirkwall
Peebleshire	1814–1900	SC.42	Peebles	
Perthshire	1824–1900	SC.49	Perth	(typed index 1824–1900)
	1824–1900	SC.44	Dunblane	(typed index 1824–1900)
Renfrewshire	1824–1900	SC.58	Paisley	(typed index 1824–99)
Ross & Cromarty	1824–1900	SC.25	Dingwall	(typed index 1824–1900)
	1826–1840	SC.33	Stornoway	Isle of Lewis only (index with SC.25)
Roxburghshire	1827–1900	SC.62	Jedburgh	Prior to 1827 see CC.18 Peebles
Selkirkshire	1824–1900	SC.63	Selkirk	
Stirlingshire	1809–1900	SC.67	Stirling	(typed index 1809–1900)
Shetland	1827–1900	SC.12	Lerwick	Records held at Shetland Archives, Lerwick
Sutherland	1799–1900	SC.9	Dornoch	Not indexed prior to 1851
West Lothian	1831–1900	SC.41	Linlithgow	Prior to 1831 included with Midlothian (typed index 1831–97)
Wigtownshire	1826–1900	SC.19	Wigtown	Prior to 1826 see CC.22 Wigtown

Note: For persons dying outside Scotland, or with no fixed residence within Scotland check indexes for SC.70 Edinburgh.

FOR 1846–67 THERE ARE PRINTED INDEXES COVERING ALL COURTS:- These should be used in conjunction with the photocopied indexes.

Fig 8. Index to Sheriff Court Commissary Records (*reproduced courtesy of the National Archives of Scotland*)

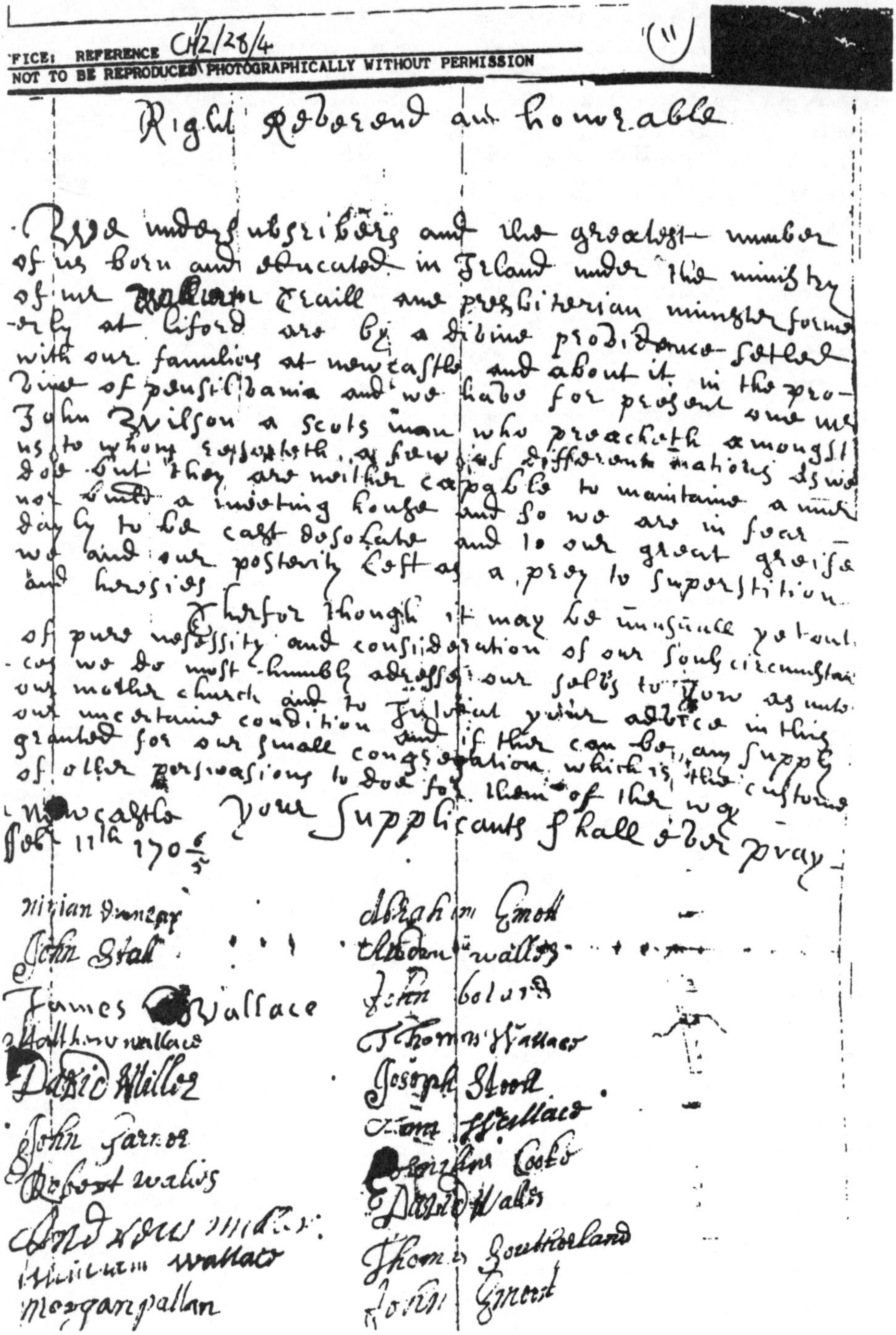

Fig. 9 Letter to the General Assembly from Pennsylvania (*reproduced courtesy of the National Archives of Scotland*)

N.B.—This Half Sheet to be kept by the Applicant.

NEW SOUTH WALES.

WILLIAM BOWIE
AGENT
17 So. St. David Street
EDINBURGH

GOVERNMENT EMIGRATION OFFICE,
PARK STREET, WESTMINSTER.

REGULATIONS

FOR THE SELECTION OF EMIGRANTS, AND CONDITIONS ON WHICH PASSAGES ARE GRANTED.

QUALIFICATIONS OF EMIGRANTS.

1. The Emigrants must be of those callings which, from time to time, are most in demand in the Colony. They must be sober, industrious, and of general good moral character ;—of all of which decisive certificates will be required. They must also be in good health, free from all bodily or mental defects ; and the Adults must, in all respects, be capable of labour, and going out to work for wages. The Candidates most acceptable are young Married Couples without Children.

2. The separation of husbands and wives, and of parents from children under 18 will in no case be allowed.

3. Single women cannot be taken without their parents, unless they go under the immediate care of some near relatives.

4. Single men can be taken except in a number not exceeding that of the Single women by the same ship.

5. Persons who intend to buy land, or to invest capital, in trade ;—or who are in the habitual receipt of parish relief ;—or who have not been vaccinated, or had the small-pox ;—or whose families comprise many young Children, cannot be accepted.

APPLICATION AND APPROVAL.

6. Applications must be made to the Commissioners in the Form annexed. The filling up of the Form, however, confers no claim to a passage ; and implies no pledge that the Candidates, though apparently within the Regulations, will be accepted.

7. If approved of, the Applicants will receive a printed "Approval Circular," calling for the Contribution required by Article 8, and pointing out how it is to be paid. After it is paid, they will, as soon as practicable, receive an Embarkation Order (which is not transferrable), naming the Ship in which they are to embark, and the time and place of joining her.

PAYMENTS TOWARDS PASSAGES.

8. The Contributions above-mentioned, out of which the Commissioners will provide Bedding and Mess Utensils, &c., for the Voyage, will be as follows :—

CLASSES	Age		
	Under 40	40 and under 50	50 and upwards
	£	£	£
I. Married Agricultural Labourers, Shepherds, Herdsmen, and their Wives ; also Female Domestic and Farm Servants—per Head...	2	6	11
II. Married Country Mechanics, such as Blacksmiths, Bricklayers, Carpenters, Masons, Sawyers, Wheelwrights, and Gardeners, and their Wives also Females of the Working Class, not being Domestic or Farm Servants—(when they can be taken) per Head	5	8	15
III. Children under 14—per Head.......	2		
But if there be more than two Children under 14 in any Family, at the time of Embarkation, for each additional Child there must be paid, instead of £2	5		

IV. Single Men of 18 years and upwards, of any of the above callings and whether part of a family or not, £1 additional. *Gratuitous*

The expense of reaching the Port of embarkation must also be paid by the Emigrants *from which place they are forwarded free.*

CAUTIONS TO APPLICANTS.

9. *No preparations must on any account be made by the Applicants, either by withdrawing from employment or otherwise, until they receive the "Approval Circular."* Applicants who fail to attend to this warning will do so at their own risk, and will have no claim whatever on the Commissioners.

10. The Selecting Agents of the Board have no authority to promise passages in any case, nor to receive money. *If, therefore, Applicants wish to make their payments through the Agents, instead of in the manner pointed out in the "Approval Circular," they must understand that they do so at their own risk, and that the Commissioners will be in no way responsible.*

11. Should any Signatures attached to an Applicant's paper prove to be not genuine, or should any false representations be made in the papers, not only will the application be rejected, but the offenders will be liable, under the Passengers' Act, 12 & 13 Vic. cap. 38, to a PENALTY NOT EXCEEDING £50.

12. Should any Applicants be found on personal examination at the Depôt, or on Board, to have made any mis-statement in their papers, or to have any infectious disorder, or otherwise not to be in a fit state of health to embark, or to have any mental or bodily defect likely to impair their usefulness as labourers, or to have left any of their young Children behind, or to have brought with them more Children than are mentioned in their Application Form, or expressly sanctioned by the Commissioners ; or to have attempted any deception whatever, or evasion of these Rules, they will be refused admission on board the Ship, or if embarked, will be landed, without having any claim on the Commissioners.

13. If Applicants fail to attend at the appointed time and place for embarkation, without having previously given to the Commissioners timely notice, and a satisfactory reason,—or if they fail to proceed in the Ship,—or are rejected for any of the reasons specified in the preceding article, they will forfeit all of their contributions the Sum of £2 for each person, and will have no claim to a passage at any future time.

OUTFIT, &c.

14. The Commissioners supply Provisions, Medical Attendance, and Cooking Utensils at their Depôt and on board the Ship. Also, new Mattresses, Bolsters, Blankets, and Counterpanes, Canvas Bags to contain Linen, &c., Knives and Forks, Spoons, Metal Plates, and Drinking Mugs, which articles will be given after arrival in the Colony to the Emigrants who have behaved well on the voyage.

15. The Emigrants must bring their own Clothing, which will be inspected at the Port by an Officer of the Commissioners ; and they will not be allowed to embark unless they have a sufficient stock for the voyage, not less, for each Person, than—

FOR MALES.	FOR FEMALES.
Six Shirts	Six Shifts
Six pairs Stockings	Two Flannel Petticoats
Two ditto Shoes	Six pairs Stockings
Two complete suits of exterior Clothing.	Two ditto Shoes
	Two Gowns.

With Sheets, Towels, and Soap. But the larger the stock of Clothing the better for health and comfort during the voyage, which usually lasts about four months, and as the Emigrants have always to pass through very hot and very cold weather, they should be prepared for both ; 2 or 3 Serge Shirts for Men, and Flannel for Women and Children, are strongly recommended.

16. The Emigrants should take out with them the necessary tools of their Trades that are not bulky. But the whole quantity of baggage for each Adult must not measure more than 20 cubic or solid feet, not exceed half a ton in weight. It must be closely packed in one or more boxes ; but no box must exceed in size 10 cubic feet. Large packages and extra baggage, if it can be taken at all, must be paid for. Mattresses and feather beds will in no case be taken.

17. On arrival in the Colony the Emigrants will be at perfect liberty to engage themselves to any one willing to employ them, and to make their own bargain for wages ; *but if they quit the Colony within 4 years after landing, they must repay to the Colonial Government a proportionate part of their Passage-money, at the rate of £3 per Adult, for each year wanting to complete four years' residence.*

18. All Applications should be addressed, Post-paid, to S. Walcott, Esquire, No. 9, Park Street, Westminster.

By Order of the Board,

STEPHEN WALCOTT,
Secretary.

Fig. 10 Regulations for Emigrants from England, Wales and Scotland (*reproduced courtesy of the National Archives of Scotland*)

1922–1965

Extract of an entry in a REGISTER of MARRIAGES
Registration of Births, Deaths and Marriages (Scotland) Act 1965

No.	When, where and how married	Names in full of parties with signature. Rank or profession and whether bachelor, spinster, widower, widow or divorced	Age	Usual residence	Name, surname and rank or profession of father. Name and maiden surname of mother	If a regular marriage, signature and designation of minister or registrar and signatures and addresses of witnesses. If an irregular marriage, date of decree of declarator or of Sheriff's warrant	When and where registered and signature of registrar
	1922. on the Nineteenth day of July at 11 Hillside Crescent Edinburgh After Banns according to the forms of the United Congregational Church	(Signature) *Archibald Young* (Signature) *Archibald Young* Ironmonger Bachelor	53	Dudley Terrace Leith	Thomas Young Ordained Minister Maria Long Young M.S. Lindsay	Signed J.G. Taylor United Free Congl Church Wm Scott 8 Arden Street Edinburgh Witness Evelyn Scott 31 Mannington Terrace Edinburgh Witness	1922. July 20th A. Edinburgh
196		Barbara Wilkinson Henderson Barbara W Henderson Spinster	51	Mattiewoode Street Edinburgh	James Grant Henderson Factor (deceased) Margaret Craig Henderson M.S. Wilkinson	M. Campbell Registrar.	

The above particulars are extracted from a Register of Marriages for the _Distrct_ of _Cannogate_ in the _City_ of _Edinburgh_

Given under the Seal of the General Register Office, New Register House, Edinburgh on _2nd February 2004_

The above particulars incorporate any subsequent corrections or amendments to the original entry made with the authority of the Registrar General.

This extract is valid only if it has been authenticated by the seal of the General Register Office. If the particulars in the relevant entry in the statutory register have been reproduced by photography, xerography, or some other similar process the seal must have been impressed after the reproduction has been made. The General Register Office will authenticate only those reproductions which have been produced by that office.

Warning

It is an offence under section 53(3) of the Registration of Births, Deaths and Marriages (Scotland) Act 1965 for any person to pass as genuine any copy or reproduction of this extract which has not been made by the General Register Office and authenticated by the Seal of that office.

Any person who falsifies or forges any of the particulars on this extract or knowingly uses, gives or sends as genuine any false or forged extract is liable to prosecution under section 53(1) of the said Act.

This extract is evidence of an event recorded in a Register of Marriages. It is NOT evidence of the identity of the person(s) presenting it.

RXM6(C)
2/2003

Fig. 11 Marriage Certificate

RECORDS FROM 1855

SU 12A 07/02

SELF SERVICE MARKER SLIP FOR THE MICROFICHE

A separate slip must be completed for **each** item required.
Please write in pencil; and **do not fold** the marker slip.
Only three microfiche may be out at any one time.
Return microfiche to the **trays** provided and **do not re-file.**

EVENT	YEAR	REGISTRATION DISTRICT No.	ENTRY No.	
Birth				TO ASSIST IN YOUR SEARCH, PLEASE WRITE THE ENTRY No. BELOW AND RETAIN THIS PORTION.
Death				
Marriage				
Divorce				
Other (Please specify)				

The details required above are shown on the computer screen

Reader's Name (BLOCK CAPITALS)	Date	Seat No.	**Dome**	Delete as applicable
			East	
			West	

Fig. 12 Statutory Register Order Form (orange)

RECORDS FROM 1841 - 1901

**ORDER SLIP
CENSUS**

A separate slip must be completed for **each** item required. Please write in pencil.

**REFERENCE
YEAR**

DISTRICT No

**ENUMERATION
BOOK No** *

TO ASSIST IN YOUR SEARCH, PLEASE WRITE THE REFERENCE No. BELOW AND RETAIN THIS PORTION.

* Please quote this number only if a street index is available. Where the list of census records indicates that a street index exists the index should be consulted for the precise reference number of the enumeration book required.

Reader's name	Date	Seat No.
(BLOCK CAPITALS)		SU 12C 04/03

Fig. 13 Census Order form (pale yellow)

RECORDS FROM 1553-1854

**ORDER SLIP
OLD PARISH REGISTER (OPR)**

A separate slip must be completed for **each** item required. Please write in pencil.

Reference

TO ASSIST IN YOUR SEARCH, PLEASE WRITE THE REFERENCE No. BELOW AND RETAIN THIS PORTION.

The details required above are shown on the computer screen or in the "List of OPRs"

Reader's name (BLOCK CAPITALS)	Date	Seat No.
		SU 12B 04/03

Fig. 14 Old Parish Register Order Form (pale pink)

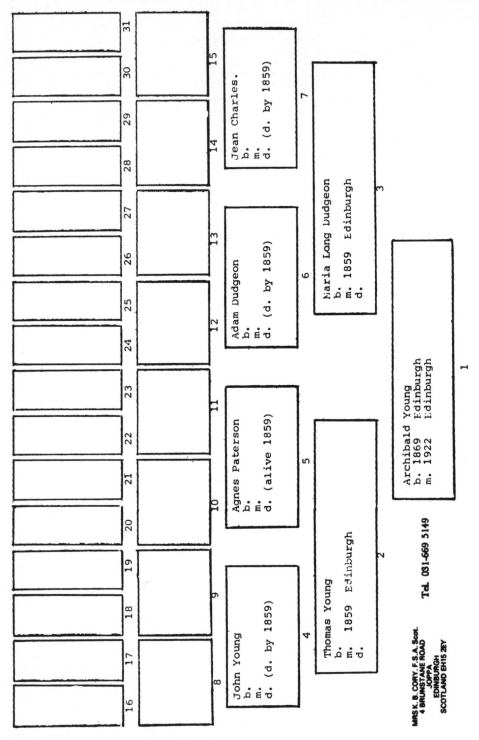

Fig. 15 Family Tree Chart (Squared)

No.	Name	Details
16		
17		
18		
19		
20		
21		
22		
23		
24		
25		
26		
27		
28		
29		
30		
31		

8 — John Young
b.
m.
d. (d. by 1859)

9 —

10 — Agnes Paterson
b.
m.
d. (alive 1859)

11 —

12 — Adam Dudgeon
b.
m.
d. (d. by 1859)

13 —

14 — Jean Charles.
b.
m.
d. (d. by 1859)

15 —

4 — Thomas Young
b.
m. 1859 Edinburgh
d.

5 —

6 — Maria Long Dudgeon
b.
m. 1859 Edinburgh
d.

7 —

2 —

3 —

1 — Archibald Young
b. 1869 Edinburgh
m. 1922 Edinburgh

MRS K. B. CORY. F.S.A. Scot.
4 BRUNSTANE ROAD
JOPPA
EDINBURGH
SCOTLAND EH15 2EY

Tel. 031-669 5149

Parish of *Inveresk*

1			2			3	4	
PLACE	HOUSES		NAME and SURNAME, SEX and AGE, of each Person who abode in each House on the Night of 6th June.			OCCUPATION	WHERE BORN	
Here insert Name of Village, Street, Square, Close, Court, &c.	Uninhabited or Building	Inhabited	NAME and SURNAME	AGE		Of what Profession, Trade, Employment, or whether of Independent Means.	If Born in Scotland, state whether in County or otherwise.	Whether Foreigner, or whether Born in England or Ireland.
				Male	Female			
Smeat's Wynd			William Currie	70		Lab.	Y	
do.			Helen Scott		60	Ind.	Y	
do.		1	John Tinto	50		Mill Wright	Y	
			Jane do.		35		Y	
			Robert do. jun	40		hawker		J
do.		—	Robert Borthwick	40		Potter J.	Y	
do.		—	William Sinclair	60		Tailor J.		E
			Elizabeth do.		50		R	
			Thomas do.	15		Shoe M. ap	Y	
do.		1	Rebecca Raver		60			J
			Catharine do.		20	Flax Spinner		J
			Rebecca do.		15	do.		J
			Samuel Kinley	60		Potter J.	R	
			James do.	18		do. J.	R	
do.		—	Adam Dudgeon	20		Flesher	Y	
			Jane do.		20		Y	
			Maria L. do.		1		Y	
			William R. Hazart	6 mos			Y	
do.			Alexander Cameron	20		Hatter J.	Y	
			Jane do.		20		Y	
			Jane do.		1 mo		Y	
			John McGregor	60		do.	R	
do.		1	Janet Clark		55	Ind.	Y	
			Adam do.	30		Tailor	Y	
			Mary do.		28		Y	
TOTAL Page 29	—	3		13	12			

Fig. 16 1841 Census for Inveresk

Extract of entries in an OLD PAROCHIAL REGISTER

Registration of Births, Deaths and Marriages (Scotland) Act 1965, s.47

Parish of Edinburgh **County of** Midlothian

Edinburgh 6th April 1835 (Proclaimed 5th) (433

Young	John Young Wright residing in Grass Market here Greyfriars Parish & Agnes Paterson residing in same place & Parish 3 Procla &no Objections
Dickson	Alexander Dickson Labourer residing in Frederick St St Georges Parish & Grace Harcus residing in same place & Parish 3 Procla &no Objections
Duncan	13 April (Proclaimed 12th) David Duncan Cabinet maker residing in Greenside place St Andrews Parish & Jean Pitcathly residing in same place & Parish 3 Procla &no Objections
Nicholson	John Nicholson Warehouseman residing in the Parish of Canongate & Mary McNaughton daughter of John McNaughton Joiner in Leith residing in 67 York Place St Andrews Parish 3 Procla &no Objections

The above particulars are extracted from a Register of Proclamations of Banns & Marriages dated 6th April 1835

Given under the Seal of the General Register Office, New Register House, Edinburgh on 3rd February 2004

Fig. 17 Marriage Entry (Old Parish Register)

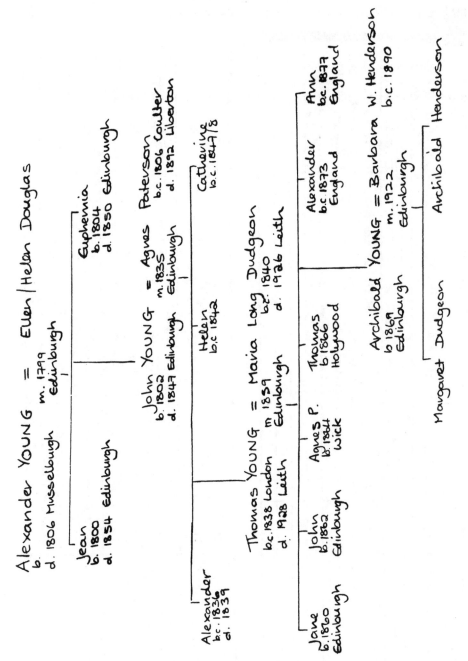

Fig. 18 Family Tree (Drop-line)

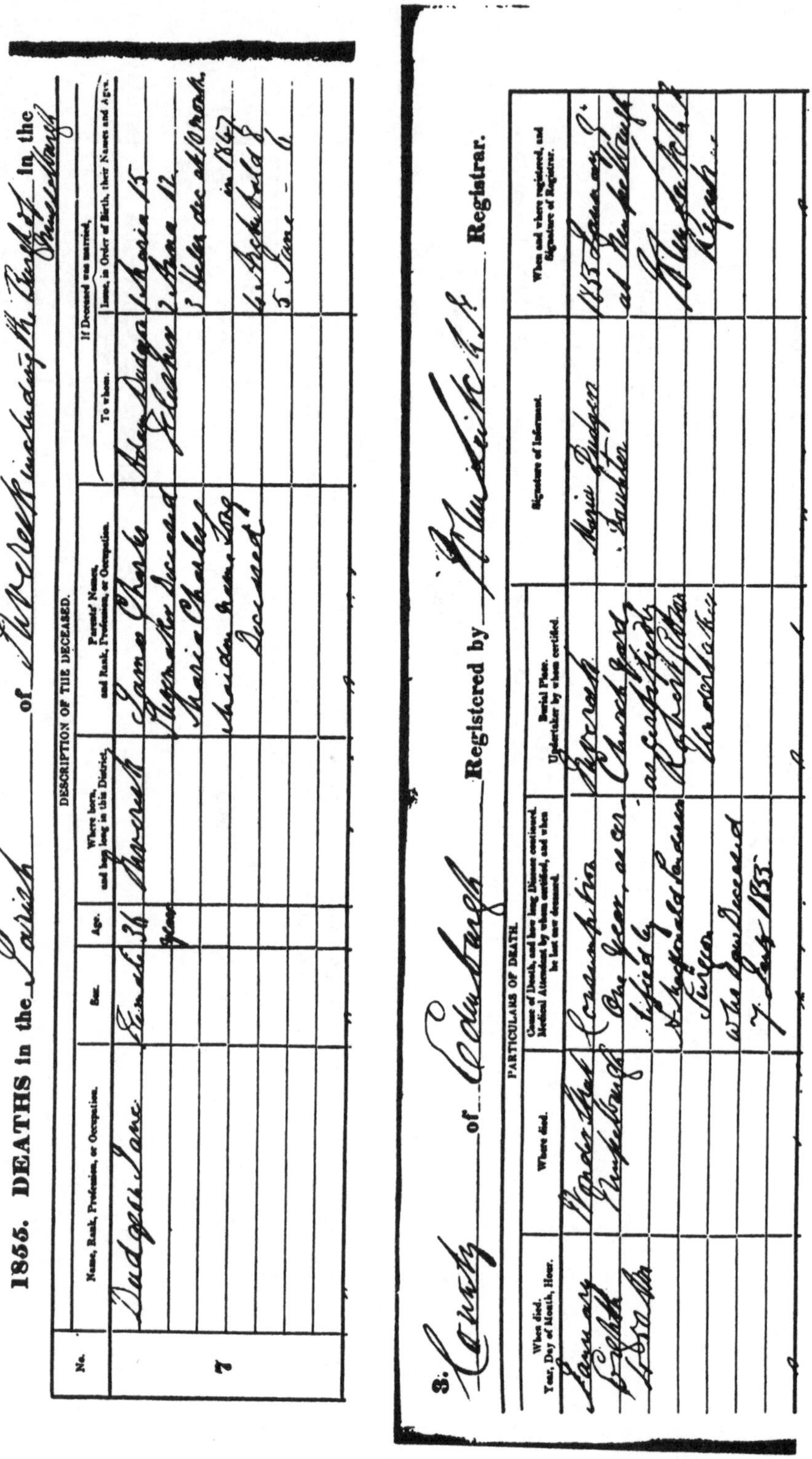

1855. DEATHS in the Parish ... of ...

DESCRIPTION OF THE DECEASED.

No.	Name, Rank, Profession, or Occupation.	Sex.	Age.	Where born, and how long in this District.	Parents' Name, and Rank, Profession, or Occupation.	If Deceased was married. To whom.	Issue, in Order of Birth, their Names and Ages.
7							

PARTICULARS OF DEATH.

When died. Year, Day of Month, Hour.	Where died.	Cause of Death, and how long Disease continued. Medical Attendant by whom certified, and when he last saw deceased.	Burial Place. Undertaker by whom certified.	Signature of Informant.	When and where registered, and Signature of Registrar.

Registered by _____ Registrar.

Fig. 19 1855 Death Certificate

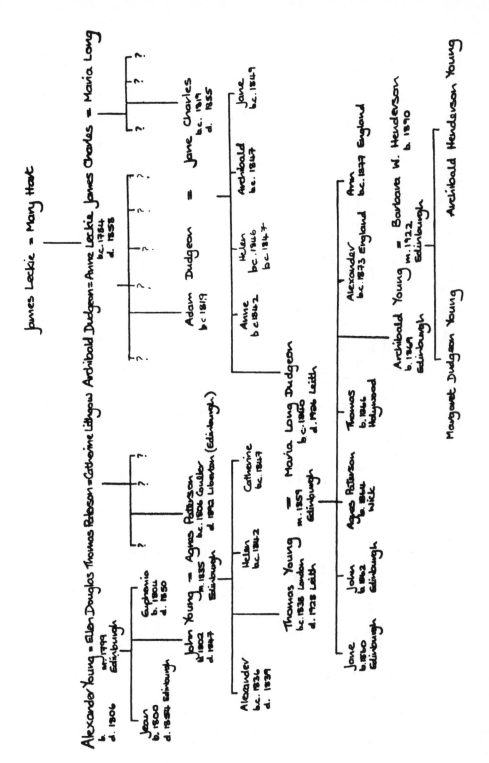

Fig. 20 Family Tree Chart (Drop-line)

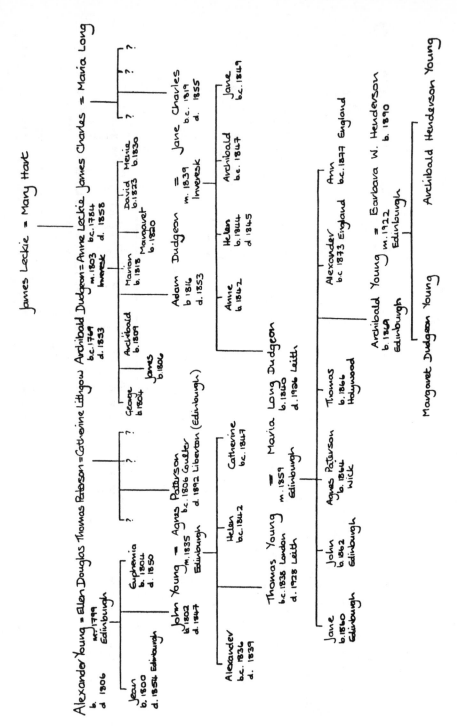

Fig. 21 Family Tree Chart (Drop-line)

Appendix I

Glossary of occupations, terms and contractions found in Scottish records and census returns

adjudication	where a seller of land refuses to give a conveyance to the buyer or the taking of a debtor's land to satisfy his creditor's claim for debt
ag. Lab.	agricultural labourer
agnate	agnates are persons related through the father
allenarly	solely, exclusively (when associated with a life-rent, prevents this from being construed as a fee)
annual rent	interest on money which has been lent
annuit.	annuitant (has yearly fixed sum)
app.	apprentice
assig(nation)	assigning of rights, as of rents or writs in disposition
assize	jury or sitting of a court
assoilzie	absolve or decide finally in favour of a defender (pronounced 'assoilie')
B. or Bach.	bachelor
bailie	magistrate in a Scottish Burgh
bairn	child
bairns' part of gear	the part of a parent's moveables to which children are entitled on parent's death: one-third when the other parent survives, one-half otherwise
barony	the right of a baron or person holding land directly from the Crown or the land itself
baxter	baker
bigging	building
bond	written obligation to do some act or pay some money
bond of provision	providing for the future of others, i.e., children and dependants
Books of Adjournal	books or records of the justiciary Court
Books of Council & Session	registers of deeds and probative writs
boll	measure of grain (six bushels)
bro.	brother
burgh	A Scottish town whose inhabitants were incorporated by Royal Charter or by statute. Since 1975 burghs have ceased to have distinct local government functions, being absorbed in local authority districts

c.	*circa* (about); c.1800 = about 1800
Candlemas	a term-day (was 2 now 28 Feb)
cautioner	surety; sponsor (pronounced 'kayshoner'-'kay' as in 'day')
cen.	census
cess	land tax (now abolished)
Charter of Novodamus	is used to make some change in the incidents of a feudal holding, or to correct a mistake, or to regrant a charter when the original has been lost
Chelsea P.	Chelsea pensioner (sometimes Chelsea out-pensioner)
clare constat	Precept of Acknowledgement by the superior that it 'clearly appears' to him that the heir of a deceased vassal is the lawful heir
close	street; alley
cognate	cognates are persons related through the mother
commissariot	court mainly concerned with wills
compear (of a defender)	appear in an action; to appear before the kirk session for censure
compt.	account
conjunct	joint
consanguine	a brother or sister is consanguine with another where they have a common father but different mother
cordiner\ cordwainer	shoemaker
courtesy	the life-rent enjoyed by a widower of the heritage of his late wife
croft	smallholding
cur. or curr.	current; now
curator	person appointed to administer the estate of another as in the case of a minor
D. or dau. or daur.	daughter
dead's part of gear	the part of moveable estate that a person can leave in their will to whomsoever they please
decree	a final judgement
discharge	termination of a liability
dispone	to assign, make over or grant
disposition	a unilateral deed by which heritable or moveable property is alienated or transferred
disposition & settlement	inheritance bequeathed in testament
dissenter	non-conformist
ditto, do.	a repeat of what was previously written
dom.	domicile
dom. servt.	domestic servant
Edin.	Edinburgh
effeiring	relating or pertaining to
eik	an addition
emp.	employing; employed

entail	designation of heritage to a prescribed line of heirs
eodem die	same day
estate	person's whole assets including both heritable and moveable property
charter of excambion	contract under which one piece of land is exchanged for another
executor	person appointed to administer property of a deceased person
F.	Father
factor	strictly speaking, someone appointed to act for a person in a particular capacity, but more usually an estate manager
factory	a deed where A allows B to act for them as their factor, particularly in the management of an estate
Fasti	*Fasti Ecclesiae Scoticanae:* Brief biographies of ministers in the Church of Scotland from the Reformation
feal & divot	the right of cutting turf; feal & divot are old words for turf
fee	full right of property in heritage; wage-agreement for employment on farm
feuar	see vassal
feu duty	a perpetual lease; annual payment for use of ground. Abolished 1974 by land tenure reform
fiar	owner of a fee
fiars' prices	prices of grain
filiation	determination of the paternity of a child, usually illegitimate
fiscal	pertaining to national revenue
flesher	butcher
flitting	moving house
F.S.	female servant
furth of	outside the borders of
General Assembly	the highest court in the Church of Scotland or the Free Church of Scotland
GD	Gifts and Deposits collection
glebe	land to the use of which a minister in a landward parish has a right, over and above his stipend
grieve	farm overseer
guid	good
guidsire or gudesir	grandfather
gutcher or gowcher etc.	grandfather, a relation, cousin
H.	head of household
haill	all, the whole of
hamesucken	an assault committed upon a person in his own house
HEICS	Honourable East India Company Service
heirs portioners	women succeeding to heritage jointly where there are no male heirs
heritor	landowner
H.L.W	hand loom weaver
horning	the charging of a debtor to pay

Ilk	same (name, place or landed estate, particularly in 'of that Ilk' used after a surname; e.g., 'Dalziel of that Ilk' means his name and his lands are both Dalziel)
illeg.	illegitimate
ind.	independent (of independent means)
indweller	inhabitant; resident
inf.	infant; informant
infeftment	a person was infeft when put into possession of heritable property
inst.	instant; this month or week
instrument	formal document
intestate	having left no will at death
interregnum	time between; between reigns of kings and queens, but mainly found as time between departure of one minister and the appointment of the next
inventory	list of deceased's moveable goods
J.\Jour.	journeyman; the stage between being apprentice and a master of a trade
J.P.	Justice of the Peace
Justiciary, High Court of	the supreme criminal court of Scotland
kin\kindred	relations
Kirk Session	the church court consisting of the minister and elders of a parish
kye	cattle, cows
L.	lawful; e.g., l.s. or l.d. = lawful son or lawful daughter
lab.	labourer
Lady Day	a term-day (25 March) when contracts were made and terminated
laigh	low
lair	a grave; a burial plot in a graveyard
laird	a landowner
Lammas	a term-day (was 1 now 28 August)
liege	a subject of the monarch
liferent	the right to enjoy for life the use of another's property
liferent sasine ex proprius manibus	'by his own hands'. No other person was employed to mediate in the granting of the sasine
litster	a dyer
locum tenens	person acting as a substitute or a deputy
Lord Lyon King of Arms	the principal administrative officer (also a judge), in Scottish heraldic matters, and also adjudicates on chiefs of clans/family names
loun	a boy
M. or mar.	married
m. or min.	a miner; a minister

mail	rent
major	a person of full legal age
mandate	authority given to one person to act for another
manse	dwelling provided for parish ministers
manufactory	a factory
march	boundary
Mark or Merk	an old Scottish coin
Martinmas	a term-day (was 11 now 28 November)
Michaelmas	a term-day (29 September)
minor	a young person between the ages of 12 and 18 if a girl, or between 14 and 18 if a boy
minute	record of a meeting
monie	many
mort-cloth	the pall placed over the coffin at a funeral
mortification	a bequest of property, usually for charitable purposes
moveable estate	property which is not heritable, and which passes to the next-of-kin
mournings	mourning clothes to which a widow has legal rights out of her husband's estate
moyr	mother
M. S.	maiden surname; Merchant Service (merchant navy); male servant
multure	a duty/payment in the form of grain taken by the tenant or proprietor of a mill, on all corn ground in it
multurer	tacksman of a mill; a miller
nat.	natural, i.e., illegitimate; a natural son or daughter is an illegitimate son or daughter
nevoy	nephew
o/oe/oi/oy/ oye/oey	grandson or nephew
outside plenishings	implements kept out of doors, as of husbandry
outwith	outside; beyond
P.	pensioner (usually Army or Navy)
pand or pawn	pledge (usually a sum of money, found in an OPR marriage entry)
panel or pannel	prisoner at the bar
pendicle	small piece of ground
pendicler	an inferior tenant
penny wedding	a wedding at which guests gave money towards the food and drink, any balance being given to the bride and groom
penult.	penultimate, last but one
plenishings	moveable property, furniture etc.
poind	take away debtor's moveables by way of execution (pronounced 'pind')
policies	grounds of a house
portioner	proprietor of a small feu

Precept of Sasine	a written order for the delivery of land or property
prestable	payable, enforceable
procurator fiscal	public prosecutor in the Sheriff Court
pupil	a child up to the age of 12 for a girl and 14 for a boy. Abolished by law in 1991
putative	believed, reputed
qu-, or quh	wh-
queynie	a little girl. Diminutive from quean, a young woman (pronounced 'quynie')
quha	who
quhilk	which
quhytt	white
quoad sacra	as far as concerns sacred matters (of a parish disjoined for ecclesiastical purposes only)
relict	widow or widower
residenter	someone who is a resident in a place
RCE	Register of Corrected Entries
RNE	Register of Neglected Entries
riever	robber
roup	auction (pronounced 'rowp' – 'ow' as in now)
runrig or runrig lands	a plan of land ownership in which alternate ridges of a field belong to different people
sasine/seisin	a method of investiture in lands, originally involving the giving of earth and/or other symbols, now by registration of the conveyance itself (pronounced 'saysin')
Session, Court of	supreme civil court in Scotland
set; sett	an old-fashioned word meaning to let
sic	reported exactly as found written
sickerly	surely, certainly
sister-bairn	the child of a sister or the child of an aunt; a cousin
steading or stedding	ground on which a house stands
superior	a grantor of land to a person who became his vassal in return for perpetual payment of feu duty
tack	lease
tacksman	holder of a lease; in the Highlands, tends to be a tenant of higher class
tailzie or tailye	see entail (pronounced 'tailie')
teind	tithe
tenantry	tenants or land occupied by tenants
term	date at which rent or interest is due
testament	will
testate	having left a will at death

tinsel	forfeiture
tocher	bride's dowry
tutor	guardian of children in pupillarity (see pupil)
udal tenure	land tenure in Orkney & Shetland, now rare
ult.	ultimate; last month, week, etc.
ultimus haeres	last heir; the Crown takes as ultimes haeres for want of other heirs
umquhile	former, late or deceased
uterine	born of the same mother but of different fathers
vassal	tenant holding land under a lord
wadset	pledge of land with right of recovery by the debtor on payment
wain	child
Whitsunday	a term-day; (15 May from c. 1696 now 28 May)
writer	a solicitor
W.S.	Writer to the Signet; a solicitor
yett	gate
yor or yr.	younger
Zetland	Shetland

Appendix II
List of useful addresses

This appendix consists of:
- National Institutions
- Archives, Libraries and Record Offices
- University Archives
- Scottish Association of Family History Societies
- Societies
- Adoption
- Addresses in England
- Addresses in Northern Ireland
- Addresses in Ireland
- Local History

NATIONAL INSTITUTIONS

Court of the Lord Lyon
HM New Register House
Edinburgh EH1 3YT

tel: 0131 556 7255

General Register Office for Scotland
New Register House
Edinburgh EH1 3YT

tel: 0131 334 0380
Certificate Order: tel: 0131 314 4411
email: records@gro-scotland.gov.uk
website: www.gro-scotland.gov.uk

National Archives of Scotland
HM General Register House
2 Princes Street
Edinburgh EH1 3YY

tel: 0131 535 1334
email: enquiries@nas.gov.uk
website: www.nas.gov.uk

National Archives of Scotland
West Search Room
West Register House
Charlotte Square
Edinburgh EH2 4DJ
(all correspondence to NAS, HM General Register House above)

tel: 0131 535 1413
email: wsr@nas.gov.uk
website: www.nas.gov.uk

National Library of Scotland
Main Library
George IV Bridge
Edinburgh EH1 1EW

tel: 0131 226 4531
email: enquiries@nls.uk
website: www.nls.uk

National Library of Scotland
Department of Manuscripts
George IV Bridge
Edinburgh EH1 1EW

tel: 0131 466 2812
email: mss@nls.uk
website: www. nls.uk

National Library of Scotland
Map Library
33 Salisbury Place
Edinburgh EH9 1SL

tel: 0131 226 4531
email: maps@nls.uk

National Monuments Record
of Scotland
Royal Commission on the Ancient
& Historical Monuments of Scotland
John Sinclair House
16 Bernard Terrace
Edinburgh EH8 9NX

tel: 0131 662 1456
email: nmrs@rcahms.gov.uk
website: www.rcahms.gov.uk

National Register of Archives
(Scotland)
The Secretary
HM General Register House
2 Princes Street
Edinburgh EH1 3YY

tel: 0131 535 1405
  0131 535 1430
email: nra@nas.gov.uk
website: www.nas.gov.uk

Register of Companies
Postal Search Section
37 Castle Terrace
Edinburgh EH1 2EB

tel: 0131 535 5800
(this will put you through to the
centralised Office for the U.K. in Cardiff.
Perhaps better to write)

Scottish Archive Network
Thomas Thomson House
99 Bankhead Crossway North
Edinburgh EH11 4DX
(known as SCAN)

tel: 0131 242 5800
email: enquiries@scan.org.uk
website: www.scan.org.uk

ARCHIVES, LIBRARIES AND RECORD OFFICES

The addresses in the following section are arranged under counties, although these thirty-three counties were superseded by nine regions and fifty-three districts in 1975. Another wholesale reorganisation of local government took place in April 1996 and thirty-two Local Government Areas were put in their place.

In most instances you will be searching in parishes in counties, which existed prior to 1975.

Co. Aberdeen

Aberdeen City Archives
Aberdeen City Council
Town House
Broad Street
Aberdeen AB10 1AQ

tel: 01224 522 513
email: archives@legal.aberdeen.net.uk
website: www.aberdeencity.gov.uk

Aberdeen Central Library
Reference and Local Studies
Rosemount Viaduct
Aberdeen AB25 1GW

tel: 01224 652 511
email: refloc@arts-rec.aberdeen.net.uk

Aberdeenshire Library &
Information Service
The Meadows Industrial Estate
Meldrum Meg Way
Oldmeldrum AB51 0GN

tel: 01651 872 707
email: ALIS@aberdeenshire.gov.uk
website: www.aberdeenshire.gov.uk

Co. Angus

Angus Archives
Montrose Library
214 High Street
Montrose DD10 8PH

tel: 01674 671 415
email: angus.archives@angus.gov.uk
website:www.angus.gov.uk/history/
history

Arbroath Library
Hill Terrace
Arbroath DD11 1AH

tel: 01241 872 248

Dundee Central Library
Local Studies Library
The Wellgate
Dundee DD1 1DB

tel: 01382 434 377
email:local.studies@dundeecity.gov.uk
website: www.dundeecity.gov.uk/
centlib/locindex.html

Dundee City Archives
Dept of Support Services
21 City Square
Dundee DD1 3BY
(Personal callers enter by 1 Shore Terrace)

tel: 01382 434 494
email: archives@ dundeecity.gov.uk
website: www.dundeecity.gov.uk/
archives

Dundee City Council
Genealogy Unit
89 Commercial Street
Dundee DD1 2AF

tel: 01382 435 222
email: grant.law@dundeecity.gov.uk
website: www.dundeecity.gov.uk/
registrar/genindex.htm

Forfar Library
50 West High Street
Forfar DD8 2EG

tel: 01307 466 071

Co. Argyll

Argyll & Bute Archives
Kilmory
Manse Brae
Lochgilphead PA31 8QU

tel: 01546 604 120

Argyll & Bute Council Archives
Highland Avenue
Sandbank
Dunoon PA23 8PB

tel: 01369 703 214

Argyll & Bute Library Service
Local Collection
Library Headquarters
Highland Avenue
Sandbank
Dunoon PA23 8PB

tel: 01369 703 214
email: andyewan@abc-libraries.
demon.co.uk

Co. Ayr

Ayrshire Archives
Ayrshire Archives Centre
Craigie Estate
Ayr KA8 0SS

tel: 01292 287 584
email: archives@south-ayrshire.gov.uk
website: www.ayrshirearchives.org.uk

East Ayrshire Council
Library Service
Ayrshire Collection
Dick Institute
Elmbank Avenue
Kilmarnock KA1 3BU

tel: 01563 554 310

East Ayrshire Council
Library Service
Local Archives
Baird Institute
3 Lugar Street
Cumnock KA18 1AD

tel: 01290 421 701
email: Baird.institute@east-ayrshire.
                                    gov.uk

North Ayrshire Libraries
Local History Library
39–41 Princes Street
Ardrossan KA22 8BT

tel: 01294 469 137
email: reference@naclibhq.prestel.gov.uk

South Ayrshire Libraries
Scottish and Local History
Carnegie Library
12 Main Street
Ayr KA8 8ED

tel: 01292 286 385
email: carnegie@south-ayrshire.gov.uk

Co. Berwick   see Co. Selkirk

Co. Caithness   see also Co. Inverness

North Highland Archive
Wick Library
Sinclair Terrace
Wick KW1 5AB

tel: 01955 606 432

Co. Clackmannan

Clackmannanshire Archives
   and Local Studies
Alloa Library
26-28 Drysdale Street
Alloa FK10 1JL

tel: 01259 722 262
email: libraries@clacks.gov.uk
website: www.clacksweb.org.uk/dyna/
                                    archives

Co. Dumfries

Dumfries & Galloway Council
   Archives
Archive Centre
33 Burns Street
Dumfries DG1 2PS
(also includes Counties Kirkcudbright and Wigtown)

tel: 01387 269 254
email: libarchive@dumgal.gov.uk
website: www.dumgal.gov.uk

Dumfries & Galloway Health Board
   Archives
Crichton Royal Museum
Easterbrook Hall
Crichton Royal Hospital
Bankhead Road
Dumfries DG1 1SY

tel: 01387 244 000

Dumfries & Galloway Libraries
Local Studies Collection
Ewart Library
Catherine Street
Dumfries DG1 1JB
(also includes counties Kirkcudbright and Wigtown)

tel: 01387 252 070
01387 253 820
email: libs&l@dumgal.gov.uk

Co. Dunbarton

East Dunbartonshire Libraries   tel: 0141 776 8090
Reference & Local Studies Library   email: libraries@eastdunbarton.gov.uk
The William Patrick Library
2 West High Street
Kirkintilloch G66 1AD

West Dunbartonshire Libraries   tel: 01389 733 273
Dumbarton Public Library   email: wdlibs@hotmail.com
Local Studies Library
Strathleven Place
Dumbarton G82 1BD

Co. East Lothian (earlier known as Co. Haddington)

East Lothian Council   tel: 01620 823 307
Library Service   email: hq@elothlib.demon.co.uk
Local History Centre
Haddington Library
Newton Port
Haddington EH41 3NA

Co. Elgin   see Co. Moray

Co. Fife

Fife Council Archives Centre   tel: 01592 416 504
Carleton House
Balgonie Road
Markinch
Glenrothes KY6 7AH

Fife Council Central Area Libraries   tel: 01592 412 878
Local History Collection   email: info@kirkcaldy.fifelib.net
Central Library
War Memorial Grounds
Kirkcaldy KY1 1YG

Fife Council East Area Libraries   tel: 01334 412 285
Local History Collection   email: cupar.library@fife.gov.uk
Cupar Library   website: www.fife.gov.uk
33 Crossgate   fif/cupar-lib.htm
Cupar KY15 5AS

Fife Council West Area Libraries   tel: 01383 312 994
Local History Department   email: dunfermline.library@fife.gov.uk
Dunfermline Library
Abbot Street
Dunfermline KY12 7NL

The Hay Fleming Reference Library   tel: 01334 412 685
St Andrews Library
Church Street
St Andrews KY16 9NN

Co. Forfar   see Co. Angus

Co. Haddington   see Co. East Lothian

Co. Inverness

Clan Donald Centre Library	tel: 01471 844 389
Armadale	email: library@cland.demon.co.uk
Ardvasar	
Isle of Skye IV45 8RS	

Co Leis Thu?	tel: 01859 520 258
Bill Lawson – Consultant Genealogist	email: seallam@aol.com
Seallam! Visitor Centre	website: www.seallam.com
Northton	
Isle of Harris HS3 3JA	

Highland Council Archive Service   tel: 01463 220 330
Inverness Library
Farraline Park
Inverness IV1 1NH
(covers former Counties of Inverness, Ross & Cromarty, Sutherland & Caithness, and Inverness Burgh)

Highland Council Genealogy Centre   tel: 01463 236 463
Inverness Public Library
Farraline Park
Inverness IV1 1NH

Co. Kinloss   see Co. Perth

Co. Kirkcudbright   see Co. Dumfries

Co. Lanark

Glasgow City Archives   tel: 0141 287 2910
Mitchell Library   email: archives@cls.glasgow.gov.uk
North Street   website: www.glasgowlibraries.org/
Glasgow G3 7DN   archives.htm
(includes former Glasgow Corporation and the Counties of Dunbarton, Lanark, Renfrew and Bute, and the former Strathclyde Region, and City of Glasgow District Council)

Glasgow City Libraries and Archive   tel: 0141 287 2937
Glasgow Collection   email: history_and_glasgow@cls.glasgow.
Mitchell Library   gov.uk
North Street   website: www.glasgowlibraries.org
Glasgow G3 7DN

Greater Glasgow Health Board   tel: 0141 330 5516
     Archive   website: www.archives.gla.ac.uk/gghb
Glasgow University Archives
77-81 Dumbarton Road
Glasgow G11 6TP

Royal College of Physicians and   tel: 0141 221 6072
     Surgeons of Glasgow   email: library@rcpsglasg.ac.uk
232–234 St Vincent Street   website: www.rcpsglasg.ac.uk
Glasgow G2 5RJ

Scottish Jewish Archives Centre   tel: 0141 332 4911
127 Hill Street   email: archives@sjac.fsbusiness.co.uk
Garnethill   website: www.sjac.org.uk
Glasgow G3 6UB

North Lanarkshire Libraries   tel: 01236 763 221
Airdrie Library
Wellwynd
Airdrie ML6 0AG

South Lanarkshire Libraries   tel: 01555 661 144
Lanark Library
Reference & Local Studies Dept.
Lindsay Institute
16 Hope Street
Lanark ML11 7LZ

South Lanarkshire Libraries   tel: 01698 452 403
Local Studies Department   email: hamilton.reference@south.
Hamilton Central Library   lanarkshire.co.uk
Cadzow Street
Hamilton ML3 6HQ

North Lanarkshire Libraries   tel: 01698 251 000
Motherwell Heritage Centre
High Road
Motherwell ML1 3HU

Co. Linlithgow   see Co. West Lothian

Co. Midlothian (earlier known as Co. Edinburgh)

Bank of Scotland Archive   tel: 0131 529 1288
Operational Services Division   email: archives@hbosplc.com
12 Bankhead Terrace
Sighthill
Edinburgh EH11 4DY

Edinburgh City Archives   tel: 0131 529 4616
City of Edinburgh Council
City Chambers
High Street
Edinburgh EH1 1YJ

Edinburgh City Libraries   tel: 0131 242 8030
Edinburgh Room   email: edinburgh.room@edinburgh.
Central Library   gov.uk
George IV Bridge
Edinburgh EH1 1EG

Edinburgh City Libraries   tel: 0131 242 8070
Scottish Library   email: central.scottish.library@edinburgh.
Central Library   gov.uk
George IV Bridge
Edinburgh EH1 1EG

Midlothian Archives and   tel: 0131 271 3976
   Local Studies Centre   email: local.studies@midlothian.gov.uk
2 Clark Street   website: www.midlothian.gov.uk/library/
Loanhead EH20 9DR   local.htm

The Royal Bank of Scotland   tel: 0131 523 3976
Group Archives   email: archives@rbs.co.uk
26 St Andrew Square   website: www.rbs.co.uk/group
Edinburgh EH2 1AF   information/memory_bank/

Royal College of Physicians
  of Edinburgh
9 Queen Street
Edinburgh EH2 1JQ

tel: 0131 225 7324
email: library@rcpe.ac.uk
website: www.rcpe.ac.uk

Royal College of Surgeons
  of Edinburgh
Nicolson Street
Edinburgh EH8 9DW

tel: 0131 527 1630
email: library@rcsed.ac.uk
website: www.rcsed.ac.uk

Co. Moray (or Co. Elgin)

Moray Local Heritage Centre
Grant Lodge
Cooper Park
Elgin IV30 1HS

tel: 01343 562 644
email: graeme.wilson@techleis.moray.
                     gov.uk
website: www.moray.org/heritage/roots.
                     html

Co. Orkney

Orkney Library and Archive Service
The Orkney Library
Laing Street
Kirkwall KW15 1NW

tel: 01856 873 166
email: alison.fraser@orkney.gov.uk

Co. Peebles   see Co. Selkirk

Co. Perth (includes Co. Kinross)

Clan Donnachaidh (Robertson)
  (Museum)
Bruar
Pitlochry PH18 5TW

tel: 01796 483 264
    01796 483 338
email: clandonnachaidh@compuserve.
                     com
website: www.donnachaidh.co.uk

Perth & Kinross Council Archives
A.K. Bell Library
2–8 York Place
Perth PH2 8EP

tel: 01738 477 022
email: archives@pkc.gov.uk
website: www.pkc.gov.uk/library/
                   archive.htm

Perth & Kinross Libraries
Local Studies Section
A.K. Bell Library
2–8 York Place
Perth PH2 8EP

tel: 01738 477 062
email: library@pkc.gov.uk
website: www.pkc.gov.uk/library/
                local studies.htm

Co. Renfrew

East Renfrew Library
Giffnock Library
Station Road
Giffnock
Glasgow G46 6JF

tel: 0141 577 4976
email: library@eastrenfrewshire.co.uk

HM Customs & Excise
Custom House
Custom House Quay
Greenock PA15 1EQ

tel: 01475 881 452

(shipping registers of ports of Clyde estuary 1785 onwards; and information on
Customs & Excise 1600 onwards)

Renfrewshire Archives
Central Library & Museum Complex
High Street
Paisley PA1 2BB

tel: 0141 889 2350
email: local-studies.library@renfrewshire.
gov.uk

Watt Library
9 Union Street
Greenock PA16 8JH

tel: 01475 715 628

Co. Ross & Cromarty   see also Co. Inverness

Comhairle Nan Eilean Siar
Stornoway Library
Keith Street
Stornoway HS1 2QG

tel: 01851 703 064

Comhairle Nan Eilean Siar
(formerly Western Isles Council)
Stornoway Record Office
Town Hall
2 Cromwell Street
Stornoway HS1 2BD

tel: 01851 709 438
email: emacdonald@cne-siar.gov.uk

Highland Libraries
Dingwall Library
Old Academy Buildings
Tulloch Street
Dingwall IV15 9JZ

tel: 01349 863 163

Co. Selkirk

Scottish Borders Archive & Local
   History Centre
Library Headquarters
St Mary's Mill
Selkirk TD7 5EW
(covers Counties Berwick, Selkirk, Roxburgh and Peebles)

tel: 01750 20842
email: archives@scotborders.gov.uk
website: www.scotborders.gov.uk/libraries

Co. Shetland (also known as Co. Zetland)

Shetland Archives
44 King Harald Street
Lerwick ZE1 0EQ

tel: 01595 696 247
email: shetland.archives@zetnet.co.uk

Shetland Library
Lower Hillhead
Lerwick ZE1 0EL

tel: 01595 693 868
email: info@shetland-library.gov.uk
website: www.shetland-library.gov.uk

Co. Stirling

Dunblane Library
High Street
Dunblane FK15 0ER

tel: 01786 823 125
email: dunblanelibrary@stirling.co.uk

Falkirk Council Library Services
Falkirk Library
Hope Street
Falkirk FK1 5AU

tel: 01324 503 605
email: falkirk-library@falkirk-library.
demon.co.uk
website: www.falkirk.gov.uk

Falkirk Museum History Research
  Centre
Callendar House
Callendar Park
Falkirk FK1 1YR

tel: 01324 503 779
email: callendarhouse@falkirkmuseums.
                              demon.co.uk
website: www.falkirkmuseums.demon.
                                    co.uk

Stirling Council Archives
Unit 6
Burghmuir Industrial Estate
Stirling FK7 7PY

tel: 01786 450 745
email: archive@stirling.gov.uk

Stirling Council Libraries
Local History Collection
Stirling Central Library
Corn Exchange Road
Stirling FK8 2HX

tel: 01786 432 106
email: centrallibrary@stirling.gov.uk

Co. West Lothian (earlier known as Co. Linlithgow)

West Lothian Council Archives
Archives & Record Management
7 Rutherford Square
Brucefield Industrial Estate
Livingston EH54 9BU

tel: 01506 460 020

West Lothian Council Library Service
Local History Collection
Connolly House
Hopefield Road
Blackburn EH47 7HZ

tel: 01506 776 331
email: localhistory@westlothian.org.uk
website: www.wlonline.org

Co. Wigtown   see also Co. Dumfries

Stranraer Museum
Old Town Hall
55 George Street
Stranraer DG9 7JP
(includes archives and records of county)

tel: 01776 705 088
email: JohnPic@dumgal.gov.uk

UNIVERSITY ARCHIVES

University of Aberdeen DISS
Heritage Division Special
  Collections & Archives
Kings College
Aberdeen AB24 3SW

tel: 01224 272 598
email: speclib@abdn.ac.uk
website: www.abdn.ac.uk/diss/heritage

University of Abertay Dundee
Library
Bell Street
Dundee DD1 1HG

tel: 01382 308 866
email: libdesk@abertay.ac.uk
website: www.iserv.tay.ac.uk

Dundee University Archives
Tower Building
University of Dundee
Dundee DD1 4HN

tel: 01382 344 095
email: archives@dundee.ac.uk
website: www.dundee.ac.uk/archives

Edinburgh University Library   tel: 0131 650 3412
Special Collections Department   email: special.collections@ed.ac.uk
University of Edinburgh   website: www.lib.ed.ac.uk
George Square
Edinburgh EH8 9LJ

Edinburgh University New College   tel: 0131 650 8957
    Library   email: new.college.library@ed.ac.uk
University of Edinburgh   website: www.lib.ed.ac.uk
Mound Place
Edinburgh EH1 2LU

Glasgow Caledonian University   tel: 0141 331 3920
    Library   email: j.powles@gcal.ac.uk
Special Collections & Archives   website: www.lib.gcal.ac.uk/archives
Cowcaddens Road
Glasgow G4 0BA

Archives & Business Records Centre   tel: 0141 330 5515
University of Glasgow   email: dutyarch@archives.gla.ac.uk
13 Thurso Street   website: www.archives.gla.ac.uk
Glasgow G11 6PE
(includes Scottish Brewing Archive)

Glasgow University Library   tel: 0141 330 6767
Special Collections Department   email: special@lib.gla.ac.uk
University of Glasgow   website: www.special.lib.gla.ac.uk
Hillhead Street
Glasgow G12 8QE

Heriot-Watt University Archive   tel: 0131 451 3218
Heriot-Watt University   email: a.e.jones@hw.ac.uk
Riccarton   website: www.hw.ac.uk/archive
Edinburgh EH14 4AS

Paisley University   tel: 0141 848 3759
Local & Special Collection Library
High Street
Paisley PA1 2BE

St Andrews University Library   tel: 01334 462 339
Special Collections Department   email: speccoll@st-andrews.ac.uk
University of St Andrews   website: www.specialcollections.st-and.
North Street   ac.uk
St Andrews KY16 9TR

Stirling University Library   tel: 01786 467 235
University of Stirling   website: www.library.stir.ac.uk
Stirling FK9 4LA

Strathclyde University   tel: 0141 950 3300
Jordanhill Campus Library   email: jordanhill.library@strath.ac.uk
76 Southbrae Drive   website: www.lib.strath.ac.uk/
Glasgow G13 1PP   Departments/JHLibrary
(records relate to Glasgow and region teacher training)

Strathclyde University Archives   tel:0141 548 2397
McCance Building   website: www.strath.ac.uk/archives
16 Richmond Street
Glasgow G1 1XQ

SCOTTISH ASSOCIATION OF FAMILY HISTORY SOCIETIES

The Scottish Association of
   Family History Societies
Hon. Secretary
Family History Research Centre
9 Glasgow Street
Dumfries DG2 9AF

tel: 01387 248093
email: marjoriemoore@belaniey.fsnet.
                                          co.uk
website: www.safhs.org.uk

Addresses of Societies

Aberdeen & North-East Scotland FHS
Hon. Secretary
The Family History Shop
164 King Street
Aberdeen AB24 5BD

tel: 01224 646323
fax: 01224 639096
email: enquiries@anesfhs.org.uk
website: www.anesfhs.org.uk

Alloway & Southern Ayrshire FHS
Hon. Secretary
c/o Alloway Public Library
Doonholm Road
Alloway
Ayr KA7 4QQ

email: ASAFHS@mtcharlesayr.fsnet.
                                          co.uk
website: www.asafhs.co.uk

Anglo-Scottish FHS
Hon. Secretary
Clayton House
59 Piccadilly
Manchester MR1 2AQ

tel: 0161 236 9750
fax: 0161 237 3812
email: office@mlfhs.org.uk
website: www.mlfhs.org.uk/AngloScots

Association of Scottish Genealogists
   & Record Agents
Hon. Secretary
93 Colinton Road
Edinburgh EH10 5DF

tel: 0131 313 1104
email: hazelweir@sea-insite.org.uk
website: www.asgra.co.uk

Borders FHS
Hon. Secretary
2 Fellowhills
Ladykirk
Berwickshire TD15 1XN

website: www.bordersfhs.org.uk

Caithness FHS
Hon. Secretary
Mill Cottage
Dunnet
Corsback
Caithness KW14 8XQ

website: www.caithnessfhs.org.uk

Central Scotland FHS
Hon. Secretary
11 Springbank Gardens
Dunblane
Perthshire FK15 9JX

website: www.csfhs.org.uk

Dumfries & Galloway FHS
Hon. Secretary
Family History Research Centre
9 Glasgow Street
Dumfries DG2 9AF

tel: 01387 248093
email: secretary@dgfhs.org.uk
website: www.dgfhs.org.uk

East Ayrshire FHS
Hon. Secretary
c/o The Dick Institute
Elmbank Avenue
Kilmarnock
East Ayrshire KA1 3BU

tel: 01563 5248798
email: sec@eastayrshirefhs.org.uk
website: www.eastayrshirefhs.org.uk

Fife FHS
Hon. Secretary
Glenmoriston
Durie Street
Leven
Fife KY8 4HF

email: chairman@fifefhs.org
website: www.fifefhs.org

The Genealogical Society of Utah
Family History Support Office
185 Penns Lane
Sutton Coldfield
West Midlands B76 1JU

website: www.familysearch.org

Glasgow & West of Scotland FHS
Hon. Secretary
Unit 5, 22 Mansfield Street
Glasgow G11 5QP

tel: 0141 339 8303
website: www.gwsfhs.org.uk

Guild of One-Name Studies
Box G, 14 Charterhouse Buildings
Goswell Road
London EC1M 7BA

email: guild@one-name.org
website: www.one-name.org

The Heraldry Society of Scotland
SAFHS Representative
40 Morningside Drive
Edinburgh EH10 5LZ

website: www.heraldry-scotland.co.uk

Highland FHS
Hon. Secretary
c/o Reference Room
Public Library
Farraline Park
Inverness IV1 1NH

tel: 01463 236463
fax: 01463 711128
website: www.genuki.org.uk/big/
         scot/Highland.FHS.home.html

Lanarkshire FHS
Hon. Secretary
c/o Local History Room
Motherwell Heritage Centre
1 High Road
Motherwell
North Lanarkshire ML1 3HU

email: infoLFHS@aol.com
website: www.lanarkshirefhs.org.uk

Largs & North Ayrshire FHS
Hon. Secretary
Bogriggs Cottage
Carlung
West Kilbride
Ayrshire KA23 9PS

email: agillan@walkerston.freeserve.co.uk

The Lothians FHS
Hon. Secretary
Lasswade High School Centre
Eskdale Drive
Bonnyrigg
Midlothian EH19 2LA

email: lothiansfhs@hotmail.com
website: www.lothiansfhs.org.uk

Orkney FHS
Hon. Secretary
The Community Room
The Strynd
Kirkwall
Orkney KW15 1HJ

email: secretary@orkneyfhs.co.uk
website: www.orkneyfhs.co.uk

Renfrewshire FHS
The Secretary
c/o Paisley Museum & Art Gallery
High Street
Paisley PA1 2BA

website: www.renfrewshirefhs.org.uk

The Scottish Genealogy Society
Hon. Secretary
15 Victoria Terrace
Edinburgh EH1 2JL

tel: 0131 220 3677
fax: 070707 13411
email: info@scotsgenealogy.com
website: www.scotsgenealogy.com

Shetland FHS
Hon. Secretary
6 Hillhead
Lerwick
Shetland ZE1 0ED

email: secretary@shetland-fhs.org.uk
website: www.shetland-fhs.org.uk

The Society of Genealogists
14 Charterhouse Buildings
Goswell Road
London EC1M 7BA

tel: 020 7251 8799
fax: 020 7250 1800
email: genealogy@sog.org.uk
website: www.sog.org.uk

Tay Valley FHS
Hon. Secretary
Research Centre
179–181 Princes Street
Dundee
Angus DD4 6DQ

tel: 01382 461845
fax: 01382 455532
email: tvfhs@tayvalleyfhs.org.uk
website: www.tayvalleyfhs.org.uk

Troon & Ayrshire FHS
Hon. Secretary
c/o MERC, Troon Library
South Beach
Troon
Ayrshire KA10 6EF

email: info@troonayrshirefhs.org.uk
website: www.troonayrshirefhs.org.uk

West Lothian FHS
Hon. Secretary
23 Templar Rise
Livingston EH54 6PJ

email: honsec@wlfhs.org.uk
website: www.wlfhs.org.uk

SOCIETIES

Association of Scottish Genealogists
  & Record Agents
(ASGRA)
Hon. Secretary
93 Colinton Road
Edinburgh EH10 5DF

tel: 0131 313 1104
email : hazelweir@sea -insite.org.uk
website: www.asgra.co.uk

The Heraldry Society of Scotland
c/o Stuart G. Emerson
25 Craigentinny Crescent
Edinburgh EH7 6QA

website: www.heraldry-scotland.co.uk

Scottish Genealogy Society
Library and Family History Centre
15 Victoria Terrace
Edinburgh EH1 2JL

tel: 0131 220 3677
email: info@scotsgenealogy.com
website: www.scotsgenealogy.com

Scottish Tartans Authority
The Administrator
Fraser House
Commissioner Street
Crieff PH7 3AY

tel: 01764 655 444
email: BrianWilton@tartansauthority.
                  com
website: www.tartansauthority.com

ADOPTION

Birth Link
Adoption Counselling Centre
Family Care
21 Castle Street
Edinburgh EH2 3DN

tel: 0131 225 6441
email: mail@birthlink.org.uk

British Association of Adoption
  and Fostering
40 Shandwick Place
Edinburgh EH2 4RT

tel: 0131 225 9285
email: Scotland@baaf.org.uk

National Organisation for Counselling
  Adoptees and their Parents
(NORCAP)
112 Church Road
Wheatley
Oxfordshire OX33 1LU

tel: 01865 875 000
email: enquiries@norcap.org
website: www.norcap.org.uk

Talkadoption

freephone: 0808 808 1234
website: www.talkadoption.org.uk

ADDRESSES IN ENGLAND

Anglo-Scottish FHS
Hon. Secretary
Clayton House
59 Piccadilly
Manchester MR1 2AQ

tel: 0161 236 9750
email: office@mlfhs.org.uk
website: www.mlfhs.org.uk

British Library
Oriental and India Office Collections
96 Euston Road
London NW1 2DB

tel: 0207 412 7873
email: oioc-enquiries@bl.uk
website: www.bl.uk/collections/
                          orientaloffice.html

Family Records Centre
1 Myddleton Street
London EC1R 1UW

tel: 0208 392 5300
email: enquiries@pro.gov.uk
website: www. familyrecords.gov.uk

General Register Office
  for England & Wales
PO Box 2
Southport
Merseyside PR8 2JD

tel: 0870 243 7788
email: certificate.services@ons.gov.uk
website: www.statistics.gov.uk

Guild of One-Name Studies
The Secretary
Box G
Society of Genealogists
14 Charterhouse Buildings
Goswell Road
London EC1M 7BA
(known as GOONS)

email: guild@one-name.org
website: www.one-name.org

The National Archives
Public Records Office
Ruskin Avenue
Kew
Richmond
Surrey TW9 4DU

tel: 0208 876 3444
email: enquiries@pro.gov.uk
website: www.pro.gov.uk
Census help desk: tel: 0208 392 500
email: 1901census@pro.gov.uk
website: www.census.pro.gov.uk

(in April 2003 the PRO merged with the Historical Manuscripts Commission in
Chancery Lane, London, to become The National Archives)

Principal Registry of the Family
  Division
First Avenue House
42–49 High Holborn
London WC1V 6NP

Probate Searchroom:
tel: 0207 947 7022
website: www.courtservice.gov.uk/
                          cms/3800.htm

Society of Genealogists
14 Charterhouse Buildings
Goswell Road
London EC1M 7BA

tel:0207 251 8799
email: library@sog.org.uk
website: www.sog.org.uk

Traceline
PO Box 106
Southport
Merseyside PR8 2WA

tel: 0151 471 4811

ADDRESSES IN NORTHERN IRELAND

Belfast Central Library
Irish & Local Studies Dept
Royal Avenue
Belfast BT1 1EA

tel: 028 9024 3233
email: info@libraries.belfast-elb.gov.uk
website: www.belb.org.uk

General Register Office   tel: 028 9025 2000
  (Northern Ireland)   email: gro.nisra@dfpni.gov.uk
Oxford House   website: www.groni.gov.uk
49-55 Chichester Street
Belfast BT1 4HL

Irish Genealogical Research Society
(see Ireland)

North of Ireland Family
  History Society   email: R.Sibbett@tesco.net
c/o Graduate School of Education   website: www.nifhs.org
69 University Street
Belfast BT7 1HL

Public Record Office of   tel: 028 9025 5905
  Northern Ireland   email:proni@dcalni.gov.uk
66 Balmoral Avenue   website: www.proni.nics.gov.uk
Belfast BT9 6NY

Ulster Historical Foundation   tel: 028 9033 2288
12 College Square East   email: enquiry@uhf.org.uk
Belfast BT1 6DD   website. www.ancestryireland.co.uk

ADDRESSES IN THE REPUBLIC OF IRELAND

Church of Ireland Archives   tel: 01 492 3979
Representative Church Body   email: library@ireland.anglican.org
  Library   website: www.ireland.anglican.org
Braemor Park
Churchtown
Dublin 14

Council of Irish Genealogical
  Organisations
186 Ashcroft
Raheny
Dublin 5

Genealogical Office/Office of the tel: +353 1 6030 200
  Chief Herald   email: herald@nli.ie
Kildare Street   website: www.nli.ie
Dublin 2

Genealogical Society of Ireland   tel: 353 1 280 2711
11 Desmond Avenue   email: GenSocIreland@iol.ie
Dun Laoghaire   website: www.gensocireland.org
Co. Dublin

General Register Office of Ireland tel: 003531 635 4000
8–11 Lombard Street East
Dublin 2   website: www.groireland.ie

Irish Genealogical Research Society
c/o 82 Eaton Square
London SW1W 9AJ   website: www.igrsoc.org

National Archives of Ireland   tel: 01 407 2300
Bishop Street   email: mail@nationalarchives.ie
Dublin 8   website: www.nationalarchives.ie

LOCAL HISTORY

British Association for
  Local History   tel: 01283 585 947
PO Box 6549   website: www.balh.co.uk
Somersal Herbert
Ashbourne DE6 5WH

Scottish Local History Forum   tel: 01506 844 649
The Secretary   fax: 0131 260 6610
45 High Street   email: chantal.hamill@dial.pipex.com
Linlithgow
West Lothian EH54 6EW

Appendix III

List of Parishes, Counties and Commissariots

This list is arranged in alphabetical order showing the registration district number and the date of the earliest birth or marriage record extant for that parish to be found in an Old Parish Register.

In some instances the place listed has no OPR, being a district under the Registration Act of 1854. Where these places are incorporated in a parish, the number of the parish is shown, otherwise the numbers shown are those of parishes which would be worth searching. In some parishes the records for the early years are sparse.

This list also shows the county and the commissariot as an aid to finding testaments or inventories. Where possible, the earliest date of the testament or inventory is listed. In some cases the places mentioned were not found in a gazetteer and so it was not possible to assign them to any particular parish. From 1823, testaments and inventories are to be found in Sheriff Court Records. These have not been consulted for this list.

The Scottish Record Society has produced indexes to testaments and inventories arranged by commissariot and person's name. Some parishes may be found in more than one commissariot.

Note: County Forfar = County Angus
County Moray = County Elgin
County Haddington = County East Lothian
County Linlithgow = County West Lothian
County Edinburgh = County Midlothian

In the Dome Search Room at New Register House, near to the entrance from both the East and West Search Rooms, there is a binder containing the lists of the Old Parishes with their registration numbers and the range of years for each births/baptisms, marriages and deaths/burials register.

These are also given in *The Parishes, Registers & Registrars of Scotland* (reprinted 1995; SAFHS). This publication includes maps of the pre-1975 counties with each parish shown.

Parish	District number	County	Commissariot	OPR	Testament or inventory
Abbey (or Abbey Paisley)	559	Renfrew	Glasgow	1676	1552
Abbey St Bathans	726	Berwick	Lauder	1715	1709
Abbotrule (also Southdean 806)	806	Roxburgh	Peebles Dumfries	1755	1682 1736
Abbotshall (incl. Kirkcaldy in 1876)	399	Fife	St Andrews	1650	1615
Abdie	400	Fife	St Andrews Edinburgh	1620	1549 1597
Abercorn	661	Linlithgow W. Lothian	Dunkeld Edinburgh	1585	1735 1576
Abercrombie (see St Monance 454)	454	Fife	St Andrews Edinburgh		1551 1585
Aberdalgic	323	Perth	Dunkeld Dunblane Edinburgh St Andrews	1615	1688 1654 1575 1662
Aberdeen	168a	Aberdeen	Aberdeen Edinburgh	1563	1715 1600
Aberdour	169	Aberdeen	Aberdeen Edinburgh	1698	1722 1564
Aberdour	401	Fife	Dunkeld St Andrews Edinburgh	1663	1682 1656 1564
Aberfeldy (see Dull, 346 & Logierait, 376)	324	Perth	Dunkeld		1697
Aberfoyle	325	Perth	Dunblane	1692	1661
Aberlady	702	Haddington E. Lothian	Dunkeld Edinburgh	1632	1570
Aberlemno	269	Forfar	St Andrews Edinburgh	1706	1606 1598
Aberlour (also Glenrinnes 155b)	145	Banff	Moray Edinburgh	1708	1685 1599
Aberluthnot (see Marykirk 265)	265	Kincardine Edinburgh	St Andrews	1577	1597
Abernethy	326	Perth	Dunblane Edinburgh St Andrews	1690	1539 1584 1607
Abernethy & Kincardine	90a	Inverness	Inverness Moray	1730	1631 1699
Abernyte	327	Perth	Dunkeld Dunblane	1667	1701 1655
Abertarff or Fort Augustus (also Boleskine 92/1)	92/2	Inverness	Inverness	1737	1630

Parish	District number	County	Commissariot	OPR	Testament or inventory
Aboyne	170	Aberdeen	Aberdeen Moray	1752	1743 1738
Acharacle	505/1	Argyll	Argyll	1829	
(also Arisaig, Sunart/Strontian & W. Ardnamurchan 505)					
Advie	128b	Moray	Moray		
(see Cromdale, Inverallan & Advie 128b)			Edinburgh		1594
Airlie	270	Forfar	St Andrews Edinburgh	1682	1598 1576
Airth	469	Stirling	Stirling Edinburgh	1660	1608 1585
Aithsting	9	Shetland	Orkney & Shetland		1613
(see Sandsting & Aithsting 9)					
Alford	171	Aberdeen	Aberdeen Moray	1717	1742 1747
Alloa	465	Clackmannan	Stirling Glasgow Dunblane Edinburgh	1609	1615 1604 1547 1586
Alness	57	Ross & Cromarty	Ross	1783	1803
Alva	470	Stirling c. 1600-1832	Stirling Edinburgh	1655	1665 1593
otherwise Co. Clackmannan					
Alvah	146	Banff	Aberdeen	1718	
Alves	125	Moray	Moray Ross Edinburgh	1648	1688 1803 1586
Alvie	90b	Inverness	Inverness	1713	1820
Alyth	328	Perth	Dunkeld Dunblane Edinburgh Stirling	1623	1688 1653 1583 1608
Ancrum	780	Roxburgh	Peebles Edinburgh	1703	1682 1574
Annan	812	Dumfries	Dumfries	1703	1638
Anstruther-Easter	402	Fife	St Andrews Edinburgh	1641	1550 1575
Anstruther-Wester	403	Fife	St Andrews Edinburgh	1577	1550 1567
Anwoth	855	Kirkcudbright	Kirkcudbright Edinburgh	1727	1667 1600
Appin	525/2	Argyll	Argyll	1751	1677
(also Lismore 525/1, Glencoe & Ballachulish 525/3, Duror 525/4)					
Applecross	58	(see Shieldaig & Kishorn 58)			
Applegarth & Sibbaldie	813a	Dumfries	Dumfries	1749	1639

Parish	District number	County	Commissariot	OPR	Testament or inventory
Arbirlot	271	Forfar	St Andrews	1632	1583
			Edinburgh		1595
Arbroath	272	Forfar	St Andrews	1653	1591
(anciently Aberbrothock)			Brechin		1657
			Edinburgh		1592
Arbuthnot	250	Kincardine	St Andrews	1631	1605
			Brechin		1657
			Edinburgh		1582
Ardchattan	504	Argyll	Argyll	1758	1677
Ardclach	120	Nairn	Moray	1652	1688
Ardersier	91	Inverness	Inverness	1719	
Ardgour, Corran of & Ballachulish *(also Kilmalie 520)*	506	Argyll	Argyll	1835	
Ardnamurchan *(also Aharacle, Arisaig, Sunart/Strontian 505)*	505/4	Argyll	Argyll	1777	1686
Ardrossan	576	Ayr	Glasgow	1734	1603
Arisaig (as *above*)	505/2	Argyll	Argyll		
Arngask	404	Fife	Dunkeld	1688	1728
	part	Kinross	Edinburgh		1595
	part	Perth	St Andrews		1551
Arrochar	492	Dunbarton	Glasgow	1759	1720
Ashkirk	781	Roxburgh	Peebles	1630	1823
Assynt *(also known as Inchnadamff)*	44	Sutherland	Caithness	1798	
Athelstaneford	703	Haddington E. Lothian	Edinburgh	1664	1581
Auchindoir & Kearn (prior *to 1811 Kearn was united with Forbes: see Tullynessle & Forbes 246)*	172	Aberdeen	Aberdeen	1694	
Auchinleck	577	Ayr	Glasgow	1693	1571
			Brechin		1671
			Hamilton & Campsie		1574
			Dumfries		1626
			Edinburgh		1577
Auchterarder	329	Perth	Dunblane	1661	1602
			Dunkeld		1714
			Edinburgh		1589
Auchterderran	405	Fife	St Andrews	1664	1613
			Edinburgh		1594
Auchtergaven	330	Perth	Dunkeld	1741	1688
			Edinburgh		1570
			Dunblane		1658
Auchterhouse	273	Forfar	Dunkeld	1645	1695
			Brechin		1657
Auchterless	173	Aberdeen	Aberdeen	1680	1723

Parish	District number	County	Commissariot	OPR	Testament or inventory
Auchtermuchty	406	Fife	St Andrews Edinburgh	1649	1550 1577
Auchtertool	407	Fife	St Andrews Edinburgh	1708	1656 1568
Auldearn	121	Nairn	Moray Edinburgh	1687	1695 1583
Avoch	59	Ross & Cromarty	Ross Edinburgh	1727	1804 1596
Avondale	621	Lanark	Glasgow Edinburgh	1698	1603 1576
Ayr	578	Ayr	Glasgow Edinburgh	1664	1547 1569
Ayton	727	Berwick	Lauder Edinburgh	1743	1564 1582
Baldernock	471	Stirling	Hamilton & Campsie also Glasgow Stirling (1649–1660) Edinburgh	1624	1612 1656 1582
Balfron	472	Stirling	Glasgow Stirling	1687	1617 1654
Ballachulish & Corran of Ardgour *(also Kilmallie 520)*	506	Argyll	Argyll	1830	
Ballachulish	525/3	*(see Glencoe & Ballachulish 525/3)*			
Ballantrae	579	Ayr	Glasgow	1731	1617
Ballingry	408	Fife	St Andrews Edinburgh	1670	1597 1597
Balmaclellan	856	Kirkcudbright	Kirkcudbright Edinburgh	1747	1675 1583
Balmaghie	857a	Kirkcudbright	Kirkcudbright Edinburgh	1768	1707 1575
Balmerino	409	Fife	St Andrews Edinburgh	1632	1587 1573
Balquhidder	331	Perth	Dunblane	1696	1622
Banchory-Devenick	251	Kincardine	Aberdeen Edinburgh	1713	1727 1588
Banchory-Ternan	252	Kincardine	Aberdeen Edinburgh	1670	1728 1588
Banff	147	Banff	Aberdeen	1620	1722
Bannockburn *(see St Ninians & Bannockburn 488)*	488	Stirling	Stirling Edinburgh		1607 1589
Bargrennan *(see Minnigaff 876 & Penninghame 895)*	857b	Wigtown	Wigtown		
Barony *(also Glasgow 644[1], Gorbals 644[2] & Govan 646)*	622	Lanark	Glasgow Hamilton & Campsie	1672	1603 1676

Parish	District number	County	Commissariot	OPR	Testament or inventory
Barr	580	Ayr	Glasgow	1689	1661
Barra	108	Inverness	The Isles	1836	
			Aberdeen		1816
Barry	274	Forfar	St Andrews	1704	1591
			Edinburgh		1583
Barvas (Lewis)	86a	Ross & Cromarty	The Isles	1810	
Bathgate	662	Linlithgow W. Lothian	Edinburgh	1672	1568
Beath	410	Fife	St Andrews	1643	1650
Bedrule	782	Roxburgh	Peebles	1690	1682
Beith	581	Ayr	Glasgow	1661	1605
			Edinburgh		1582
Belhelvie	174	Aberdeen	Aberdeen	1624	1727
Bellie	126	Moray	Moray	1709	1687
Benbecula (also S. Uist 118)	118	Inverness	The Isles	1848	1815
Bendochy	332	Perth	St Andrews	1642	
			Dunkeld		1766
			Dunblane		1653
			Edinburgh		1587
Benholm	253	Kincardine	St Andrews	1684	1614
			Edinburgh		1565
Benvie	301	Forfar	St Andrews	1655	
			Edinburgh		1579
Bervie (or Inverbervie)	254	Kincardine Brechin	St Andrews	1698 1657	1681
			Edinburgh		1585
Berwick North (see North Berwick 713)					
Biggar	623	Lanark	Lanark	1730	1621
			Edinburgh		1577
Birnie	127	Moray	Moray	1712	1688
Birsay	13	Orkney	Orkney & Shetland	1645	1612
Birse	175	Aberdeen	Aberdeen	1758	1726
Blackford	333	Perth	Dunblane	1738	1612
Blair Atholl & Strowan (also Tenandry 394c)	334	Perth	Dunkeld Dunblane	1718	1688 1654
Blairgowrie (also Persie 386b)	335	Perth Dunblane	St Andrews	1647 1653	1591
			Edinburgh		1583
Blantyre	624	Lanark	Glasgow	1677	1618
			Edinburgh		1586
Boharm	128a	Banff	Moray	1634	1686

Parish	District number	County	Commissariot	OPR	Testament or inventory
Boleskine (also Abertarff or Fort Augustus 92/2)	92/1	Inverness	Inverness	1777	1630
Bolton	704	Haddington E. Lothian	Edinburgh	1686	1584
Bonhill	493	Dunbarton	Glasgow Edinburgh	1676	1606 1594
Borgue	858	Kirkcudbright	Kirkcudbright Edinburgh	1742	1682 1587
Bo'ness (Borrowstounness)	663	Linlithgow W. Lothian	Edinburgh	1656	1575
Borthwick (also Stobhill 689b) Midlothian	674	Edinburgh	Edinburgh	1706	1583
Bothkennar	473	Stirling	Stirling Edinburgh	1723	1608 1569
Bothwell	625	Lanark	Glasgow Edinburgh	1671	1547 1578
Botriphnie	148	Banff	Moray	1683	1686
Bourtie	176	Aberdeen	Aberdeen Edinburgh	1709	1728 1594
Bowden	783	Roxburgh	Peebles	1697	1693
Bower	34	Caithness	Caithness	1740	1663
Bowmore (or Kilarrow)	536	Argyll	The Isles	1763	1726
Boyndie	149	Banff	Aberdeen	1700	1741
Bracadale (Skye)	109	Inverness	The Isles	1802	1785
Braemar & Crathie	183	Aberdeen	Aberdeen	1771	1783
Brechin	275	Forfar	Brechin Edinburgh	1612	1578 1569
Bressay (also Burra & Quarff 1/2)	1/1	Shetland	Orkney & Shetland	1737	1613
Bridekirk (see Brydekirk 813b)					
Broughton (also Kilbucho 763 & Glenholm 761)	758	Peebles	Peebles Edinburgh	1697	1584
Brydekirk (also Annan 812, Cummertrees 817 & Hoddam 829)	813b	Dumfries	Dumfries	1836	
Buchanan	474	Stirling	Glasgow	1646	1614
Buittle	859	Kirkcudbright	Kirkcudbright Edinburgh	1736	1710 1572
Bunkle & Preston	728	Berwick	Lauder Edinburgh	1704	1655 1578

Parish	District number	County	Commissariot	OPR	Testament or inventory
Burness & Lady 26 (also Sanday 26)		Orkney Shetland	Orkney &	1758	1615
Burntisland 411		Fife	St Andrews Edinburgh	1672	1589 1575
Burra & Quarff 1/2 (also Bressay 1/1)		Shetland Shetland	Orkney &	1755	
Burray 29 (also S. Ronaldsay 29)		Orkney	Orkney & Shetland	1657	1624
Cabrach	177	Aberdeen	Aberdeen	1711	1812
Cadder	626	Lanark	Hamilton & Campsie also Glasgow Edinburgh	1662	1564 1587
Caddonfoot (see Stow 699 & Galashiels 775)					
Caerlaverock	815	Dumfries	Dumfries	1749	1638
Cairney	178	Aberdeen	Aberdeen Moray	1738	1717
Calder, East 690 (also Kirknewton & East Calder 690)		Edinburgh Midlothian	Edinburgh	1642	1567
Calder, Mid 694 (see Mid Calder 694)					
Calder, West 701 (see West Calder 701)					
Callander	336	Perth	Dunblane Dunkeld	1710	1543 1706
Cambuslang	627	Lanark	Glasgow Edinburgh	1657	1604 1582
Cambusnethan	628	Lanark	Glasgow Lanark Edinburgh	1634	1552 1626 1578
Cameron 412 (disjoined from St Andrews 1645)		Fife	St Andrews	1695	1649
Campbeltown	507	Argyll	Argyll Kincardine Glasgow	1659	1676 1722 1608
Campsie	475	Stirling	Hamilton & Campsie Dunkeld Dunblane Stirling (1649–1660) Edinburgh Glasgow	1646	1564 1769 1653 1653 1581 1625
Canisbay	35	Caithness	Caithness	1652	1664
Canonbie	814	Dumfries	Dumfries	1693	1676

Parish	District number	County	Commissariot	OPR	Testament or inventory
Canongate	685[3]	Edinburgh Midlothian	Edinburgh	1564	1568
(also Edinburgh 685[1] and St Cuthbert's 685[2])					
Canna	116	Inverness	Small Isles	1855	1717
(also Small Isles 116)					
Caputh	337	Perth	Dunkeld	1670	1688
			Dunblane		1653
			Edinburgh		1581
Cardross	494	Dunbarton	Hamilton & Campsie	1681	1564
			Dunblane		1617
			Glasgow		1655
			Edinburgh		1592
Careston	277	Forfar	Brechin	1714	1600
Cargill	338	Perth	Dunkeld	1652	1690
			Dunblane		1652
			Edinburgh		1582
Carlaverock	815				
(see Caerlaverock 815)					
Carloway	86b				
(see Barvas 86a & Lochs 87)					
Carluke	629	Lanark	Lanark	1690	1620
			Edinburgh		1586
Carmichael	630	Lanark	Lanark	1695	1599
Carmunnock	631	Lanark	Glasgow	1654	1607
Carmyllie	276	Forfar	Brechin	1684	1610
			St Andrews		1615
Carnbee	413	Fife	St Andrews	1646	1550
			Edinburgh		1565
Carnock	414	Fife	Stirling	1652	1641
			St Andrews		1591
			Edinburgh		1599
Carnwath	632	Lanark	Lanark	1709	1601
			Edinburgh		1577
Carriden	664	Linlithgow W. Lothian	Edinburgh	1687	1583
			St Andrews		1617
Carrington or Primrose	675	Edinburgh Midlothian	Edinburgh	1653	1596
Carsphairn	860	Kirkcudbright	Kirkcudbright	1758	1674
Carstairs	633	Lanark	Lanark	1672	1596
			Hamilton & Campsie		1564
			Edinburgh		1584
Castleton	784	Roxburgh	Peebles	1749	1770
			Kirkcudbright		1680

Parish	District number	County	Commissariot	OPR	Testament or inventory
Cathcart	560 part	Renfrew Lanark	Hamilton & Campsie	1701	1620
			Glasgow		1550
			Edinburgh		1572
Catterline (see Kinneff & Catterline 262)	262	Kincardine	St Andrews Brechin Edinburgh		1605 1623 1597
Cavers	785	Roxburgh	Peebles	1694	1685
Cawdor	122	Nairn	Moray	1716	1791
Ceres	415	Fife	St Andrews Edinburgh	1620	1550 1580
Channelkirk	729	Berwick	Lauder Edinburgh	1651	1561 1575
Chapel of Garioch	179	Aberdeen	Aberdeen	1763	1823
Chirnside	730	Berwick	Lauder Edinburgh	1660	1636 1583
Clackmannan	466	Clackmannan	Stirling Edinburgh	1595	1610 1577
Clatt	180	Aberdeen	Aberdeen	1680	1739
Cleish	460	Kinross	St Andrews Edinburgh	1700	1597 1597
Closeburn	816	Dumfries	Dumfries	1765	1642
Clova (also Cortachy 278)	278	Forfar St Andrews	Brechin	1697 1595	1681
Clunie	339	Perth	Dunkeld Dunblane Edinburgh	1702	1688 1653 1583
Cluny	181	Aberdeen	Aberdeen	1751	1729
Clyne	45	Sutherland	Caithness Inverness	1782	1784
Cockburnspath	731	Berwick	Lauder Edinburgh	1642	1641 1580
Cockpen (also Stobhill 698b)	676	Edinburgh Midlothian	Edinburgh	1690	
Coldingham	732	Berwick	Lauder Lanark Edinburgh	1690	1628 1683 1578
Coldstream (formerly Lennel)	733	Berwick Edinburgh	Lauder	1690 1573	1653
Colinton or Hailes	677	Edinburgh Midlothian	Edinburgh	1654	1578
Coll (also Tyree 551/1)	551/2	Argyll	The Isles	1776	1772

Parish	District number	County	Commissariot	OPR	Testament or inventory
Collace	340	Perth	St Andrews	1713	1584
			Dunkeld		1781
			Edinburgh		1597
Collessie	416	Fife	St Andrews	1696	1550
			Edinburgh		1583
Colmonell	582	Ayr	Glasgow	1759	1607
			Edinburgh		1677
Colonsay (also Jura 539/1)	539/2	Argyll	The Isles	1796	1776
Colvend (incl. Southwick)	861	Kirkcudbright	Dumfries	1781	1639
		Edinburgh		1582	
Comrie	341	Perth	Dunblane	1693	1543
			Edinburgh		1569
Contin	60	Ross & Cromarty	Ross	1778	
Conveth (see Laurencekirk 263)	263	Kincardine	St Andrews		1606
			Edinburgh		1580
			Inverness		1632
Corgarff (see Strathdon 240)	240				
Corran of Ardgour (also Ballachulish 506)	506	Argyll	Argyll	1835	
Corrie (see Hutton & Corrie 831)	831	Dumfries	Dumfries		1661
Corsock-Bridge (see Parton 878)	862	Kirkcudbright	Kirkcudbright		1679
Corstorphine	678	Edinburgh Midlothian	Edinburgh	1634	1564
Cortachy (also Clova 278)	278	Forfar	Brechin	1662	1610
Coull	182	Aberdeen	Aberdeen	1752	
Coupar-Angus	279 part	Perth Forfar	Dunkeld Dunblane Edinburgh	1683	1696 1653 1588
Covington & Thankerton	634	Lanark	Lanark	1772	1621
Coylton	583	Ayr	Glasgow	1723	1759
Craig (anciently Inchbrayock)	280	Forfar	St Andrews Edinburgh	1657	1615 1591
Craigie	584	Ayr	Glasgow Brechin Edinburgh	1679	1606 1583 1571
Craignish	508	Argyll	Argyll	1755	1676
Crail	417	Fife	St Andrews Edinburgh	1684	1549 1565

Parish	District number	County	Commissariot	OPR	Testament or inventory
Crailing	786	Roxburgh	Peebles	1708	1681
Cramond	679	Edinburgh	Edinburgh	1651	1574
Cranshaws (also Longformacus 750)	734	Berwick	Lauder	1731	1636
Cranston	680	Edinburgh Midlothian	Edinburgh Lauder	1682	1578 1679
Crathie & Braemar	183	Aberdeen	Aberdeen	1717	1751
Crawford (incl. Leadhills)	635	Lanark	Lanark	1741	1626
Crawfordjohn	636	Lanark	Lanark Edinburgh Glasgow	1694	1601 1583 1550
Creich	46	Sutherland	Caithness Sutherland	1785	1821
Creich	418	Fife	St Andrews Edinburgh	1695	1550 1578
Crichton	681	Edinburgh Midlothian	Edinburgh	1682	1580
Crieff	342	Perth	Dunkeld Dunblane Edinburgh	1692	1695 1653 1586
Crimond	184	Aberdeen	Aberdeen	1743	1754
Cromarty	61	Ross & Cromarty	Ross Edinburgh	1675	1803 1594
Cromdale, Inverallan & Advie	128b	Moray Edinburgh	Moray	1702 1590	1712
Cross, Burness & Lady (also Sanday 26)	26	Orkney	Orkney & Shetland	1758	1615
Crossmichael	863	Kirkcudbright	Kirkcudbright Edinburgh	1751	1679 1576
Croy & Dalcross	94	Inverness	Inverness	1719	1630
Cruden	185	Aberdeen	Aberdeen	1707	1723
Cullen	150	Banff	Aberdeen	1668	1722
Cullicudden (also Resolis 79)	79				
Culross	343	Perth	Dunblane Edinburgh	1641	1543 1569
Culsamond	186	Aberdeen	Aberdeen	1735	1733
Culter	637	Lanark	Lanark Edinburgh	1700	1621 1597
Cults	419	Fife	St Andrews Edinburgh	1693	1550 1586
Cumbernauld	495	Dunbarton	Glasgow	1688	1765

Parish	District number	County	Commissariot	OPR	Testament or inventory
Cumbraes	552	Bute	The Isles	1730	
Cumlodden	509				
(see Glassary 511 & Inveraray 513)					
Cummertrees	817	Dumfries	Dumfries	1753	1624
Cumnock, New	608				
(see New Cumnock 608)					
Cumnock, Old	610				
(see Old Cumnock 610)					
Cunningsburgh	3/2	Shetland	Orkney & Shetland	1746	
(also Dunrossness 3/1, Sandwick 3/2 & Fair Isle 3/4)					
Cupar	420	Fife	St Andrews Edinburgh	1654	1549 1567
Currie	682	Edinburgh Midlothian	Edinburgh	1638	1576
Dailly	585	Ayr	Glasgow Edinburgh	1691	1607 1582
Dairsie	421	Fife	St Andrews Edinburgh	1645	1550 1581
Dalarossie	105	Inverness	Inverness		1633
(see Mey & Dalarossie 105)					
Dalavich	517	Argyll	Argyll		1676
(see Kilcrechan & Dalavich 517)					
Dalbeattie	864	Kirkcudbright	Kirkcudbright Dumfries		1685
(see Urr 884)					
Dalcross	94	Inverness	Inverness	1747	1666
(also Croy & Dalcross 94)					
Dalgain	613	Ayr	Glasgow		1668
(see Sorn 613)					
Dalgety	422	Fife	St Andrews Edinburgh	1644	1655 1570
Dalkeith	683	Edinburgh Midlothian	Edinburgh	1609	1564
Dallas	129	Moray	Moray	1742	1684
Dalmellington	586	Ayr	Glasgow Edinburgh	1641	1609 1578
Dalmeny	665	Linlithgow W. Lothian	Edinburgh	1679	1568
(pre 1636 Queensferry)					
Dalry	587	Ayr	Glasgow Edinburgh	1680	1605 1584
Dalry	865	Kirkcudbright	Kirkcudbright Edinburgh	1691	1677 1575
Dalrymple	588	Ayr	Glasgow	1699	1610

Parish	District number	County	Commissariot	OPR	Testament or inventory
Dalserf	638	Lanark	Hamilton & Campsie	1738	1564
			Edinburgh		1589
			Glasgow		1654
Dalton	810	Dumfries	Dumfries	1723	
			Edinburgh		1581
			Glasgow		1795
Dalziel	639	Lanark	Glasgow	1648	
			Hamilton & Campsie		1612
			Edinburgh		1578
Daviot	187	Aberdeen	Aberdeen	1723	1630
Daviot & Dunlichty	95	Inverness	Inverness	1774	1630
Deerness	14	Orkney	Orkney & Shetland	1754	1612
Delting	2	Shetland	Orkney & Shetland	1751	1613
Denny	476	Stirling	Stirling	1679	1612
Deskford	151	Banff	Aberdeen	1660	1730
Dingwall	62	Ross & Cromarty	Ross	1662	1805
			Edinburgh		1591
Dipple (see Speymouth 143)	143	Moray	Moray		
			Edinburgh	1592	
Dirleton	705	Haddington E. Lothian	Edinburgh	1664	1575
Dollar	467	Clackmannan	Stirling	1701	1610
			Edinburgh		1581
Dolphinton	640	Lanark	Lanark	1717	1624
Dores	96a	Inverness	Inverness	1734	1723
Dornoch	47	Sutherland	Caithness	1730	1817
			Edinburgh		1599
Dornock	819	Dumfries	Dumfries	1773	1658
Douglas	641	Lanark	Lanark	1691	1597
			Glasgow		1608
			Edinburgh		1583
Dowally	344	Perth	Dunkeld	1705	1690
			Dunblane		1653
			Edinburgh		1590
Down (see Gamrie 155a)	155a	Banff	Aberdeen		1769
Drainie (formerly Kineddar 130)	130	Moray	Moray	1631	1789
Dreghorn	589	Ayr	Glasgow	1749	1603
			Edinburgh		1577

Parish	District number	County	Commissariot	OPR	Testament or inventory
Dron	345	Perth	Dunblane	1682	1616
			Edinburgh		1589
			St Andrews		1641
Drumblade	188	Aberdeen	Aberdeen	1702	1740
Drumelzier	759	Peebles	Peebles	1649	1823
			Edinburgh		1573
Drumoak	189	Aberdeen	Aberdeen	1692	1724
Dryfesdale	820	Dumfries	Dumfries	1732	1630
Drymen	477	Stirling	Glasgow	1672	1610
			Stirling		1654
			Dunblane		1621
			Edinburgh		1589
Duddingston	684	Edinburgh Midlothian	Edinburgh	1631	1575
Duffus	131	Moray	Moray	1629	1684
Duirinish	110	Inverness	The Isles	1817	1715
Dull (also Foss 355b & Tenandry 394c)	346	Perth	Dunkeld	1703	1688
			Dunblane		1656
			Edinburgh		1592
Dumbarton	496	Dunbarton	Glasgow	1666	1603
			Edinburgh		1594
Dumbennan (see Huntly 202)	202	Aberdeen Edinburgh	Aberdeen	1588	1680
Dumfries	821	Dumfries	Dumfries	1605	1625
			Edinburgh		1568
Dun	281	Forfar	St Andrews	1642	1587
			Edinburgh		1579
Dunbar	706	Haddington E. Lothian	Edinburgh	1672	1564
Dunbarney	347	Perth	St Andrews	1594	1593
			Dunblane		1655
			Edinburgh		1586
Dunblane	348	Perth	Dunblane	1658	1539
			Edinburgh		1574
Dunbog	423	Fife	St Andrews	1695	1549
			Edinburgh		1596
Dundee	282	Forfar	Brechin	1645	1578
			Edinburgh		1567
			St Andrews		1584
Dundonald	590	Ayr	Glasgow	1673	1603
			Edinburgh		1576
Dundurcas (also Rothes 141)	141	Moray	Moray	1698	1696
Dunfermline	424	Fife	St Andrews	1561	1613
			Edinburgh		1574

Parish	District number	County	Commissariot	OPR	Testament or inventory
Dunino	425	Fife	St Andrews Edinburgh	1643	1596 1580
Dunipace	478	Stirling	Stirling Edinburgh	1594	1619 1581
Dunkeld	349	Perth	Dunkeld Dunblane Edinburgh	1672	1688 1653 1578
Dunlichty (see Daviot & Dunlichty 95)	95	Inverness	Inverness		1631
Dunlop	591	Ayr	Glasgow Edinburgh	1701	1606 1592
Dunnet	36	Caithness	Caithness	1751	1819
Dunnichen	283	Forfar	Brechin St Andrews	1683	1576 1600
Dunning	350	Perth	Dunblane Edinburgh	1708	1598 1586
Dunnottar	255	Kincardine	St Andrews Brechin Edinburgh	1672	1606 1656 1576
Dunoon & Kilmun	510	Argyll	Argyll Edinburgh	1744	1675 1584
Dunrossness (incl. Sandwick & Cunningsburgh 3/2 & Fair Isle 3/4)	3/1	Shetland	Orkney & Shetland	1753	1612
Dunscore	822	Dumfries	Dumfries Edinburgh	1777	1638 1577
Dunse (or Duns)	735	Berwick	Lauder Edinburgh	1615	1627 1574
Dunsyre	642	Lanark	Lanark Edinburgh	1687	1621 1576
Durness	48	Sutherland	Caithness	1764	
Duror (also Lismore 525/1, Appin 525/2, Glencoe & Ballachulish 525/3)	525/4	Argyll	Argyll	1833	1738
Durris	256	Kincardine	St Andrews Inverness	1716	1613 1630
Durrisdeer	823	Dumfries	Dumfries Edinburgh	1758	1624 1582
Duthil (also Rothiemurchus 96b²)	96b¹	Inverness	Inverness Moray Edinburgh	1766	1632 1710 1588
Dyce	190	Aberdeen	Aberdeen	1646	1737
Dyke	133	Moray	Moray Edinburgh	1635	1710 1590
Dysart	426	Fife	St Andrews Dunkeld Edinburgh	1582	1549 1695 1565

Parish	District number	County	Commissariot	OPR	Testament or inventory
Eaglesham	561	Renfrew	Glasgow	1659	1602
			Edinburgh		1592
Earlston	736	Berwick	Lauder	1694	1628
			Kirkcudbright		1665
			Edinburgh		1565
Eassie & Nevay	284	Forfar	St Andrews	1728	1597
East Calder	690				
(see Kirknewton & East Calder 690)					
East Kilbride	643	Lanark	Hamilton & Campsie	1688	
East Kilpatrick	500				
(see New or East Kilpatrick 500)					
Eastwood	562	Renfrew	Glasgow	1674	1604
			Edinburgh		1592
Eccles	737	Berwick	Lauder	1699	1635
			Edinburgh		1578
Ecclesgreig	267	Kincardine	St Andrews		1595
(see St Cyrus 267)		Edinburgh		1576	
Ecclesmachen	666	Linlithgow W. Lothian	Edinburgh	1717	1582
Echt	191	Aberdeen	Aberdeen	1678	1722
Eckford	787a	Roxburgh	Peebles	1694	1682
Eday & Pharay	15	Orkney	Orkney & Shetland	1789	
Edderton	63	Ross & Cromarty	Ross	1799	1821
Eddleston	760	Peebles	Peebles	1713	1823
			Edinburgh		1586
Eddrachillis	49	Sutherland	Caithness	1808	
Edgerston	787b	Roxburgh	Peebles		1682
(see Jedburgh 792, Oxnam 802 & Southdean 806)					
Edinburgh	685[1]	Edinburgh	Edinburgh	1595	1528
(also Canongate 685[3] & St Cuthbert's 685[2])			Glasgow		1611
			St Andrews		1648
			Peebles		1821
Edinkillie	134	Moray	Moray	1702	1700
Ednam	788	Roxburgh	Peebles	1666	1683
			Edinburgh		1573
Edrom	738	Berwick	Lauder	1721	1628
			Edinburgh		1578
Edzell	285	Forfar	St Andrews	1684	1606
			Edinburgh		1571
Egilshay	24	Orkney	Orkney & Shetland		1612
(see Rousay & Egilshay 24)					
Eigg	116				
(see Small Isles 116)					

Parish	District number	County	Commissariot	OPR	Testament or inventory
Elgin	135	Moray	Moray	1609	1684
			Edinburgh		1573
Elie	427	Fife	St Andrews	1639	1584
			Edinburgh		1597
Ellon	192	Aberdeen	Aberdeen	1640	1732
Enzie	152	Banff	Moray	1835	1764
Errol	351	Perth	St Andrews	1553	1594
			Dunblane		1653
			Edinburgh		1577
Erskine	563	Renfrew	Glasgow	1705	1605
			Edinburgh		1572
Eskdalemuir	824	Dumfries	Dumfries	1724	1681
Essie (see Rhynie & Essie 237a)	237a	Aberdeen	Aberdeen Edinburgh		1577
Essil (also Speymouth 143)	143	Moray	Moray	1654	
Ettrick (also Kirkhope 776 & Yarrow 779)	774b	Selkirk	Peebles	1693	1819
Evie & Rendall	16	Orkney	Orkney & Shetland	1725	1612
Ewes	825	Dumfries	Dumfries	1700	1661
Eyemouth	739	Berwick	Lauder	1710	1628
			Edinburgh		1574
Fair Isle	3/3	Shetland	Orkney & Shetland	1767	
(also Dunrossness 3/1, Sandwick & Cunningsburgh 3/2)					
Fala & Soutra	686	Edinburgh Midlothian	Edinburgh Peebles	1673	1586 1691
Falkirk	479	Stirling	Stirling	1611	1610
			Dunblane		1619
			Edinburgh		1576
			Glasgow		1799
Falkland	428	Fife	St Andrews	1669	1550
			Brechin		1595
			Edinburgh		1577
Farnell	286	Forfar	Brechin	1699	1602
			Edinburgh		1594
Farr	50	Sutherland	Caithness	1790	
Fearn	287	Forfar	Dunkeld	1762	1688
			Brechin		1578
			Edinburgh		1586
Fearn	64	Ross & Cromarty	Ross	1749	
Fenwick	592	Ayr	Glasgow	1644	1605
Ferry-Port-on- Craig (Leuchars pre 1606)	429	Fife	St Andrews	1634	1591

Parish	District number	County	Commissariot	OPR	Testament or inventory
Fetlar (also North Yell 4/2)	4/1	Shetland Shetland	Orkney &	1754	1613
Fettercairn	257	Kincardine	St Andrews Brechin Edinburgh	1720	1605 1657 1576
Fetteresso	258	Kincardine	St Andrews Brechin Edinburgh	1620	1597 1656 1578
Findo-Gask	352	Perth	Dunblane Edinburgh	1669	1604 1564
Fintray	193	Aberdeen	Aberdeen	1728	1723
Fintry	480	Stirling	Glasgow Stirling Edinburgh	1659	1617 1607 1586
Firth & Stennes (also Stennes 17)	17	Orkney	Orkney & Shetland	1732	1612
Flisk	430	Fife	St Andrews Edinburgh	1697	1550 1594
Flotta (also Walls 32/1)	32/2	Orkney Shetland	Orkney &	1708	1619
Fodderty	65	Ross & Cromarty	Ross	1735	1815
Fogo	740	Berwick	Lauder Edinburgh	1660	1653 1582
Forbes & Kearn (also Tullynessle 246)	246	Aberdeen	Aberdeen	1718	1791
Fordoun	259	Kincardine	St Andrews Brechin Edinburgh	1693	1605 1657 1576
Fordyce	153	Banff	Aberdeen Brechin Edinburgh	1665	1732 1680 1582
Forfar	288	Forfar	St Andrews Brechin Edinburgh	1633	1587 1658 1576
Forgan (also Wormit 431 & Newport-on-Tay 431)	431	Fife	St Andrews Dunkeld Edinburgh	1695	1549 1688 1587
Forgandenny	353	Perth	Dunkeld Dunblane Edinburgh St Andrews	1695	1684 1656 1582 1591
Forglen	154	Banff	Aberdeen	1647	1738
Forgue	194	Aberdeen	Aberdeen	1684	1738
Forres	137	Moray	Moray Edinburgh	1675	1696 1697

Parish	District number	County	Commissariot	OPR	Testament or inventory
Fort Augustus or Abertarff (also Boleskine 92/1)	92/2	Inverness	Inverness	1737	1737
Forteviot	354	Perth	St Andrews Dunblane Edinburgh	1710	1599 1653 1592
Fortingall (also Kinloch-Rannoch 367)	355a	Perth	Dunkeld Dunblane	1748	1688 1656
Foss (see Dull 346)	355b				
Fossoway & Tullibole (united in 1614)	461	Kinross Edinburgh	St Andrews Dunblane	1609 1588	1655 1547
Foula (also Walls 12/1)	12/4	Shetland	Orkney & Shetland	1783	1631
Foulden	741	Berwick	Lauder	1682	1653
Foveran	195	Aberdeen	Aberdeen	1658	1733
Fowlis (see Lundie & Fowlis 306)	306	Forfar	St Andrews Edinburgh		1596 1565
Fowlis-Easter	356	Perth	St Andrews Edinburgh	1701	1690 1565
Fowlis-Wester	357	Perth	Dunblane Edinburgh	1674	1553 1565
Fraserburgh	196	Aberdeen	Aberdeen	1733	1727
Fyvie	197	Aberdeen	Aberdeen	1685	1724
Gairloch (also Poolewe 66)	66	Ross & Cromarty	Ross	1781	
Galashiels (also Caddonfoot 774a)	775	Selkirk	Peebles Edinburgh	1714	1698 1588
Galston	593	Ayr	Glasgow Edinburgh	1670	1604 1576
Gamrie (incl. Macduff & Down 155a)	155a	Banff	Aberdeen	1704	1819
Gargunnock	481	Stirling	Stirling	1615	1616
Gartly	198	Aberdeen	Moray	1709	1688
Garvald	707	Haddington E. Lothian	Edinburgh	1694	1582
Garvock	260	Kincardine	St Andrews Dunblane Brechin Edinburgh	1703	1606 1622 1657 1582
Gifford (see Yester 725)	725				
Gigha	537	Argyll	The Isles	1792	1787
Girthon	866	Kirkcudbright	Kirkcudbright	1699	1718

Parish	District number	County	Commissariot	OPR	Testament or inventory
Girvan	594	Ayr	Glasgow Edinburgh	1733	1605 1577
Gladsmuir	708	Haddington E. Lothian	Edinburgh	1688	
Glamis	289	Forfar	St Andrews Brechin Edinburgh	1677	1600 1659 1565
Glasgow (also Gorbals 644², Govan 646 & Barony 622)	644¹	Lanark	Glasgow Hamilton & Campsie Edinburgh	1609	1547 1609 1564
Glass	199	Aberdeen	Moray	1736	1684
Glassary (also Cumlodden 509 & Lochgilphead 526)	511	Argyll	Argyll	1750	1674
Glasserton	885	Wigtown	Wigtown	1700	1710
Glassford	645	Lanark	Glasgow Edinburgh	1692	1605 1586
Glenaray (see Inveraray & Glenaray 513)	513	Argyll	Argyll		1705
Glenbervie	261	Kincardine	Brechin Edinburgh	1721	1582 1581
Glenbucket (or Glenbuchat)	200	Aberdeen Moray	Aberdeen	1719 1754	1747
Glencairn	826	Dumfries	Dumfries Edinburgh	1693	1624 1577
Glencoe & Ballachulish (see Lismore 525/1, Appin 525/2, Duror 525/4)	525/3	Argyll	Argyll		1686
Glencorse (formerly Woodhouselee 687)	687	Edinburgh	Edinburgh	1672	1570
Glendevon	358	Perth	Dunblane Edinburgh St Andrews	1710	1611 1583 1729
Glenelg	97	Inverness	Argyll	1792	1749
Glengairn (see Glenmuick, Tullich & Glengairn 201)	201				
Glenholm (see Kilbucho 753 & Broughton 758)	761	Peebles	Peebles		1823
Glenisla	290	Forfar	Brechin	1719	1579
Glenluce (see Old Luce 894)	894	Wigtown	Wigtown		1713
Glenmoriston (also Urquhart & Glenmoriston 107)	107	Inverness	Inverness	1785	
Glenmuick, Tullich & Glengairn	201	Aberdeen	Aberdeen	1744	1751
Glenorchy & Inishail	512	Argyll	Argyll	1753	

Parish	District number	County	Commissariot	OPR	Testament or inventory
Glenrinnes 155b (see Mortlach 162 & Aberlour 145)					
Glenshiel	67	Ross & Cromarty	Ross	1785	
Golspie	51	Sutherland	Caithness	1739	
Gorbals 644² (also Glasgow 644¹, Govan 646 &Barony 622)		Lanark	Hamilton & Campsie Glasgow	1771	1612 1657
Gordon	742	Berwick	Lauder Edinburgh	1652	1561 1598
Govan 646 (also Glasgow 644¹, Gorbals 644² & Barony 622)		Lanark	Hamilton & Campsie Glasgow	1690	1564 1615
Graemsay 20 (also Hoy & Graemsay 20)		Orkney	Orkney & Shetland	1777	1614
Graitney/Gretna 827		Dumfries	Dumfries	1730	1662
Grange	156	Banff	Moray	1684	1693
Greenlaw	743	Berwick	Lauder Kirkcudbright Edinburgh	1699	1630 1687 1583
Greenock	564	Renfrew	Glasgow Dunblane		1607 1618
Greenock, Middle or New	564¹			1741	
Greenock, East	564²			1809	
Greenock, Old or West	564³			1698	
Gretna (see Graitney)					
Guthrie	291	Forfar	Brechin St Andrews	1664	1583 1618
Haddington	709	Haddington E. Lothian	Edinburgh	1619	1564
Hailes 677 (see Colinton 677)					
Halfmorton	828	Dumfries	Dumfries	1787	
Halkirk	37	Caithness	Caithness	1772	1819
Hamilton	647	Lanark	Hamilton & Campsie Edinburgh Glasgow	1645	1564 1564 1652
Harray	18	Orkney	Orkney & Shetland	1784	1612
Harris 111 (also St Kilda 111)		Inverness	The Isles	1823	1810

Parish	District number	County	Commissariot	OPR	Testament or inventory
Hawick	789	Roxburgh	Peebles	1634	1682
			Edinburgh		1583
Heriot	688	Edinburgh Midlothian	Edinburgh	1685	1569
Hilton (see Whitsome & Hilton 757)	757				
Hobkirk	790	Roxburgh	Peebles	1726	1818
Hoddam	829	Dumfries	Dumfries	1746	1625
			Kirkcudbright		1687
Holm & Paplay	19	Orkney	Orkney & Shetland	1654	1611
Holywood	830	Dumfries	Dumfries	1687	1638
			Edinburgh		1576
			Glasgow		1549
Houston & Killellan	565	Renfrew	Glasgow	1720	1606
			Peebles		1686
			Edinburgh		1591
Hownam	791	Roxburgh	Peebles	1689	1685
			Edinburgh		1596
Hoy & Graemsay (combined 1651)	20	Orkney	Orkney & Shetland	1776	1612
Humbie	710	Haddington E. Lothian	Edinburgh	1648	1577
Hume (see Stitchell 808)	744	Roxburgh Lauder	Peebles	1564	
			Edinburgh		1600
Huntly (formerly Dumbennan & Kinnoir)	202	Aberdeen	Aberdeen	1680	
			Moray		1693
Hutton	745	Berwick	Lauder	1700	1637
			Edinburgh		1600
Hutton & Corrie	831	Dumfries	Dumfries	1745	1775
Hyskier (see Small Isles 116)	116				
Inch	886	Wigtown	Wigtown	1729	1700
			Edinburgh		1581
Inchbrayock (see Craig 280)	280	Forfar	St Andrews		1613
Inchinnan	566	Renfrew	Glasgow	1722	1603
			Edinburgh		1589
Inchnadamff (see Assynt 44)	44				
Inchture	359	Perth	St Andrews	1619	1615
			Edinburgh		1583
Inishail (see Glenorchy & Inishail 512)	512	Argyll	Argyll		1677

Parish	District number	County	Commissariot	OPR	Testament or inventory
Innerkip or Inverkip	567	Renfrew	Glasgow Edinburgh	1694	1602 1583
Innerleithen or Inverleithen	762	Peebles	Peebles Edinburgh	1643	1798 1579
Innerwick	711	Haddington E. Lothian	Edinburgh	1614	1576
Insch	203	Aberdeen	Aberdeen	1683	1734
Insh *(see Kingussie & Insh 102)*	102	Inverness	Inverness		1808
Inverallan *(see Cromdale etc. 128b)*	128b	Moray	Moray Inverness		1631
Inveraray & Glenaray *(also Cumlodden 509)*	513	Argyll	Argyll Glasgow	1653	1677 1781
Inverarity & Methy	292	Forfar	St Andrews Brechin Edinburgh	1710	1596 1657 1577
Inveravon	157	Banff	Moray	1630	1772
Inverchaolin	514	Argyll	Argyll	1737	1675
Inveresk	689	Edinburgh Midlothian	Edinburgh	1607	1567
Invergowrie *(see Liff, Benvie & Invergowrie 301)*	301	Forfar	St Andrews Edinburgh		1598 1596
Inverkeillor	293	Angus	St Andrews Edinburgh	1717	1599 1575
Inverkeithing	432	Fife	St Andrews Edinburgh	1676	1587 1577
Inverkeithny	158	Banff	Moray Edinburgh	1721	1597
Inverness	98	Inverness	Inverness Moray Edinburgh	1604	1630 1798 1587
Invernochtie *(see Strathdon 240)*	240				
Inverurie	204	Aberdeen	Aberdeen	1611	1736
Iona (Mull)	538	Argyll	The Isles	1829	
Irongray (Kirkpatrick-Irongray)	867	Kirkcudbright	Dumfries Edinburgh	1757	1624 1580
Irvine	595	Ayr	Glasgow Edinburgh	1645	1602 1576
Jedburgh *(also Edgerston 787b)*	792	Roxburgh Lauder	Peebles Edinburgh	1639 1763	1681 1582
Johnstone	832	Dumfries	Dumfries	1734	1680

Parish	District number	County	Commissariot	OPR	Testament or inventory
Jura 539/1 *(also Colonsay 539/2)*		Argyll	The Isles	1704	1728
Kearn 246 *(see Forbes & Kearn 246, Auchindoir 172)*					
Keig	205	Aberdeen	Aberdeen	1750	1751
Keir	833	Dumfries	Dumfries	1722	1639
Keith	159	Banff	Moray Edinburgh	1686	1688 1600
Keithhall & Kinkell	206	Aberdeen	Aberdeen	1678	1723
Kells	868	Kirkcudbright	Kirkcudbright Dumfries Wigtown Edinburgh	1698	1663 1638 1736 1582
Kelso	793	Roxburgh	Peebles Lauder Edinburgh	1598	1682 1653 1574
Kelton	869	Kirkcudbright	Kirkcudbright Edinburgh	1717	1668 1582
Kemback	433	Fife	St Andrews	1649	1591
Kemnay	207	Aberdeen	Aberdeen	1660	1726
Kenmore	360	Perth	Dunkeld Dunblane	1636	1698 1656
Kennoway	434	Fife	St Andrews Edinburgh	1638	1550 1576
Kettins 294 *(previously Lathrisk)*		Forfar Edinburgh	St Andrews	1650 1580	1588
Kettle 435 *(also Kingskettle 435)*		Fife	St Andrews	1633	1590
Kilarrow or Bowmore	536	Argyll	The Isles	1763	1726
Kilbarchan	568	Renfrew	Glasgow Edinburgh	1651	1602 1579
Kilberry 516 *(see Kilcalmonell & Kilberry 516)*		Argyll	Argyll		1676
Kilbirnie	596	Ayr	Glasgow Edinburgh	1688	1607 1590
Kilblane with Kilcolmkill *(see Southend 532)*		Argyll	Argyll		1676
Kilbrandon & Kilchattan	515	Argyll	Argyll	1733	1674
Kilbride (Arran)	553	Bute	The Isles	1723	1662
Kilbride 523 *(see Kilmore & Kilbride 523)*		Argyll	Argyll Glasgow		1676 1608

Parish	District number	County	Commissariot	OPR	Testament or inventory
Kilbucho	763	Peebles	Peebles	1749	1823
(also Broughton 758 & Glenholm 761)			Edinburgh		1587
Kilcalmonell &	516	Argyll	Argyll	1777	1676
Kilberry (also Tarbert 535)					
Kilchattan	515				
(see Kilbrandon & Kilchattan 515)					
Kilchenzie	519	Argyll	Argyll		1684
(see Killean & Kilchenzie 519)					
Kilchoman	540	Argyll	The Isles	1821	1727
Kilchrenan &	517	Argyll	Argyll	1751	1676
Dalavich			The Isles		1795
Kilcolmkill		Argyll	Argyll		1694
(united with Kilblane to form Southend 532)					
Kilconquhar	436	Fife	St Andrews	1637	1549
			Edinburgh		1580
Kildalton	541	Argyll	The Isles	1723	1738
(Islay)			Argyll		1700
Kildonan	52	Sutherland	Caithness	1791	
			Edinburgh		1579
Kildrummy	208	Aberdeen	Aberdeen	1681	1723
Kilfinan	518	Argyll	Argyll	1728	1674
Kilfinichen &	542	Argyll	The Isles	1804	1711
Kilvickeon (Mull)					
Kilgour (see Falkland 428)			St Andrews		1549
Killean &	519	Argyll	Argyll	1762	1676
Kilchenzie			The Isles		1723
Killearn	482	Stirling	Glasgow	1694	1611
			Stirling		1658
Killearnan	68	Ross & Cromarty	Ross	1744	1803
Killellan	565	Renfrew	Glasgow		1602
(see Houston & Killellan 565)					
Killin	361	Perth	Dunkeld	1689	1712
Kilmacolm	569	Renfrew	Glasgow	1710	1647
			Edinburgh		1586
Kilmadock	362	Perth	Dunblane	1623	1603
			Edinburgh		1587
Kilmallie	520	Argyll	Argyll	1773	1676
(also Ballachulish & Corran of Ardgour 506)					
Kilmany	437	Fife	St Andrews	1706	1549
			Edinburgh		1575
Kilmarnock	597	Ayr	Glasgow	1640	1602
			Edinburgh		1575
Kilmaronock	497	Dunbarton	Glasgow	1686	1607
			Edinburgh		1596

Parish	District number	County	Commissariot	OPR	Testament or inventory
Kilmartin	521	Argyll	Argyll	1747	1674
Kilmaurs	598	Ayr	Glasgow	1688	1603
			Edinburgh		1583
Kilmelford *(set Kilninver & Kilmelford 524)*	524	Argyll	Argyll		1676
Kilmeny	543	Argyll	The Isles	1802	1709
Kilmodan	522	Argyll	Argyll	1737	1675
Kilmonivaig	99	Inverness	Argyll	1730	1678
Kilmorack	100	Inverness	Inverness	1674	1802
Kilmore & Kilbride *(incl. Oban 523)*	523	Argyll	Argyll	1782	1676
Kilmore & Kilninian	544	Argyll	The Isles	1766	1709
Kilmorich *(also Lochgoilhead 527/1)*	527/2	Argyll	Argyll	1750	1676
Kilmory (Arran) *(see Shisken 554 and Lochranza 554)*	554	Bute	The Isles Argyll		1763 1675
Kilmuir (Skye)	112	Inverness	The Isles	1823	1729
			Edinburgh		1592
Kilmuir-Easter	69	Ross & Cromarty	Ross	1738	1814
Kilmuir-Wester *(see Knockbain 73)*	73	Ross & Cromarty Moray	Ross	1753	
Kilmun *(see Dunoon & Kilmun 510)*	510	Argyll	Argyll		1675
Kilninian & Kilmore (Mull) *(also Ulva 544)*	544	Argyll	The Isles	1766	1707
Kilninver & Kilmelford	524	Argyll	Argyll	1758	1676
Kilpatrick, New or East, *(see New or East Kilpatrick 500)*					
Kilpatrick, Old or West, *(see Old or West Kilpatrick 501)*					
Kilrenny	438	Fife	St Andrews	1647	1550
			Edinburgh		1577
Kilspindie	363	Perth	St Andrews	1656	1598
			Dunblane		1652
			Edinburgh		1577
Kilsyth *(formerly Monyabroch 483)*	483	Stirling	Stirling also Glasgow	1619	1671
Kiltarlity	101	Inverness	Inverness	1714	1630
Kiltearn	70	Ross & Cromarty	Ross	1702	1813
			Edinburgh		1597
Kilwinning	599	Ayr	Glasgow	1699	1603
			Edinburgh		1581

Parish	District number	County	Commissariot	OPR	Testament or inventory
Kilvickeon (see Kilfinichen & Kilvickeon 542)	542	Argyll	The Isles		1712
Kincardine	364	Perth	Dunblane Brechin Edinburgh St Andrews	1691	1604 1593 1597 1635
Kincardine	71	Ross & Cromarty	Ross	1804	1821
Kincardine (see Abernethy 90a)	90a	Inverness	Inverness		1669
Kincardine O'Neil	209	Aberdeen	Aberdeen Edinburgh	1706	1734 1578
Kinclaven	365	Perth	Dunkeld Edinburgh	1726	1680 1581
Kineddar (see Drainie 130)	130		Moray		1789
Kinfauns	366	Perth	St Andrews Edinburgh	1624	1605 1577
Kingarth	555	Bute	The Isles	1727	1661
King-Edward	210	Aberdeen	Aberdeen	1701	1821
Kinghorn	439	Fife	St Andrews Edinburgh	1576	1549 1568
Kinglassie	440	Fife	St Andrews Edinburgh	1627	1550 1588
Kingoldrum	295	Forfar	Brechin Edinburgh St Andrews	1700	1581 1591 1776
Kingsbarns	441	Fife	St Andrews	1642	1592
Kingskettle (see Kettle 435)	435				
Kingussie & Insh	102	Inverness	Inverness	1724	1630
Kinkell (see Keithhall & Kinkell 206)	206	Aberdeen	Aberdeen Dunblane St Andrews		1633 1553 1740
Kinloch (see Lethendy & Kinloch 372)	372	Perth	Dunkeld St Andrews		1685 1593
Kinloch-Rannoch (see Fortingall 355a)	367		Dunkeld		1693
Kinlochspelvie (Mull) (also Toronsay 549)	545	Argyll	The Isles	1842	
Kinloss	138	Moray	Moray Edinburgh	1699	1751 1591
Kinnaird	368	Perth	St Andrews Brechin Edinburgh	1632	1598 1601 1581

Parish	District number	County	Commissariot	OPR	Testament or inventory
Kinneff & Catterline	262	Kincardine	St Andrews Edinburgh	1616	1582
Kinnell	296	Forfar	St Andrews Brechin Edinburgh	1657	1605 1582 1594
Kinnellar	211	Aberdeen	Aberdeen	1697	1725
Kinnethmont	212	Aberdeen	Aberdeen Edinburgh	1728	1728 1575
Kinnettles	297	Forfar	St Andrews	1696	1595
Kinnoir (see Huntly 202)	202		Moray		1685
Kinnoull	369	Perth	St Andrews Dunblane Edinburgh	1618	1584 1657 1573
Kinross	462	Kinross	St Andrews Edinburgh	1676	1614 1573
Kintail	72	Ross & Cromarty	Ross	1776	
Kintore	213	Aberdeen	Aberdeen Moray	1717	1736 1685
Kippen	484 part	Stirling Perth	Dunblane Stirling Edinburgh	1700	1600 1607 1588
Kirkbean	870	Kirkcudbright	Dumfries Edinburgh	1714	1638 1584
Kirkcaldy	442	Fife	St Andrews Edinburgh	1614	1549 1570
Kirkcolm	887	Wigtown	Wigtown Edinburgh	1779	1758 1584
Kirkconnel	834	Dumfries	Dumfries Kirkcudbright Edinburgh Glasgow St Andrews	1742	1638 1725 1567 1617 1551
Kirkcowan	888	Wigtown	Wigtown	1788	1736
Kirkcudbright	871	Kirkcudbright	Kirkcudbright Dumfries Edinburgh	1743	1667 1643 1564
Kirkden	298	Forfar	St Andrews Brechin	1650	1600 1652
Kirkgunzeon	872	Kirkcudbright	Kirkcudbright Dumfries Edinburgh	1702	1657 1590
Kirkhill	103	Inverness	Inverness	1726	1814
Kirkhope (also Ettrick 774b & Yarrow 779)	776	Selkirk	Peebles	1852	1691

Parish	District number	County	Commissariot	OPR	Testament or inventory
Kirkinner	889	Wigtown	Wigtown	1694	1709
			Edinburgh		1576
Kirkintilloch (formerly Lenzie)	498	Dunbarton	Glasgow	1656	1605
Kirkliston	667	Linlithgow	Edinburgh	1675	1581
		W. Lothian	St Andrews		1711
Kirkmabreck	873	Kirkcudbright	Kirkcudbright	1703	1674
			Wigtown		1769
			Edinburgh		1581
Kirkmahoe	835	Dumfries	Dumfries	1720	1625
			Edinburgh		1586
Kirkmaiden	890	Wigtown	Wigtown	1716	1718
			Edinburgh		1594
Kirkmichael (see Resolis 79)	79	Ross & Cromarty	Ross		1823
Kirkmichael	370	Perth	Dunkeld	1650	
			Dunblane		1652
Kirkmichael	600	Ayr	Glasgow	1638	1605
			Edinburgh		1581
Kirkmichael	160	Banff	Moray	1725	1594
Kirkmichael	836	Dumfries	Dumfries	1727	1658
Kirknewton & East Calder	690	Edinburgh	Edinburgh	1642	1587
Kirkoswald	601	Ayr	Glasgow	1694	1604
			Edinburgh		1581
Kirkpatrick-Durham	874	Kirkcudbright	Dumfries	1693	1638
			Edinburgh		1587
Kirkpatrick-Fleming	837	Dumfries	Dumfries	1748	1657
Kirkpatrick-Irongray (see Irongray 867)	867	Kirkcudbright	Dumfries		
			Edinburgh		1580
			Glasgow		1548
Kirkpatrick-Juxta	838	Dumfries	Dumfries	1694	1661
Kirktown	794	Roxburgh	Peebles	1707	1682
Kirkurd	764	Peebles	Peebles	1705	1823
			Edinburgh		1576
Kirkwall & St Ola	21	Orkney	Orkney & Shetland	1657	1611
			Edinburgh		1574
Kirriemuir	299	Forfar	St Andrews	1716	1589
			Brechin		1658
			Edinburgh		1576
Kishorn (also Applecross & Shieldaig 58)	58	Ross & Cromarty	Ross	1808	

Parish	District number	County	Commissariot	OPR	Testament or inventory
Knapdale North, *(see North Knapdale 530)*					
Knapdale South, *(see South Knapdale 533)*					
Knockando	139	Moray	Moray	1757	1701
Knockbain *(formerly Kilmuir Wester & Suddy 73)*	73	Ross & Cromarty	Ross	1749	1823
Lady *(or Cross Burness & Lady, see Sanday 26)*	26				
Ladykirk	746	Berwick	Lauder Edinburgh	1697	1631 1582
Laggan	104	Inverness	Inverness	1775	1633
Lairg	53	Sutherland	Caithness	1768	1677
Lamington & Wandell *(see Wandell & Lamington 659)*	659	Lanark	Lanark Edinburgh Glasgow		1622 1594 1548
Lanark	648	Lanark	Lanark Glasgow Edinburgh	1647	1596 1550 1582
Langholm *(formerly Staplegortoun 839)*	839	Dumfries	Dumfries	1668	1656
Langton	747	Berwick	Lauder Peebles Edinburgh	1728	1628 1686 1568
Larbert	485	Stirling	Stirling Edinburgh St Andrews	1663	1614 1582 1743
Largo	443	Fife	St Andrews Edinburgh	1636	1550 1576
Largs	602	Ayr	Glasgow Edinburgh	1723	1603 1590
Lasswade	691	Edinburgh Midlothian	Edinburgh	1617	1569
Latheron	38	Caithness	Caithness	1740	1663
Lathrisk *(see Kettins 294)*	294	Forfar Edinburgh	St Andrews	1594	1549
Lauder	748	Berwick	Lauder Edinburgh	1680	1561 1568
Laurencekirk *(formerly Conveth)*	263	Kincardine Brechin	St Andrews	1702 1657	1715
Leadhills *(also Crawford 635)*	635	Lanark	Lanark	1698	1629
Lecropt	371 part	Perth Stirling	Dunblane Stirling Edinburgh	1720	1601 1607 1599
Legerwood	749	Berwick	Lauder	1689	1564
Leith (North)	692[1]	Edinburgh	Edinburgh	1615	1564

Parish	District number	County	Commissariot	OPR	Testament or inventory
Leith (South)	692²	Edinburgh	Edinburgh	1599	1564
Lennel	733	Berwick	Lauder		1635
(see Coldstream 733)		Edinburgh		1598	
Lenzie	498	Dunbarton	Glasgow		1666
(see Kirkintilloch 498)			Edinburgh		1587
Leochel-Cushnie	214	Aberdeen	Aberdeen	1669	
Lerwick	5	Shetland	Orkney & Shetland	1728	1648
Leslie	215	Aberdeen	Aberdeen	1699	1739
Leslie	444	Fife	Dunkeld	1673	1684
			Edinburgh		1576
			St Andrews		1650
Lesmahagow	649	Lanark	Lanark	1692	1620
			Edinburgh		1576
Lessudden	804	Roxburgh	Peebles		
(see St Boswells 804)		Lauder		1562	
Leswalt	891	Wigtown	Wigtown	1729	1715
			Edinburgh		1598
Lethendy & Kinloch	372	Perth	Dunkeld	1698	1689
			Dunblane		1655
			Moray		1796
			Edinburgh		1589
			Inverness		1666
			St Andrews		1725
Lethnott & Nevar	300	Forfar	Brechin	1728	1597
			St Andrews		1620
Leuchars	445	Fife	St Andrews	1665	1550
			Edinburgh		1576
Lhanbryde	142	Moray	Moray	1723	
(also St Andrews Lhanbryde 142)					
Libberton	650	Lanark	Lanark	1717	1597
			Edinburgh		1581
Liberton	693	Edinburgh Midlothian	Edinburgh	1624	1578
Liff, Benvie & Invergowrie	301	Angus	St Andrews	1651	1598
			Brechin		1640
Lilliesleaf	795	Roxburgh	Peebles	1737	1811
Linlithgow	668	Linlithgow W. Lothian	Edinburgh	1613	1564
Linton	796	Roxburgh	Peebles	1732	1683
			Lauder		1668
			Edinburgh		1575
Lintrathen	302	Forfar	St Andrews	1717	1613
Lismore	525	Argyll	Argyll	1758	1679
(also Appin 525/2, Duror 525/4, Glencoe & Ballachulish 525/3)					

Parish	District number	County	Commissariot	OPR	Testament or inventory
Little Dunkeld	373	Perth	Dunkeld	1759	1688
			Dunblane		1653
Livingston	669	Linlithgow W. Lothian	Edinburgh	1639	1578
Lochalsh	74	Ross & Cromarty	Ross	1755	1802
Lochbroom	75	Ross & Cromarty	Ross	1798	1817
Lochcarron	76	Ross & Cromarty	Ross	1819	1821
Lochgilphead (see Glassary 511)	526	Argyll	Argyll		1675
Lochgoilhead (also Kilmorich 527/2)	527/1	Argyll	Argyll	1692	1675
Lochlee	303	Forfar	Brechin	1731	1626
Lochmaben	840	Dumfries	Dumfries	1741	1629
Lochranza (also Kilmory 554)	556	Bute	The Isles	1732	
Lochrutton	875	Kirkcudbright	Dumfries	1698	1678
			Edinburgh		1590
Lochs (also Carloway 86b)	87	Ross & Cromarty	The Isles	1831	
Lochwinnoch	570	Renfrew	Glasgow	1718	1602
			Edinburgh		1597
Logie	446	Fife	St Andrews	1660	1597
			Edinburgh		1587
Logie	374	Perth	Dunblane	1688	1617
	part	Stirling	also Stirling		
	part	Clackmannan	Dunkeld		1742
	part	Clackmannan	Brechin		1597
			Edinburgh		1596
Logiealmond (see Monzie 382, Fowlis-Wester 357, Methven 380 & Redgorton 390)	375				
Logie-Buchan	216	Aberdeen	Aberdeen	1698	
Logie-Coldstone	217 Aberdeen		Aberdeen	1716	1731
Logie-Easter	77	Ross & Cromarty	Ross	1665	
Logie-Wester (see Urquhart & Logie-Wester 84)	84				
Logie-Pert	304	Forfar	St Andrews	1717	1773
			Edinburgh		1598
Logierait (also Aberfeldy 324)	376	Perth Dunblane	Dunkeld	1673 1685	1683
			Edinburgh		1584
Longforgan	377	Perth	St Andrews	1634	1588
			Dunblane		1656
			Edinburgh		1573

Parish	District number	County	Commissariot	OPR	Testament or inventory
Longformacus (also Cranshaws 734)	750	Berwick	Lauder	1654	1636
Longside (disjoined from Peterhead in 1640)	218	Aberdeen	Aberdeen	1621	
Lonmay	219	Aberdeen	Aberdeen	1687	1730
Loth	54	Sutherland	Caithness	1795	1822
Loudoun	603	Ayr	Glasgow Edinburgh	1673	1551 1579
Lumphannan	220	Aberdeen	Aberdeen	1740	1722
Lunan	305	Forfar	St Andrews	1654	1614
Lundie & Fowlis	306	Forfar	St Andrews Brechin	1667	1588 1622
Lunnasting (also Nesting 7/1, Whalsay & Sherries 7/3)	7/2	Shetland	Orkney & Shetland	1781	1613
Luss	499	Dunbarton	Glasgow Edinburgh	1698	1549 1565
Lyne & Megget	765	Peebles	Peebles Edinburgh	1649	1823 1588
Macduff (also Gamrie & Down 155a)	155a	Banff	Aberdeen	1786	1798
Madderty	378	Perth	Dunkeld Dunblane Edinburgh	1701	1713 1656 1582
Mains (also Strathmartine 307)	307	Forfar	St Andrews Edinburgh	1635	1596 1595
Makerston	797	Roxburgh	Peebles Lauder	1692	1691 1559
Manor	766	Peebles	Peebles Edinburgh	1663	1823 1583
Markinch	447	Fife	St Andrews Edinburgh Inverness	1635	1549 1586 1630
Marnoch	161	Banff	Moray	1676	1751
Maryculter	264	Kincardine	Aberdeen Edinburgh	1696	1746 1599
Marykirk (formerly Aberluthnot 265)	265	Kincardine	St Andrews	1699	1635
Maryton	308	Forfar	Brechin Edinburgh	1727	1596 1586
Mauchline	604	Ayr	Glasgow Edinburgh	1670	1602 1576
Maxton	798	Roxburgh	Peebles	1689	1805
Maxwelltown (also Troqueer 882)	882	Kirkcudbright	Dumfries	1837	1624

Parish	District number	County	Commissariot	OPR	Testament or inventory
Maybole	605	Ayr	Glasgow	1712	1555
			Edinburgh		1576
Mearns	571	Renfrew	Glasgow	1756	1602
			Brechin		1656
			Edinburgh		1578
Megget	765				
(see Lyne & Megget 765)					
Meigle	379	Perth	Dunkeld	1727	1638
(also Persie 386b)		Dunblane	1653		
			Edinburgh		1580
Melrose	799	Roxburgh	Peebles	1642	1794
			Lauder		1560
			Edinburgh		1565
Menmuir	309	Forfar	Brechin	1701	1578
			Edinburgh		1576
Merton	751	Berwick	Lauder	1729	1634
Methlick	221	Aberdeen	Aberdeen	1670	1723
Methven	380	Perth	St Andrews	1662	1593
(also Logiealmond 375)			Dunblane		1653
			Dunkeld		1712
			Edinburgh		1576
Methy	292	Forfar	St Andrews		1595
(see Inverarity 292)					
Mid Calder	694	Edinburgh Midlothian	Edinburgh	1604	1567
Middlebie	841	Dumfries	Dumfries	1744	1640
Midmar	222	Aberdeen	Aberdeen	1717	1777
Mid Yell	6	Shetland	Orkney & Shetland	1723	
Migvy	242	Aberdeen	Aberdeen		
(see Tarland & Migvy 242)			Inverness		1807
Minnigaff	876	Kirkcudbright	Wigtown	1694	1702
			Edinburgh		1577
Minto	800	Roxburgh	Peebles	1703	1681
Mochrum	892	Wigtown	Wigtown	1720	1706
			Edinburgh		1577
Moffat	842	Dumfries	Dumfries	1723	1627
			Lanark		1673
Moneydie	381	Perth	Dunkeld	1655	1684
			Edinburgh		1591
			Dunblane		1659
Monifieth	310	Forfar	St Andrews	1562	1599
			Edinburgh		1580
Monikie	311	Forfar	Brechin	1613	1610
			Edinburgh		1596
			St Andrews		1599

Parish	District number	County	Commissariot	OPR	Testament or inventory
Monimail	448	Fife	St Andrews	1656	1549
			Edinburgh		1573
Monkton & Prestwick	606	Ayr	Glasgow	1702	1607
			Edinburgh		1591
Monkland, New 651 *(see New Monkland 651)*					
Monkland, Old 652 *(see Old Monkland 652)*					
Monquhitter	223	Aberdeen	Aberdeen	1670	1729
Montrose	312	Forfar	Brechin	1615	1579
			Dunkeld		1676
			Edinburgh		1565
			St Andrews		1606
Monyabroch *(see Kilsyth 483)*	483	Stirling Stirling	Glasgow Stirling	1654	1617
			Edinburgh		1576
Monymusk	224	Aberdeen	Aberdeen	1678	1722
Monzie *(also Logiealmond 375)*	382	Perth	Dunblane Dunkeld Edinburgh	1720	1543 1731 1584
Monzievaird & Strowan	383	Perth	Dunblane Edinburgh	1729	1663 1599
Moonzie	449	Fife	St Andrews	1713	1596
Mordington	752	Berwick	Lauder	1721	1635
Morebattle	801	Roxburgh	Peebles Edinburgh	1726	1685 1576
Morham	712	Haddington E. Lothian	Edinburgh	1712	1581
Mortlach *(also Glenrinnes 155b)*	162	Banff	Aberdeen	1741	1742
Morton	843	Dumfries	Dumfries	1692	1690
Morvern	528	Argyll	Argyll	1803	1676
Moulin *(also Tenandry 394c)*	384	Perth Dunblane	Dunkeld	1741 1655	1685
			Edinburgh		1581
Mousewald	844	Dumfries	Dumfries	1751	1673
Moy & Dalarossie	105	Inverness	Inverness Edinburgh	1788	1630 1599
Muckairn	529	Argyll	Argyll	1746	1734
Muckart	385 part	Perth Kinross	Stirling also St Andrews Dunblane Edinburgh	1698	1612 1656 1580
Muiravonside	486	Stirling	Stirling	1689	1608

Parish	District number	County	Commissariot	OPR	Testament or inventory
Muirkirk	607	Ayr	Glasgow	1659	1632
Murroes	313	Forfar	St Andrews	1698	1595
			Edinburgh		1599
Muthill	386a	Perth	Dunblane	1704	1554
			Edinburgh		1589
Nairn	123	Nairn	Moray	1705	1687
Neilston	572	Renfrew	Glasgow	1688	1610
			Edinburgh		1594
Nenthorn	753	Berwick	Lauder	1715	1563
			Peebles		1691
Nesting *(also Lunnasting 7/2, Whalsay & Skerries 7/3)*	7/1	Shetland	Orkney & Shetland	1783	1613
Nevar *(see Lethnot & Nevar 300)*	300	Forfar	Brechin Edinburgh		1610 1567
Nevay *(see Eassie & Nevay 284)*	284				
New Abbey	877	Kirkcudbright	Dumfries	1691	1628
			Edinburgh		1582
Newbattle *(also Stobhill 698b)*	695	Edinburgh	Edinburgh	1618	1572
Newburgh	450	Fife	St Andrews	1654	1591
			Dunblane		1671
			Edinburgh		1564
Newburn	451	Fife	St Andrews	1628	1550
			Edinburgh		1595
New Cumnock	608	Ayr	Glasgow	1706	1670
New Deer *(anciently called Auchreddie)*	225	Aberdeen	Aberdeen	1684	1725
New or East Kilpatrick	500	Dunbarton	Glasgow	1691	1603
			Stirling (1649–1660)		1656
			Edinburgh		1577
Newhills	226	Aberdeen	Aberdeen	1700	1725
Newlands	767	Peebles	Peebles	1677	
			Edinburgh		1576
			Dumfries		1817
New Luce	893	Wigtown	Wigtown	1695	1705
New Machar	227	Aberdeen	Aberdeen	1676	1740
			Edinburgh		1590
New Monkland	651	Lanark	Hamilton & Campsie	1693	1564
			Glasgow		1652
			Edinburgh		1579

Newport-on-Tay 431
  (see Forgan 431)

Parish	District number	County	Commissariot	OPR	Testament or inventory
New Spynie	136	Moray	Moray	1711	1688
Newton	696	Edinburgh Midlothian	Edinburgh	1629	1600
Newton-on-Ayr (also St Quivox)	612	Ayr	Glasgow	1780	1507
Newtyle	314	Forfar	St Andrews Edinburgh	1685	1591 1570
Nigg	266	Kincardine	St Andrews	1675	1614
Nigg	78	Ross & Cromarty	Ross Edinburgh	1730	1820 1589
North Berwick	713	Haddington E. Lothian	Edinburgh	1604	1576
North Bute	557	Bute	The Isles	1844	1821
North Knapdale	530	Argyll	Argyll The Isles	1779	1723 1787
Northmavine	8	Shetland	Orkney & Shetland	1758	1612
North Ronaldshay	22	Orkney	Orkney & Shetland	1800	1611
North Uist	113	Inverness	The Isles	1821	1782
North Yell (also Fetlar 4/1)	4/2	Shetland	Orkney & Shetland	1787	1613
Oa (Islay)	546	Argyll	The Isles	1833	
Oathlaw	315	Forfar	Brechin	1717	1662
Oban (see Kilmore & Kilbride 523)	523	Argyll	Argyll	1796	1790
Ochiltree	609	Ayr	Glasgow Edinburgh	1642	1605 1582
Old Cumnock	610	Ayr	Glasgow	1704	1604
Old Deer	228	Aberdeen	Aberdeen	1735	1722
Oldhamstocks	714	Haddington E. Lothian	Edinburgh	1664	1579
Old or West Kilpatrick	501	Dunbarton	Glasgow	1688	1577
Old Luce (or Glenluce 894)	894	Wigtown	Wigtown	1731	1713
Old Machar	168b	Aberdeen	Aberdeen Edinburgh	1641	1785 1590
Old Meldrum	229	Aberdeen	Aberdeen Moray	1713	1725 1695
Old Monkland	652	Lanark	Hamilton & Campsie Edinburgh Glasgow	1695	1596 1579 1652

Parish	District number	County	Commissariot	OPR	Testament or inventory
Olrig	39	Caithness	Caithness	1699	1662
Ordiquhill	163	Banff	Aberdeen	1704	1823
Ormiston	715	Haddington E. Lothian	Edinburgh Peebles	1637	1565 1683
Orphir	23	Orkney	Orkney & Shetland	1708	1612
Orwell	463	Kinross	St Andrews Edinburgh	1688	1606 1586
Oxnam (also Edgerston 787b)	802	Roxburgh	Peebles	1700	1682
Oyne	230	Aberdeen	Aberdeen	1703	
Paisley	573	Renfrew	Glasgow Edinburgh		1552 1572
Paisley High	573^1			1788	
Paisley Middle	573^2			1788	
Paisley Low	573^3			1738	
Panbride	316	Forfar	Brechin Edinburgh St Andrews	1693	1579 1576 1700
Papa-Stour (also Walls 12/1 & Sandness 12/2)	12/3	Shetland	Orkney & Shetland	1772	1630
Papa-Westray (also Westray 33/1)	33/2	Orkney Shetland	Orkney &	1784	1613
Paplay (see Holm & Paplay 19)	19	Orkney	Orkney & Shetland		1613
Parton (also Corsock-Bridge 862)	878	Kirkcudbright	Kirkcudbright Edinburgh	1714	1682 1574
Peebles	768	Peebles	Peebles Edinburgh Glasgow	1622	1823 1569 1547
Pencaitland	716	Haddington E. Lothian	Edinburgh	1598	1569
Penicuik	697	Edinburgh	Edinburgh	1654	1586
Penninghame	895	Wigtown	Wigtown Edinburgh	1695	1700 1584
Penpont	845	Dumfries	Dumfries Edinburgh	1728	1627 1581
Persie (see Blairgowrie 335 & Meigle 379)	386b				
Perth	387	Perth	St Andrews Dunblane Edinburgh Glasgow	1561	1586 1546 1569 1744
Peterculter	231	Aberdeen	Aberdeen	1643	1730

Parish	District number	County	Commissariot	OPR	Testament or inventory
Peterhead	232	Aberdeen	Aberdeen	1668	1722
Pettinain	653	Lanark	Lanark	1689	1602
			Edinburgh		1583
Petty	106	Inverness	Moray	1633	
			Inverness		1630
			Aberdeen		1743
Pharay (see Eday & Pharay 15)	15				
Pitsligo	233	Aberdeen	Aberdeen	1720	1735
Pittenweem	452	Fife	St Andrews	1611	1549
			Edinburgh		1565
Polmont	487	Stirling	Stirling	1729	1663
Polwarth	754	Berwick	Lauder	1652	1633
			Edinburgh		1598
Poolewe (also Gairloch 66)	66	Ross & Cromarty	Ross	1835	
Port-Glasgow	574	Renfrew	Glasgow	1696	1707
Port of Menteith	388	Perth	Dunblane	1697	1542
			Edinburgh		1600
Portmoak	464	Kinross	St Andrews	1701	1550
			Edinburgh		1594
Portnahaven (Islay)	547	Argyll	The Isles	1831	
Portpatrick	896	Wigtown	Wigtown	1720	1711
Portree (Skye)	114	Inverness	The Isles	1800	1795
Premnay	234	Aberdeen	Aberdeen	1718	1732
Preston (see Bunkle and Preston 728)	728	Berwick	Lauder		1653
Prestonkirk (formerly Prestonhaugh)	717	Haddington E. Lothian	Edinburgh	1658	1570
Prestonpans (formerly Saltpreston)	718	Haddington E. Lothian	Edinburgh	1596	1568
Prestwick (see Monkton & Prestwick 606)	606	Ayr	Glasgow Edinburgh		1603 1591
Primrose (see Carrington 675)	675				
Quarff (also Bressay 1/1 & Burra 1/2)	1/2	Shetland	Orkney & Shetland	1755	
Queensferry (or Queensferry South) (also Dalmeny 665)	670	Linlithgow W. Lothian	Edinburgh	1635	1568
Queensferry, North (prior to 1855 see Dunfermline 424, since 1855 see Inverkeithing 432)		Fife	St Andrews		1718

Parish	District number	County	Commissariot	OPR	Testament or inventory
Rafford	140	Moray	Moray	1682	1695
			Edinburgh		1598
Rathen	235	Aberdeen	Aberdeen	1704	1724
			Edinburgh		1578
Ratho	698a	Edinburgh	Edinburgh	1682	1576
Rathven	164	Banff	Aberdeen	1716	
(also Seafield 167)		Brechin		1581	
			Edinburgh		1594
Rattray	389	Perth	Dunkeld	1606	1684
			Dunblane		1652
			Edinburgh		1575
Rayne	236	Aberdeen	Aberdeen	1679	1738
Reay	40	Caithness	Caithness	1732	1812
Redgorton	390	Perth	Dunkeld	1706	1688
(also Logiealmond 375)			Edinburgh		1579
			St Andrews		1673
Rendall	16	Orkney	Orkney &		1611
(see Evie & Rendall 16)			Shetland		
Renfrew	575	Renfrew	Hamilton &	1673	1564
			Campsie		
			Edinburgh		1569
Rerrick	879	Kirkcudbright	Kirkcudbright	1736	1700
			Edinburgh		1571
Rescobie	317	Forfar	St Andrews	1688	1600
			Edinburgh		1597
Resolis	79	Ross & Cromarty	Ross	1731	1816
(formerly Kirkmichael & Cullicudden 79)					
Rhu (see Row)	503				
Rhum	116				
(see Small Isles 116)					
Rhynd	391	Perth	St Andrews	1698	1550
Rhynie & Essie	237a	Aberdeen	Moray	1740	1687
Riccarton	611	Ayr	Glasgow	1695	1606
			Edinburgh		1569
Roberton	777	Selkirk	Peebles	1679	1823
Roberton	660	Lanark	Lanark	1691	1620
(also Wiston 660)					
Rogart	55	Sutherland	Caithness	1795	
Ronaldshay North	22				
(see North Ronaldshay 22)					
Ronaldshay South	29				
(see South Ronaldshay 29)					
Rosemarkie	80	Ross & Cromarty	Ross	1744	1804

Parish	District number	County	Commissariot	OPR	Testament or inventory
Roseneath	502	Dunbarton Edinburgh	Glasgow	1722 1584	1606
Rosskeen	81	Ross & Cromarty	Ross Edinburgh	1783	1815 1596
Rothes (also Dundurcas 141)	141	Moray Edinburgh	Moray	1717 1564	1686
Rothesay	558	Bute	The Isles Argyll	1691	1661 1740
Rothiemay	165	Banff	Moray Aberdeen Edinburgh	1658	1687 1736 1587
Rothiemurchus (also Duthil 96b¹)	96b²	Inverness	Inverness	1774	1630
Rousay & Egilshay	24	Orkney	Orkney & Shetland	1733	1612
Row (or Rhu)	503	Dunbarton	Glasgow	1760	1675
Roxburgh	803	Roxburgh	Peebles Edinburgh	1624	1683 1600
Rutherglen	654	Lanark	Glasgow Edinburgh	1698	1606 1581
Ruthven	318	Forfar	Dunkeld Moray Edinburgh	1744	1684 1688 1587
Ruthwell	846	Dumfries	Dumfries	1723	1638
Saddell & Skipness	531	Argyll	Argyll	1756 1783	1676
St Andrews	25	Orkney	Orkney & Shetland	1657	1612
St Andrews (incl. Lhanbryde)	142	Moray	Moray	1701	1827
St Andrews & St Leonards	453	Fife	St Andrews Edinburgh	1627	1549 1565
St Boswells (formerly Lessudden 804)	804	Roxburgh	Peebles	1692	1693
St Cuthberts (also Edinburgh 685¹ & Canongate 685³)	685²	Edinburgh Midlothian	Edinburgh	1573	1590
St Cyrus (formerly Ecclesgreig 267)	267	Kincardine	St Andrews	1696	1792
St Fergus	166	Banff	Aberdeen	1658	1823
St Kilda (Skye) (also Harris 111)	111	Inverness	The Isles	1830	
St Lawrence (see Slamannan 489)	489	Stirling Edinburgh	Stirling	1598	1610

Parish	District number	County	Commissariot	OPR	Testament or inventory
St Leonards *(also St Andrews & St Leonards 453)*	453	Fife	St Andrews	1667	1550
St Madoes	392	Perth	Dunblane Dunkeld Edinburgh	1591	1612 1724 1594
St Martins	393	Perth	Dunkeld St Andrews Dunblane	1697	1586 1673 1658
St Monance *(or Abercromie)*	454	Fife	St Andrews Edinburgh	1628	1550 1581
St Mungo	847	Dumfries	Dumfries	1700	1657
St Ninians & Bannockburn *(also Stirling 490)*	488	Stirling	Stirling Edinburgh	1643	1607 1576
St Ninians *(also known as St Ringans)*			St Andrews		1599
St Ola *(see Kirkwall & St Ola 21)*	21	Orkney	Orkney & Shetland		1611
St Quivox *(also Newton-upon-Ayr 612)*	612	Ayr	Glasgow Edinburgh	1735	1612 1599
St Ringans *(see St Ninians 488)*	488				
St Vigeans	319	Forfar	St Andrews Edinburgh	1669	1599 1586
Salen (Mull)	548	Argyll	The Isles	1828	1815
Saline	455	Fife	Stirling	1746	1610
Salton	719	Haddington E. Lothian	Edinburgh	1636	1578
Saltpreston *(see Prestonpans 718)*	718				
Sanday *(see Cross & Burness and Lady 26)*	26	Orkney	Orkney & Shetland		1613
Sanday *(see Small Isles 116)*	116				
Sandness *(also Walls 12/1, Papa Stour 12/3 & Foula 12/4)*	12/2	Shetland	Orkney & Shetland	1787	1630
Sandsting & Aithsting	9	Shetland	Orkney & Shetland	1733	1612
Sandwick	27	Orkney	Orkney & Shetland	1728	1612
Sandwick *(also Cunningsburgh & Dunrossness 3/1 & Fair Isle 3/3)*	3/2	Shetland	Orkney & S.	1746	1648
Sanquhar *(also Wanlockhead 853)*	848	Dumfries	Dumfries Wigtown Glasgow Edinburgh	1693	1625 1787 1607 1565

Parish	District number	County	Commissariot	OPR	Testament or inventory
Saulseat		Wigtown	Wigtown		
(incorporated with Inch in 17th century)			Edinburgh		1593
Savoch	237b	Aberdeen	Aberdeen	1852	1774
Scone	394a	Perth	St Andrews	1620	1592
			Dunblane		1652
			Edinburgh		1586
Scoonie	456	Fife	St Andrews	1675	1550
			Edinburgh		1593
Seafield	164				
(see Rathven 164)					
Selkirk	778	Selkirk	Peebles	1697	1691
			Edinburgh		1567
Shapinsay	28	Orkney	Orkney &	1632	1612
			Shetland		
Shieldaig	58	Ross & Cromarty	Ross	1797	
(also Applecross & Kishorn 58)					
Shisken	554	Bute	The Isles	1701	
(also Lochranza 554)					
Shotts	655	Lanark	Hamilton &	1707	
			Campsie		
			Glasgow		1606
			Edinburgh		1576
Simprim	755	Berwick	Lauder	1700	1631
(also Swinton 755)					
Skene	238	Aberdeen	Aberdeen	1746	1721
Skerries	7/3	Shetland	Orkney &	1787	
(also Nesting 7/1, Lunnasting 7/2 & Whalsay 7/3)			Shetland		
Skipness	531				
(see Saddell & Skipness 531)					
Skirling	769	Peebles	Peebles	1683	1823
			Edinburgh		1594
Slains	239	Aberdeen	Aberdeen	1707	1728
Slamannan	489	Stirling	Stirling	1681	1617
(formerly St Lawrence 489)			Edinburgh		1579
Sleat (Skye)	115	Inverness	The Isles	1813	1711
Smailholm	805	Roxburgh	Peebles	1648	1682
			Dumfries		1678
			Lauder		1634
			Edinburgh		1565
Small Isles	116	Inverness	The Isles	1855	
(Rhum, Eigg, Canna, Sanday & Hyskier 116)					
Snizort (Skye)	117	Inverness	The Isles	1823	1723
Sorbie	897	Wigtown	Wigtown	1700	1730
			Edinburgh		1581

Parish	District number	County	Commissariot	OPR	Testament or inventory
Sorn *(formerly Dalgain 613)*	613	Ayr	Glasgow Edinburgh	1692	1671 1584
Southdean *(also Abbotrule 806 & Edgerston 787b)*	806	Roxburgh	Peebles Edinburgh	1696	1823 1591
Southend *(formerly Kilcolmkill & Kilblane)*	532	Argyll	Argyll	1768	1725
South Knapdale	533	Argyll	Argyll	1771	1717
South Ronaldshay & Burray *(combined in 1682)*	29	Orkney	Orkney & Shetland	1657	1611
South Uist *(also Benbecula 118)*	118	Inverness	The Isles	1839	1797
Southwick *(see Colvend 861)*	861				
South Yell	6	Shetland	Orkney & Shetland	1730	
Soutra *(see Fala & Soutra 686)*	686				
Speymouth *(formerly Essil & Dipple 143)*	143	Moray	Moray Edinburgh	1654	1786 1592
Spott	720	Haddington E. Lothian	Edinburgh	1683	1569
Sprouston	807	Roxburgh	Peebles Edinburgh	1635	1681 1580
Stair *(formed out of Ochiltree 609 in 1673)*	614	Ayr	Glasgow	1736	
Staplegortoun *(see Langholm 839)*	839				
Stennes *(also Firth & Stennes 17)*	17	Orkney	Orkney & Shetland	1732	1613
Stenton	721	Haddington E. Lothian	Edinburgh Dunkeld	1679	1581 1766
Stevenston	615	Ayr	Glasgow	1700	1605
Stewarton	616	Ayr	Glasgow Edinburgh	1693	1548 1587
Stirling *(also St Ninians & Bannockburn 488)*	490	Stirling	Stirling Edinburgh	1587	1607 1564
Stitchel & Hume (744)	808	Roxburgh	Peebles Lauder	1640	1685 1560
Stobhill *(see Borthwick 674, Cockpen 676, Newbattle 695 & Temple 700)*	698b				
Stobo	770	Peebles	Peebles Edinburgh	1783	1684 1580
Stonehouse	656	Lanark	Glasgow	1696	1600

Parish	District number	County	Commissariot	OPR	Testament or inventory
Stoneykirk	898	Wigtown	Wigtown Edinburgh	1744	1727 1592
Stornoway (Lewis)	88	Ross & Cromarty	The Isles Ross	1762	1798 1804
Stow (also Caddonfoot 774a)	699	Edinburgh	Edinburgh	1626	1575
Strathcathro	320	Forfar	Brechin	1709	1600
Strachan	268	Kincardine	Brechin	1704	1581
Strachur (also Stralachlan 534/1)	534/2	Argyll	Argyll	1745	1685
Straiton	617	Ayr	Glasgow Edinburgh	1644	1551 1576
Stralachlan (also Strachur 534/2)	534/1	Argyll	Argyll	1764	1676
Stranraer	899	Wigtown	Wigtown	1695	1701
Strath (Skye)	119	Inverness	The Isles	1820	
Strathaven (see Avondale 621)	621	Lanark Edinburgh	Glasgow	1576	
Strathblane	491	Stirling	Glasgow Edinburgh	1672	1549 1590
Strathbrock (see Uphall 672)	672	Linlithgow	Edinburgh		1592
Strathdon (formerly Invernochtie, incl. Corgarff 240)	240	Aberdeen	Aberdeen	1667	1730
Strathfillan (see Killin 361)	394b				
Strathmartine (also Mains 307)	307	Forfar Edinburgh	St Andrews	1744 1600	1598
Strathmiglo	457	Fife	Dunkeld Edinburgh St Andrews	1719	1694 1578 1595
Strichen	241	Aberdeen	Aberdeen Inverness	1672	1744 1727
Stromness	30	Orkney	Orkney & Shetland	1695	1612
Stronsay	31	Orkney	Orkney & Shetland	1743	1619
Strontian or 505/3 Sunart (also Aharacle 505/1, Arisaig 505/2 & W. Ardnamurchan 505/4)		Argyll	Argyll	1804	1686
Strowan (see Monzievaird 383)	383	Perth	Dunblane Dunkeld		1601 1706
Suddy (see Knockbain 73)	73				

Parish	District number	County	Commissariot	OPR	Testament or inventory
Swinton & Simprim	755	Berwick	Lauder Edinburgh	1700	1628 1583
Symington	618	Ayr	Glasgow Edinburgh	1642	1603 1579
Symington	657	Lanark	Lanark	1692	1626
Tain	82	Ross & Cromarty	Ross Edinburgh	1719	1817 1582
Tannadice	321	Forfar	St Andrews Edinburgh	1694	1595 1580
Tarbat	83	Ross & Cromarty	Ross The Isles Edinburgh	1801	1723 1581
Tarbert (see Kilcalmonell & Kilberry 516)	516	Argyll	Argyll Glasgow		1778 1793
Tarbolton	619	Ayr	Glasgow Edinburgh	1730	1606 1576
Tarland & Migvy	242	Aberdeen	Aberdeen	1764	
Tarves	243	Aberdeen	Aberdeen	1695	1739
Tealing	322	Forfar	Dunkeld Edinburgh	1599	1688 1568
Temple (also Stobhill 698b)	700	Edinburgh Midlothian	Edinburgh	1688	1589
Tenandry (see Blair Atholl 334, Dull 346 & Moulin 384)	394c	Perth	Dunkeld Lauder		1674
Terregles	880	Kirkcudbright	Dumfries Edinburgh	1724	1624 1564
Teviothead (formed out of Hawick & Cavers in 1850)	809	Roxburgh	Peebles	1824	
Thankerton (see Covington 634)	634	Lanark	Lanark		1601
Thurso	41	Caithness	Caithness Edinburgh	1647	1662 1598
Tibbermore	395	Perth	Dunkeld Dunblane Edinburgh	1694	1688 1656 1576
Tillicoultry	468	Clackmannan	Dunblane Stirling Edinburgh	1640	1554 1610 1597
Tingwall (also Whiteness & Weesdale 10/2)	10/1	Shetland	Orkney & Shetland	1709	1613
Tinwald	849	Dumfries	Dumfries	1789	1624
Tiree (see Tyree 551)	551				

Parish	District number	County	Commissariot	OPR	Testament or inventory
Tobermory (Mull)	549	Argyll	The Isles	1830	1803
Tongland	881	Kirkcudbright	Kirkcudbright Edinburgh	1693	1713 1577
Tongue	56	Sutherland	Caithness	1789	
Torosay (Mull) (also Kinlochspelvie 545)	550	Argyll	The Isles	1772	1730
Torphichen	671	Linlithgow W. Lothian	Edinburgh	1693	1577
Torrance (see East Kilbride 643)	643	Lanark	Hamilton & Campsie Glasgow Edinburgh		1610 1583
Torryburn	458	Fife	St Andrews Stirling	1663	1616 1664
Torthorwald	850	Dumfries	Dumfries	1696	1657
Tough	244	Aberdeen	Aberdeen	1706	1724
Towie	245	Aberdeen	Aberdeen	1751	1757
Tranent	722	Haddington E. Lothian	Edinburgh	1611	1570
Traquair	771	Peebles	Peebles Edinburgh	1694	1823 1577
Trinity-Gask	396	Perth	Dunblane Dunkeld Edinburgh	1641	1603 1719 1577
Troqueer (also Maxwelltown 882)	882	Kirkcudbright	Dumfries Edinburgh	1690	1629 1583
Tulliallan	397	Perth	Dunblane Edinburgh	1673	1618 1578
Tullibody (see Alloa 465)	465	Clackmannan	Stirling Edinburgh		1655 1565
Tullibole (see Fossoway & Tullibole 461)	461	Kinross	St Andrews Dunblane Edinburgh		1543 1592
Tullich (see Glenmuick, Tullich etc. 201)	201	Aberdeen	Aberdeen		1750
Tullynessle (also Forbes & Kearn 246)	246	Aberdeen	Aberdeen	1760	1775
Tundergarth	851	Dumfries	Dumfries	1791	1690
Turriff	247	Aberdeen	Aberdeen	1696	1731
Tweedsmuir	772	Peebles	Peebles	1644	1823
Twynholm	883	Kirkcudbright	Kirkcudbright Edinburgh	1694	1676 1574
Tynninghame (see Whitekirk & Tynninghame 723)	723	Haddington E. Lothian	Edinburgh		1564

Parish	District number	County	Commissariot	OPR	Testament or inventory
Tynron	852	Dumfries	Dumfries	1742	1637
			Edinburgh		1569
Tyree (also Coll)	551/1	Argyll	The Isles	1766	1817
Tyrie	248	Aberdeen	Aberdeen	1710	1789
Udny	249	Aberdeen	Aberdeen	1744	1755
Uig	89	Ross & Cromarty	The Isles	1824	
Uist, North *(see North Uist 113)*	113				
Ulva	544	Argyll	Argyll	1828	
Unst	11	Shetland	Orkney & Shetland	1776	1613
Uphall *(formerly Strathbrock 672)*	672	Linlithgow	Edinburgh	1600	1588
Urquhart	144	Moray	Moray	1647	
			Edinburgh		1590
Urquhart & Glenmoriston	107	Inverness	Inverness	1739	1610
			Edinburgh		1590
Urquhart & Logie-Wester	84	Ross & Cromarty	Ross	1715	1821
			Moray		1687
Urr *(also Dalbeattie 864)*	884	Kirkcudbright Dumfries	Kirkcudbright	1760 1624	1790
Urray	85	Ross & Cromarty	Ross	1756	1812
			Edinburgh		1592
Walls *(also Sandness 12/2, Papa Stour 12/3 & Foula 12/4)*	12/1	Shetland	Orkney & Shetland	1771	1620
Walls *(also Flotta 32/2)*	32/1	Orkney	Orkney & Shetland	1708	1611
Walston	658	Lanark	Lanark	1679	1621
Wamphray	853a	Dumfries	Dumfries	1709	1656
Wandell & Lamington	659	Lanark	Lanark	1656	1623
Wanlockhead *(see Sanquhar 848)*	853	Dumfries	Dumfries		1748
Watten	42	Caithness	Caithness	1714	1662
Weem	398	Perth	Dunkeld	1692	1738
Weesdale, now Weisdale *(also Tingwall 10/1 & Whiteness 10/2)*	10/2	Shetland	Orkney & Shetland	1727	1613
Wemyss	459	Fife	St Andrews	1660	1549
			Edinburgh		1568
West Calder	701	Edinburgh	Edinburgh	1645	1567
Westerkirk	854	Dumfries	Dumfries	1693	1642
West Kilbride	620	Ayr	Glasgow	1671	
West Kilpatrick *(see Old or West Kilpatrick 501)*	501				

Parish	District number	County	Commissariot	OPR	Testament or inventory
West Linton	773	Peebles	Peebles	1656	1823
Westray (also Papa-Westray 3312)	33/1	Orkney	Orkney & Shetland	1733	1615
Westruther	756	Berwick	Lauder	1657	1636
Whalsay & Skerries (also Nesting 7/1 & Lunnasting 7/2)	7/3	Shetland	Orkney & Shetland	1787	1613
Whitburn	673	Linlithgow W. Lothian	Edinburgh	1719	1597
Whitekirk & Tynninghame	723	Haddington E. Lothian	Edinburgh	1695	1597
Whiteness & Weesdale/Weisdale (also Tingwall 10/1)	10/2	Shetland	Orkney & Shetland	1727	1613
Whithorn	900	Wigtown	Wigtown Edinburgh	1712	1700 1584
Whitsome & Hilton	757	Berwick	Lauder	1724	1653
Whittinghame	724	Haddington E. Lothian	Edinburgh Lauder	1627	1582 1790
Wick	43	Caithness	Caithness	1701	1661
Wigtown	901	Wigtown	Wigtown Edinburgh	1706	1700 1587
Wilton	810	Roxburgh	Peebles	1694	1610
Wiston (also Roberton 660)	660	Lanark	Lanark	1694	1601
Woodhouselee (see Glencorse 687)	687				
Wormit (see Forgan 431)	431				
Yarrow (also Kirkhope 776 & Ettrick 774b)	779	Selkirk	Peebles	1691	1686
Yell, Mid (see Mid Yell 6)	6				
Yell, North (see North Yell (also Fetlar) 4/1)	4/2				
Yell, South (see South Yell 6)	6				
Yester, or Gifford	725	Haddington E. Lothian	Edinburgh	1654	1591
Yetholm	811	Roxburgh	Peebles	1689	

Appendix IV

BOOK LIST

GENEALOGY

Baptie, Diane, *Parish Registers in the Kirk Session Records of the Church of Scotland.* (2000; Scottish Association of Family History Societies, Glasgow)

Baptie, Diane, *Registers of the Secession Churches in Scotland.* (2000; Scottish Association of Family History Societies, Glasgow)

Bevan, Amanda, *Tracing Your Ancestors in the Public Record Office.* (6th edition, 2002; HMSO, London)

Birthlink, *Search Guide for Adopted People in Scotland.* (1997; Birthlink Adoption Counselling Centre, HMSO, Edinburgh)

Brack, Arthur A., transcriber *Marriages at Lamberton Toll, 1833–49.* (1995; Northumberland & Durham FHS)

'Claverhouse' (M.C. Smith), *Irregular Border Marriages.* (1934; Moray Press, Edinburgh & London)

Dobson, David, *Dictionary of Scottish Settlers in North America: 1625–1825*: 7 volumes. (1984–93; Genealogical Publishing Co. Inc., Baltimore)

Ferguson, Joan P.S., compiler *Family Histories.* (1986; National Library of Scotland, Edinburgh)

Hamilton-Edwards, Gerald, *In Search of Scottish Ancestry.* (1983; Phillimore, Chichester)

Sandison, Alexander, *Tracing Ancestors in Shetland.* (1985; A. Sandison, London)

Scottish Association of Family History Societies, *The Parishes, Registers & Registrars of Scotland.* (Reprinted January 1995)

Stafford, Georgina, *Where to Find Adoption Records: a guide for counsellors.* (3rd edition, 2001; British Association of Adoption & Fostering, Edinburgh)

Steel, D. J., *Sources of Scottish Genealogy and Family History*. (1970; Phillimore, London & Chichester)

Stuart, Mrs Margaret, & Paul, Sir James Balfour, *Scottish Family History*. (1930; Oliver & Boyd, Edinburgh)

The National Archives of Scotland, *Tracing Your Scottish Ancestors: The Official Guide* (3rd edition 2003; Mercat Press, Edinburgh)

Whyte, Donald, *Dictionary of Scottish Emigrants to the USA*: 2 volumes. (1972 and 1986; Magna Carta Books Co., Baltimore)

Whyte, Donald, *Dictionary of Scottish Emigrants to Canada before Confederation*: 3 volumes. (1986, 1995 and 2003; Ontario Genealogical Society, Toronto)

THE CHURCH

Anson, Peter F., *The Catholic Church in Modern Scotland*. (1937; Burns, Oates, Washbourne, London)

Beckerlegge, O. A., compiler *United Methodist Ministers & Their Church*. (1968; Epworth Press, London)

Bertie, David M., *Scottish Episcopal Clergy: 1689–2000*. (2000; T. & T. Clark, Edinburgh)

Burnet, George B., *The Story of Quakerism in Scotland*. (1952; James Clark, London)

Couper, William J., *The Reformed Presbyterian Church in Scotland: its Congregations, Ministers and Students* [a *Fasti* of this Church from 1743 to 1876]. (1925; United Free Church of Scotland Publications Dept, Edinburgh)

Daiches, Salis, *The Jew in Scotland*. Scottish Church History Society Records III (1929) pp. 196–209.

Ewing, William, *Annals of the Free Church of Scotland: 1843–1900*: 2 volumes. (1914; T. & T. Clark, Edinburgh)

Gandy, M., *Catholic Missions and Registers: 1700–1880: Volume 6: Scotland*. (1993; publ. by author, London)

Goldie, Frederick, *A Short History of the Episcopal Church in Scotland from the Restoration to the Present Time*. (2nd edition, 1976; St Andrew Press, Edinburgh)

Hutchison, Matthew, *The Reformed Presbyterian Church in Scotland: 1680–1876*. (1893; J. & R. Parlane, Paisley)

Lamb, John A., *The Fasti of the United Free Church of Scotland: 1900–1929*. (1956; Oliver & Boyd, Edinburgh)

Macdonald, Donald F. Macleod, *Fasti Ecclesiae Scoticanae: Volume 10: Ministers of the Church from 1955–1975*. (1981; St Andrew Press, Edinburgh)

MacKelvie, William, *Annals & Statistics of the United Presbyterian Church*. (1873; Oliphant & Co., Edinburgh)

Scott, Hew, *Fasti Ecclesiae Scoticanae; the succession of Ministers in the Parish Churches of Scotland from 1560*. New edition revised by W. S. Crockett and Sir Francis J. Grant (1915–61): 9 volumes. (1961; Oliver & Boyd, Edinburgh)

Small, R., *History of the Congregations of the United Presbyterian Church 1733–1900*. (1904; David M. Small, Edinburgh)

Swift, Wesley F., *Methodism in Scotland* (1947; Epworth Press, London)

HISTORY

Donaldson, Gordon, *Scotland, the Shaping of a Nation*. (1974; David & Charles, London)

Donaldson, Gordon, *Scotland: Church and Nation through Sixteen Centuries*. (2nd edition, 1972; Scottish Academic Press, Edinburgh)

Donaldson, Gordon, *Scottish Church History*. (1985; Scottish Academic Press, Edinburgh)

Donaldson, G. & Morpeth, R.S., *A Dictionary of Scottish History*. (1977; John Donald, Edinburgh)

Donnachie, Ian, & Hewitt, George, *A Companion to Scottish History: from the Reformation to the Present*. (1989; Batsford, London)

Donnachie, I., & Hewitt, G., *Collin's Dictionary: Scottish History*. (2001; reprinted 2003; Collins, Glasgow)

Dunbar, Sir Archibald H., *Scottish Kings: 1005–1625* (1909; David Douglas, Edinburgh). [With notes of principal events, tables of regnal years, pedigrees, calendars, etc.]

Smout, T.C., *A History of the Scottish People: 1580–1830*. (2nd edition, 1970; Collins, London & Glasgow)

Smout, T.C., *A Century of the Scottish People: 1830–1950*. (1986; Collins, London)

Young, Margaret D., editor *The Parliaments of Scotland; Burgh & Shire Commissioners*: 2 volumes (1992; publ. for the Scottish Committee on the History of Parliament, Scottish Academic Press). [Biographical notes, with sources, on each individual commissioner]

HERALDRY

Innes of Learney, Sir Thomas, *Scots Heraldry*. (2nd edition, 1956; Oliver & Boyd, Edinburgh & London)

Burnett, C.J., & Dennis, M.D., *Scotlands's Heraldic Heritage: The Lion Rejoicing*. (1997; Historic Scotland/The Stationery Office, Edinburgh)

Paul, Sir James Balfour, *An Ordinary of Arms Contained in the Public Register of All Arms and Bearings: 1672–1902*. (2nd edition 1903; reprinted 1991, Genealogical Publishing Co. Inc., Baltimore)

Lyon Office (compiled by David Reid of Robertland and Vivian Wilson), *An Ordinary of Arms: Volume II: 1902–1973*. (1977; Edinburgh)

CLANS

Adam, Frank (revised by Sir Thomas Innes of Learney), *The Clans, Septs, and Regiments of the Scottish Highlands*. (8th edition, 1970; reprinted 1984; Johnston & Bacon Ltd, Edinburgh & London)

Bain, R., *The Clans and Tartans of Scotland* (revised and enlarged, 1959; Collins, London & Glasgow)

Martine, Roddy, *Scottish Clan and Family Names: their arms, origins and tartans*. (1987; Bartholomew, Edinburgh)

Moncreiffe of that Ilk, Sir Iain, *The Highland Clans: dynastic origins, Chiefs and background of their clans connected with Highland history and some other families*. (1967; Barry & Rockcliff, London)

Moncreiffe, Sir Iain, and Pottinger, Don, *Map of Scotland of Old*. (1983; Bartholomew, Edinburgh). [Shows areas of distribution of clans and families at the beginning of the seventeenth century.]

Way of Plean, George, and Squire, Romilly, *Scottish Clan & Family Encyclopedia*. (1994; Harper-Collins, Glasgow)

GENERAL

Black, George F., *The Surnames of Scotland; their Origin, Meaning and History*. (1946; The New York Public Library, New York)

Camp, A.J., *Wills and their Wherabouts*. (1974; Phillimore, Canterbury)

Christian, Peter, *The Genealogist's Internet*. (2nd edition 2003; The National Archives, London)

Daiches, David, editor *A Companion to Scottish Culture*. (1981; Edward Arnold, London)

Dawes, F.V., *Not in Front of the Servants: a true portrait of upstairs, downstairs life.* (New edition 1989, reprinted 1990; National Trust Classics, Century, London)

Donaldson, Gordon, *The Scots Overseas.* (1966; Hale, London)

Filby, P.W., *American & British Genealogy: a selected list of books.* (1983; New England Historic and Genealogical Society, Boston)

Gibson, J., *Probate Jurisdictions: Where to Look for Wills.* (4th edition, 1994; reprinted 1997; Federation of Family History Societies, Bury)

Hawgood, David, *Internet for Genealogy.* (2nd edition, 1999; Federation of Family History Societies, Bury)

Mackenzie, Alice, *Newsplan (Scotland).* (Sept. 1994; Scottish Library & Information Council/National Library of Scotland, Edinburgh). [Where local Scottish newspapers are held]

McLaughlin, Eve, *Simple Latin for Family Historians.* (1986; Federation of Family History Societies, Bury)

Raymond, Stuart A., *Scottish Family History on the Web.* (2002; Federation of Family History Societies, Bury)

Scottish Records Association, *Scottish Handwriting: 1500–1700: a self-help pack.* (1994; Edinburgh)

Simpson, Grant G., *Scottish Handwriting 1150–1650: an introduction to the reading of documents.* (New edition 1998; Tuckwell Press, East Linton)

Stevenson, David & Wendy, *Scottish Texts and Calendars: an analytical guide to serial publications.* (1987; Royal Historical Society, London/ Scottish History Society, Edinburgh)

Torrance, D.R., *Scottish Trades, Professions, Vital Records and Directories – a selected bibliography,* (2nd edition, 1998; Scottish Association of Family History Societies, Glasgow)

Walker, Stephen P., *The Society of Accountants in Edinburgh: 1854– 1914.* (1987; published privately)

LAW

Bell, George J., *A Dictionary & Digest of the Law of Scotland* (7th edition by George Watson,Bell & Bradfute, 1890; Edinburgh)

Bell, Robert, *A Dictionary of the Law of Scotland* (1807; printed by John Anderson, Edinburgh). [Intended for the use of the public at large as well as the profession]

Duncan, A.G.M., *Green's Glossary of Scottish Legal Terms.* (3rd edition, 1992; W. Green/Sweet & Maxwell, Edinburgh)

Grant, Sir Francis J., editor *The Faculty of Advocates in Scotland: 1532–1943; with genealogical notes.* (1944; The Scottish Record Society, Edinburgh)

The Register of the Society of Writers to Her Majesty's Signet. (1983; Clark Constable, Edinburgh). [Details of Members from the fifteenth century to the 1980s]

MEDICAL

Appleby, J.H., *British Doctors in Russia: 1657–1807.* (1979; University of East Anglia, Norwich)

Craig, W.S., *History of the Royal College of Physicians of Edinburgh.* (1976; Blackwell, Oxford). [Includes lists of Honorary Fellows and members.]

Duncan, Alexander, *Memorials of the Faculty of Physicians and Surgeons of Glasgow: 1599–1850.* (1896; Faculty of Physicians and Surgeons of Glasgow, Glasgow)

Munk, Wm, *Roll of the Royal College of Physicians of London: 1518–1825*: 3 volumes. (2nd edition 1874; The College, London); continued as *Lives of the Fellows of the Royal College of Physicians of London (Munk's Roll): Vol. IV: 1826–1925* (1955); *Vol. V: 1926–65* (1968)

Royal College of Surgeons of Edinburgh: list of Fellows: 1581–31 Dec. 1873. (1874; Edinburgh)

Smith, R.W. Innes, *English-Speaking Students of Medicine at the University of Leyden.* (1932; Oliver & Boyd, Edinburgh & London)
See also Army & Navy; and India.

ARMY & NAVY

Dalton, C., *The Scots Army: 1661–1688.* (republished 1989; Greenhill Books, Edinburgh)

Fowler, S. & Spencer, W., *Army Records for Family Historians.* (2nd edition revised 1998; PRO, Kew)

Gibson, Jeremy, and Dell, Alan, *Tudor and Stuart Muster Rolls; a directory of holdings in the British Isles.* (1989; Federation of Family History Societies, Bury)

Gibson, Jeremy, and Medleycott, Mervyn, *Militia Lists and Musters: 1757–1876.* (3rd edition, 1994; Federation of Family History Societies, Bury). [Section on Scotland, pp. 44–8]

Hamilton-Edwards, Gerald, *In Search of Army Ancestry.* (1977; Phillimore, London & Chichester)

Henderson, Diana M. *The Scottish Regiments*. (1993; Harper-Collins, Glasgow)

Rodger, N.A.M., *Naval Records for Genealogists*. (1998; PRO, Kew)

Syrett, David & DiNardo, R.L., *The Commissioned Sea Officers of the Royal Navy: 1660–1815*. (1994; Navy Records Society, Scolar Press, Aldershot)

Watts, M.J. & Watts, C.T., *My Ancestor was in the British Army: How can I find out more about him?* (1992; Society of Genealogists, London)

Wellcome Historical Medical Library, *Medical Officers of the British Army: 1660–1960*; *Vol. I: 1660–1898* by A. Peterkin & W. Johnston (1968; London), *Vol. II: 1898–1960* by Lt. Col. Sir R. Drew (1968; London)

MERCHANT NAVY

Hogg, Peter L., *Basic Facts about . . . Using Merchant Shipping Records for Family Historians*. (1997; Federation of Family History Societies, Bury)

Smith, K., Watts, C.T. & Watts, M.J., *Records of Merchant Shipping and Seamen*. (1998; PRO, Kew)

Watts, C.T. & Watts, M.J., *My Ancestor was a Merchant Seaman: how can I find out more about him?*. (1991; Society of Genealogists, London)

INDIA

The East India Kalendar or Asiatic Register; annually 1791–1800 – each edition divided into the three presidencies.

Asiatic Journal & Monthly Register for British India; annually 1815–45 Annual Directories for each of Bengal, Bombay, Madras and Calcutta (different annual runs)

Thacker's Bengal Directory; annually 1863–84; continues as *Thacker's Indian Directory*; annually 1886–1960.

Baxter, Ian A., *A Brief Guide to Biographical Sources*, (2nd edition,1990; India Office Library & Records, London)

Crawford, Lt.-Col. D.G., *Roll of the Indian Medical Service: 1615–1930*. (200 copies only; 1930; W. Thacker & Co., London)

Dodwell, E. & Miles, J.S., *Honourable East India Company's Bengal Civil Servants: 1780–1838; Honourable East India Company's Madras Civil Servants: 1780–1838* (1839; Longman, Orme, Brown & Co.,

London). [These books give dates of various appointments, and dates of death or retirement. They include lists of Governors-General of India.]

Dodwell, E. & Miles, J.S., *Medical Officers of the Indian Army: 1764–1838*, (1839; Longman, Orme & Brown, London). [Gives positions and dates of death or retirement. Includes list of directors and chairmen of HEICo. Divided into the three presidencies.]

Hodson, Major V.C.P., *Officers of the Bengal Army: 1758–1834* (1927–47; Phillimore & Co., London: 4 volumes)

Officers of the Indian Army: 1770–1837 (1838; Wm H. Allen & Co., London). [Includes list of Commanders-in-Chief in India.]

LOCAL HISTORY

Cox, Michael, *Exploring Scottish History.* (2nd edition, 1999; Scottish Library Association, Scottish Local History Forum and Scottish Records Association, Hamilton)

Dymond, David, *Researching and Writing History: a practical guide for local historians.* (2002; British Association for Local History, London)

Groome, Francis, *Ordnance Gazetteer of Scotland*: 6 volumes. (1882–5; Thomas C. Jack, Edinburgh)

Moody, David, *Scottish Local History.* (1986; Batsford, London)

Moody, David, *Scottish Towns: a guide for local historians.* (1992; Batsford, London)

Munro, R.W., editor *Johnstone's Gazetteer of Scotland.* (1973; Johnston & Bacon, Edinburgh & London)

Richardson, J., *The Local Historian's Encyclopaedia.* (2nd edition, 1986; Historical Publications, New Barnet)

Royal Scottish Geographical Society, *The Early Maps of Scotland: to 1850* (Volume 1, 1973; Volume 2, 1983; Edinburgh)

Sinclair, Cecil, *Tracing Scottish Local History.* (1994; SRO, HMSO, Edinburgh)

Sinclair, Sir John, compiler *The Statistical Account of Scotland*: 21 volumes (1791–9) (Reprinted 1983; with all parish accounts for individual counties together for the first time: E.P. Publishing, Wakefield, England)

Williams, M.A., *Researching Local History: the human journey.* (1996; Longman, London)

The New Statistical Account of Scotland: 15 volumes (1845; William Blackwood & Sons, Edinburgh & London)

Appendix V

Sample forms for searchers

BIRTH ENTRY

District registration and entry number ....

Name and surname .... Sex (M/F) ....

Date of birth...

Place of birth ....

Place of residence (if different) ....

Name and surname of father...

Occupation of father .... if deceased ....

Name and surname of mother...

Maiden surname (M/S) of mother ....

Occupation of mother .... if deceased ....

Date and place of parents' marriage ....

Name of informant ....

Relationship to the child ....

Marriage Entry

District registration and entry number ....

Date of marriage ....

Place of marriage ....

According to forms/rites of ....

Name and surname of groom ....

Age and marital status ....

Occupation ....

Usual residence ....

Name and surname of father ....

Occupation of father .... if deceased ....

Name and surname of mother

Maiden surname of mother .... if deceased ....

Name and surname of bride ....

Age and marital status ....

Occupation ....

Usual residence ....

Name and surname of father ....

Occupation of father .... if deceased ....

Name and surname of mother ....

Maiden surname of mother .... if deceased ....

Name of minister (etc) ....

Witnesses ....

Addresses ....

DEATH ENTRY

District registration and entry number ....

Name and surname.. Sex (M/F) ....

Age at death and occupation ....

Date of death ....

Place of death ....

Place of residence (if different) ....

Marital status and name of spouse ....

Name of father..

Occupation of father .... if deceased ....

Name of mother..

Occupation, M/S of mother .... if deceased ....

Cause of death ....

Name of informant ....

Relationship to the deceased ....

Appendix VI

Internet access to indexes and for obtaining copies of digitised images

---

Scottish birth (1856–1902), marriage (1856–1927) and death (1856–1952) certificates, and 1891 and 1901 census returns

www.scotlandspeople.gov.uk

Scottish testaments and wills 1500–1901

www.scottishdocuments.com

English wills 1610–1858 of the Prerogative Court of Canterbury

www.documentsonline.pro.gov.uk

1901 census returns for England and Wales, the Channel Islands and the Isle of Man

www.census.pro.gov.uk

English and Welsh births, marriages and deaths (from 1837) [index only]

www.1837online.com

Statistical Account of Scotland (1791–8)
New Statistical Account of Scotland (1845)

www.edina.ac.uk/stat_acc_scot

Scottish newspapers on-line

www.onlinenewspapers.com/scotland.htm

Other valuable websites with databases, and for genealogical information

Commonwealth War Graves Commission

www.cwgc.org

Vital events database by the Church of Jesus Christ of Latter Day Saints (the Mormons)

www.familysearch.org

Genealogical and related information: United Kingdom and Ireland (GENUKI)

www.genuki.org.uk

English and Welsh births, marriages and deaths (not complete – an on-going programme dependent on volunteers) [index only]

www.freebmd.org.uk

Cyndis List – major gateway to international genealogical websites, including Scottish ones

www.CyndisList.com

Immigrant Ships' Transcribers' Guild: Scottish Ports

www.immigrantships.org

Harold Ralston's links to ship passenger lists

www.execpc.com/-haroldr/shiplist.htm

Handwriting – a coaching manual, interactive tutorials, and weekly quizzes to test your skills

www.scottishhandwriting.com

Part II

A STEP-BY-STEP GUIDE TO SHOW YOU
THE EASIEST WAY TO WORK OUT
YOUR OWN FAMILY TREE,
QUICKLY AND ACCURATELY

———

HOW TO DRAW A DROP-LINE CHART

A Step-by-Step Guide

To guide you through all the steps necessary in searching for birth, marriage and death entries after Statutory (Civil) Registration was introduced in 1855, and in the Old Parish Registers before that date, I have been given permission to use the family tree of Margaret Dudgeon Young. Through finding out all about the Young and the Dudgeon families, when and where they were born, married, and died, I hope to show you the easiest way to work out your family tree, quickly and accurately.

During the course of this search we shall find ourselves going down some blind alleys, but this will serve to show some of the snags you may meet when searching your own family lines.

SEARCHING FOR A BIRTH ENTRY FROM 1855 ONWARDS

1. Choose a member of the family born in Scotland, whose parents' names, or at least one parent's name you know.
2. Decide in which year you want to start your search. Using the computer index, key in the appropriate year, surname, Christian (or forename) or initial. The computer index has superseded the paper index in New Register House, Edinburgh. (See Chapter 2: 'Searching records in New Register House'.)

Probably there will be more than one entry for the name, so it will help to know the town or parish of birth. In this case I was searching for the birth of Archibald Young, and I had been given his marriage certificate as a starting point. (Illustrations: Figure 11)

From the copy of his certificate we deduce that Archibald Young, aged 53, would have been born in 1869. He was the son of Thomas Young and Maria Long Young, maiden surname (M/S) Dudgeon. The marriage took place in Edinburgh, and, according to tradition, the family originated from that area.

In the index of births for 1869, I found six entries for the name Archibald Young, but only one for Edinburgh. I wrote down in my notebook all the information from the index:

Birth Archibald Young. 1869 St Andrews Edinburgh 685^2 /326.

Always make a note of the district registration and entry numbers for the year you require, as they are vital to the search.

I now filled in an order slip for a statutory register (Illustrations: Figure 12) as illustrated. When I had collected the microfiche copy of the register, I checked the names of the parents against those recorded in the 1922 marriage entry. I then copied the information as follows:

Birth of Archibald Young

    1869 St Andrew District, Edinburgh (685^2/326) on April 10th at 5h. P.M. at 26 Maryfield Place, Edinburgh.

    Archibald Young.   son of Thomas Young, Joiner (Journeyman)
                                & Maria Young, M/S Dudgeon.

    Marriage of parents 1859 June 6th Edinburgh.

    Informant   Thomas Young. Father. Present.

Or get a print of the digitised image of the whole page.

This 1869 birth certificate of Archibald Young contained the following information:

1. Date and time of birth.
2. An address, 26 Maryfield Place, Edinburgh, which can be used for the 1871 census return. Addresses are important as they lead to census entries which in turn show the parish of birth.
3. The marriage date and place for Thomas Young and Maria Dudgeon.
4. That both parents were alive when the baby was born.
5. That the informant was the father.
6. That Thomas Young was a joiner by trade. He was a journeyman joiner, i.e., he had passed his apprenticeship but he was not as yet a master joiner.

Following item 2 on the list, I would search the 1871 census return and hope to find the Young family. This census return should show the names of other brothers and sisters born between 1869 when Archibald was born, and 1859 when his parents married. The 1871 census may show a child born in 1870 or early 1871.

Following item 3, I would search for the marriage of Thomas Young and Maria Long Dudgeon in 1859, and for the purpose of this exercise I decided to do that.

SEARCHING FOR A MARRIAGE ENTRY FROM 1855 ONWARDS

Using the computer cross-index system for marriages (see Chapter 2, 'Searching Records in New Register House') I found the appropriate entry in 1859, and noted the reference number:

Marriage of Thomas Young and Maria Dudgeon
1859 St George District, Edinburgh (685^1/84)

Beware! District Registration sub-numbers depend on the year of the event.

I again completed an order slip for a statutory register, filling in the line for a marriage register, and I noted all the information this certificate contained. I suggest that unless you are filling in your own pre-prepared certificate, you use the following form:

Marriage of Thomas Young and Maria Dudgeon

    1859 St George. Edinburgh, (685^1/84) on June 6th 1859. Marriage after Banns was solemnized between us according to the Forms of the . . .

Thomas Young.	Aged 23, Bachelor. Joiner.
	Usual residence, 27 Bread Street.
	(Edinburgh)
son of	John Young, Joiner (deceased) and Agnes
	Young M/S Paterson.

and

Maria Dudgeon	Aged 19, Spinster, Servant.
	Usual residence. Drumdryan House
	(Edinburgh)
daughter of	Adam Dudgeon, Butcher (deceased) and
	Jean Dudgeon M/S Charles (deceased)
Signed	Robert Gemmell. Minister.
Witnesses	Andrew Taylor, Helen Young.
	John Graham, William McLean.

Marriage entries are now digitised, so you can get a print of the whole page.

This 1859 marriage certificate contained the following information concerning the bridegroom:

1. Thomas Young, aged 23 in 1859, therefore born about 1836.
2. His father, John Young, a joiner and deceased by 1859.
3. His mother, Agnes Young, maiden surname (M/S) Paterson, alive in 1859.
4. His usual residence in 1859 was 27 Bread Street, Edinburgh.
5. Thomas Young was a bachelor at the time of his marriage, 1859.
6. Thomas Young was a joiner.
7. Thomas Young's religious denomination not known: entry incomplete. If necessary, this may be found by searching for the minister, Robert Gemmell, in *Fasti* or the other 'fasti-type' records for clergymen of other denominations.
8. One witness was Helen Young who may turn out to have been related to Thomas.

Similar information was recorded for Maria Dudgeon. Although her son Archibald gave her name as Marion Long Dudgeon when he married in 1922, she did not use this middle name in 1859.

Concerning the bride, there was the following information:

1. Maria Dudgeon aged 19 in 1859, therefore born about 1840.
2. Her father, Adam Dudgeon, a butcher, deceased by 1859.

3.   Her mother, Jean Dudgeon, M/S Charles, deceased by 1859.
4.   Her usual residence in 1859 was Drumdryan House, Edinburgh.
5.   Maria Dudgeon, probably in service at Drumdryan House as a maid.
6.   It should be possible to find out who owned Drumdryan House and so to ascertain the names of Maria's employers.
7.   Maria Dudgeon's religious denomination was not known: entry incomplete, but might be found through minister, Robert Gemmell.

What next?

At this point I made a chart to see how far the search had advanced. The squared chart (Illustrations: Fig. 15) is an easy one to use while the search is in progress, as it shows each generation at a glance. Once siblings have been found, it is better to draw up a drop-line chart as illustrated later in this chapter (Figs 18 and 21). Looking at the squared chart (Fig. 15) we have the following information:

1.   Thomas Young married Maria Dudgeon in Edinburgh in 1859.
2.   Archibald, their son, was born in Edinburgh in 1869.
3.   Thomas Young was the son of John Young (deceased by 1859) and his wife Agnes Paterson (alive in 1859).
4.   Maria Dudgeon was the daughter of Adam Dudgeon (deceased by 1859) and his wife Jean Charles (deceased by 1859).

What next?

A search of the 1871 census return revealed that the family were no longer at 26 Maryfield Place, Edinburgh, where Archibald Young was born in 1869. As the 1922 marriage certificate of Archibald Young recorded that his father Thomas was a surveyor, the next step was to search the most readily available copy of the *Post Office Directory for Edinburgh and Leith.* An entry in the 1888–9 issue showed:

Young, Thomas, ordained surveyor, 10 Brunton Ter. Edinburgh.

Having found a new address, the next step was to search the 1891 census return for 10 Brunton Terrace, Edinburgh, using the computer index to obtain reference numbers:

$1891/685^2$/*Book 16/page 17 at 10 Brunton Terrace, Civil Parish of*
South Leith, Burgh of Edinburgh.

Thomas Young.	Head	Mar.	53	Surveyor of Buildings.	Born England
Maria Young.	wife	Mar.	50	–	B. Musselburgh, Edinburghsh.
John Young.	son	unmar	28	Surveyor of Buildings.	B. Edinburgh. Edinburghsh.
Agnes Young.	daur.	unmar	26	Housekeeper	B. Wick, Caithness
Thomas Young.	son	unmar	24	School Teacher	B. Hollywood, Dumfriesshire.

Archibald Young.	son	unmar	21	Ironmonger's	B. Edinburgh
		unmar		Assistant	
Alexander Young.	son	unmar	18	Dental Student	B. England
Ann Young.	daur.	unmar	14	Scholar	B. England

You can also get a print of the digitised image of the page.

As the next earliest available census return was 1881, I again searched the *Edinburgh and Leith Directory* (1881–2) for an address for Thomas Young and his family. The 1881 census (now on computer) may give more detail concerning the place of birth in England of Thomas, and his children Alexander and Ann. The 1881–2 Directory gave the address 26 Maryfield Place. (This is where Archibald had been born in 1869, but the family was not there in the 1871 census return.) Using the computer index for the 1881 census return for Edinburgh and the reference number I found the following entry:

1881/685²/34/5 at 26, Maryfield Place, Greenside, Edinburgh.

Thomas Young	Head	mar.	43	Building Surveyor	B. England
Maria Young	wife	mar.	40	–	B. Musselburgh Midlothian.
John Young	son	mar.	18	App.	B. Edinburgh.
Agnes Young	daur	mar.	16	Dressmaker	B. Edinburgh.
Thomas Young	son	mar.	14	Scholar	B. Edinburgh.
Archibald Young	son	mar.	11	Scholar	B. Edinburgh.
Alexander Young	son	mar.	8	Scholar	B. England.
Annie Young	daur	mar.	4		B. England.

Unfortunately, no precise places of birth were recorded here either. Also, the places of birth for Agnes and Thomas were recorded as Edinburgh whereas in the 1891 census return they had been Wick and Holywood!

What next?

I now decided to search for the deaths of Thomas Young (aged 53 in 1891) and his wife Maria Dudgeon (aged 50 in 1891), both alive in 1922 at the marriage of their son Archibald. I searched the death index from 1922 until I found the following entries:

Death of Maria Long Young.
   1926   North Leith, Edinburgh. (685¹⁰/40) on February 5th at 18 Dudley Terrace, Leith.

Maria Long Young	Aged 85. Married to Thomas Young. Building Surveyor. (Retired).
Daughter of	Adam Dudgeon. Cattle Dealer. (deceased) and Jean Dudgeon M/S Charles (deceased).
Cause of death	Carcinoma of Pancreas. 3 Months. As Certified by A. Murray Woods. M.D.
Informant	John Young. Son. Present. 2 Bellevue Crescent. Ayr.

Death of Thomas Young
   1928   North Leith, Edinburgh (685[10]/15) on January 11th at 18 Dudley
       Terrace, Leith.
   Thomas Young.   Aged 90. Building Surveyor. (Retired)
                             Widower of Maria Long Dudgeon.
   Son of John Young. Wright (Joiner) (deceased) and
                             of Agnes Young M/S Paterson. (deceased).
   Cause of death   Myocarditis. Influenza. Cardiac Failure. As
                             Certified by A. Murray Woods. M.D.
   Informant   John Young. Son. Present 2 Bellevue
                             Crescent, Ayr

What next?

Since it is always advisable to work on one family name at a time, I decided
to complete, as far as possible, the Young line.

The 1891 census return for 10 Brunton Terrace showed siblings for
Archibald: I can now search for those who were born in Scotland and perhaps
visit the Family Records Centre in London to search for those born in England.
Civil registration started in England in 1837, so the birth entry for Thomas
Young, born in England, and aged 53 in 1891, should be there; and so should
the entries for Alexander and Ann. It will be possible to identify Thomas
Young as the names of his parents were given on his marriage certificate in
1859.

The 1891 census return recorded that Thomas and Maria had a son John
born in Edinburgh *circa* 1863 (he was aged 28 in 1891); I searched the index
to find the correct John Young entry.

   Birth of John Young.
   1862   St Andrews District Edinburgh (685[2]/334) on April 16th at 8
       Simes Court, Calton Hill, Edinburgh.
   John Young.   son of Thomas Young, Joiner (Journeyman)
                             and of Maria Young M/S Dudgeon
   Marriage of parents 1859 June 6th Edinburgh.
   Informant   Thomas Young. Father. Present.

Making use of the information contained in the above certificate, I searched
the 1861 census return for 8 Simes Court, Calton Hill, Edinburgh. The street
index provided the reference numbers for this address.

1861/685[2]/Book 93 page 12 at 8 Calton Hill, Edinburgh.

Thomas Young,	Head	married	24	Joiner J.	Born England, London.
Maria Young,	wife	married	20		Born Midlothian, Inveresk
Jane Young,	daughter		10 mos.		Born Midlothian, S. Leith

Simes Court was omitted by the enumerator.

This census return provided some information not previously known. Thomas Young was born in London, England; Jane aged 10 months in 1861 was not listed in either the 1881 or the 1891 census return.

I searched for her birth entry (she should have been born either in 1860 or 1861 in South Leith). I did not find an entry in the birth index for a Jane Young in South Leith or in North Leith for either of those years. However, I did find two entries in Edinburgh, and on examination, one of these turned out to be correct for this search; that is, the parents' names were Thomas Young and Maria Dudgeon.

Birth of Jane Young.
   1860   St Andrew, (Edinburgh) (685^2/452) on May 31st at 8 Calton Hill, Edinburgh.

Jane Young.	daughter of Thomas Young, Joiner (Journeyman) and of Maria Young M/S Dudgeon.
Informant	Thomas Young. Father. Present.

You will notice that no date and place of the parents' marriage was shown on the above certificate. This was not recorded on birth certificates for the years 1856–60 inclusive. (See Chapter 2, 'Searching Registers prior to 1855'.)

The information contained in the 1891 and 1881 census returns showed that there were other children born to Thomas and Maria Young in Scotland; so I decided to take copies of these entries to find out where the family had been living. They were Agnes, aged 26 in 1891 born in Wick, County Caithness and Thomas, aged 24, born in Holywood, County Dumfries. (The spelling in the census was given as Hollywood.) Bearing in mind that they may have been born in Edinburgh, I searched the births index and found the following entries:

Birth of Agnes Paterson Young.
   1864, Wick, County Caithness (43/298) on December 4th at Alexandra Place, Wick.

Agnes Paterson Young.	daughter of Thomas Young. Joiner, and of Maria Young M/S Dudgeon.
Marriage of parents	[Not recorded].
Informant	Thomas Young. Father.

Birth of Thomas Young.
   1866   Holywood, Co. Dumfries (830/33) on October 4th at Newton-airds.

Thomas Young.	son of Thomas Young, Journeyman Joiner and of Maria Young M/S Dudgeon.
Marriage of parents	1859 June 6th St Cuthberts, Edinburgh.
Informant	Thomas Young. Father.

So the 1891 census return was more reliable than the 1881. Agnes and Thomas were not born in Edinburgh after all. This shows the advisability of trying to find a family in more than one census return.

The Young family certainly moved around a great deal! They had children in Edinburgh, Wick, Dumfries and England. To have found these entries without the help of a census would have been a monumental task.

What next?

Still working on the Young line. The 1859 marriage certificate of Thomas Young and Maria Dudgeon recorded that Thomas' father John was deceased but that his mother Agnes Paterson was still alive at that date.

Although Thomas Young was born in London, England (according to the 1861 census return), he was in Scotland for his marriage in 1859, and for the births of most of his children; so it was worth searching for the deaths of his parents in Scottish records.

To search for the death of a John Young, age unknown, anywhere in Scotland between 1855 and 1860, promised to be a long haul; particularly as the death index for that period does not show ages at time of death.

It is nearly always best policy to search for the death of the wife first, so I started by looking for the death of Agnes Paterson, who was alive in 1859. There was a chance that she and her husband may have died in the same place.

SEARCHING FOR A DEATH ENTRY FROM 1855 ONWARDS

Using the cross-index computer programme (see Chapter 2: 'Searching Records in New Register House') I started in 1859, when Agnes Paterson or Young was known to have been alive. In 1860 the computer turned up an entry with the correct names, but with a reference number for Dundee. When I read this entry from the microfiche I found Agnes Young, widow of a slater and daughter of James Paterson, baker, London. But since death registers in Scotland from 1856 to 1861 do not record the name of the spouse I could not know for certain whether or not this was our Agnes Young M/S Paterson. However, since the subject of the entry would have been 57 years of age when her son Thomas was born, since she resided in Dundee when all the rest of the family were in Edinburgh, and since she was the widow of a slater and not a joiner, I reluctantly dismissed the entry as irrelevant. Nevertheless, this illustrates how important it is to record very carefully all the information, and not to accept an entry just because the names seem correct at first.

What next?

I went back to the index of deaths to see if I could find the death of our Agnes Young M/S Paterson. I searched under Young, Agnes, and Paterson, Agnes from 1860 up to 1892, and at last, I found the correct entry! The names Agnes Young and Agnes Paterson were both in Liberton, both entries had the same age, 86, and the same entry number, 92, so the entry came up on the computer index. I filled in the order slip, collected the microfiche of the death register, and copied out the information:

Death of Agnes Young.

1892   Liberton Co. Midlothian (693/92) on September at Park Neuk, Liberton.

Agnes Young.	aged 86. Widow of John Young, Joiner.
Daughter of	Thomas Paterson, Builder, (deceased) and of Catherine Paterson M/S Lithgow (deceased).
Cause	Old Age. Syncope caused by Diarrhoea. 1 Day. As. Cert. by W. Booth F.R.C.S.E. etc.
Informant	Thomas Young. Son present. 10, Brunton Terrace, Edinburgh.

You can now get a print of the digitised image of the whole page.

The informant on the above death certificate confirms that this time I have the correct entry. I had already found Thomas Young at that address in the 1891 census return. I searched the 1891 census return for Liberton, but found nothing applicable to this search. So Agnes Young was not there then. This census is now on computer.

Agnes Paterson's husband John Young was definitely recorded as being deceased in 1859 when his son was married, and with luck that was correct. To try to save time I consulted the Monumental Inscriptions held in New Register House for the parishes where the family had been, that is Edinburgh, Leith and Liberton, but found nothing applicable, so I returned to the death index.

No ages were recorded in the death index before 1866, and as there were so many entries for that name each year, I decided to confine the search to those entries found in the Edinburgh area. There were twelve of them, and on examination of those twelve entries, only one was a married man, the rest were children or single men.

The one married man was a John Young who died in 1858, in Edinburgh, aged about 60, Slater (Master); Married; son of James Young, Teacher (deceased) and – [blank]; Informant, William Goodlet, Brother-in-law. Was he our John Young? It seems doubtful as his occupation was recorded as Master Slater and not as Joiner; he was married but his wife's name was not recorded. How could I prove it one way or another?

What next?

The next step was to search the 1851 census return for the address given in the death certificate. So, using the index for Edinburgh, I fetched the census return and when I read the microfilm I found:

1851/685^6/49/8 at 1 Gayfield Place, Parish of St Cuthberts,
Parliamentary Burgh of Edinburgh.

John Young,	Head	married 46	Master Slater.	B. New Bannswick
Janet Young,	Wife	married 36	– –	B. Midlothian, Edinburgh.
James Young,	Nephew unmar 23		Slater	B. England.
Janet Wilson,	Servant unmar 24		Dom. Servt.	B. Fife, Kirkcaldy.

The Edinburgh person's index for the 1851 census has been published in three volumes.

From this entry it was seen that John Young had a wife named Janet (although this was not shown on the 1858 death certificate), and the John I needed for this search had a wife named Agnes, so, reluctantly, this entry could not be accepted. But it took a lot of work, and a great deal of time to prove that it was wrong for our search!

What next?

I decided to go back to Margaret Young, who had been the source of my original information. I expressed to her my frustration at not finding any MIs (Monumental Inscriptions) for John Young, and was promptly told of a family grave with tombstones in Inveresk Cemetery!

We visited Inveresk and saw three tombstones; two of them had names and dates I had found, but the third was a goldmine of information and took the family back another generation. On this stone was inscribed:

> Also in Memory of his Grandfather
> Alexander Young
> Wright Musselburgh
> Died 1806
> And his Wife
> Ellen Douglas
> Died 1865 (?) aged 85 (?) (not clear)
> And their daughters
> Jean & Euphemia
>
> _____
>
> Also of his Father
> John Young
> Wright in Musselburgh
> Died 1847
> and his Wife
> Agnes Paterson
> Died 1892 aged 86 years
> and their son
> Alexander
> Died 1839 (?) aged 4 years.

From one of the other stones it would appear that Thomas Young, son of John Young and Agnes Paterson, had had them erected. If I had found this MI earlier I would not have taken so long to search for the deaths of John Young and Agnes Paterson. All this was news to Margaret Young who had never read the tombstones, and had never heard of Alexander Young!

You can see how important such a Monumental Inscription is. John Young died prior to 1855, and it would have been difficult to prove his parentage with any certainty.

Nothing in the search had indicated that John Young came from Musselburgh.

What next?

A return to New Register House and to the 1841 census return and the OPRs for Musselburgh.

As John Young died in 1847, possibly in Musselburgh, I decided to search the 1841 census return for him and his family. Inveresk, the parish which contains Musselburgh, is not a large town, and there is a street index available for the 1841 and 1851 census returns. Using an order slip of the type shown (Illustrations: Fig. 13), I fetched the microfilm for 1841. Not having an address for John Young in Musselburgh I had to read through the microfilm until I found him. Extending the search to the 1851 census return I also found Agnes as a widow.

To make full use of the information gained from the census returns and the Monumental Inscriptions, I searched the OPRs for Inveresk.

SEARCHING IN OLD PARISH REGISTERS' ENTRIES PRIOR TO 1855

Before searching the OPR, I listed all the events I hoped to find, thereby obviating the possibility of forgetting to search for an entry, and of having to re-order the microfilm.

OPR Inveresk, Co. Midlothian (689).
Search for:
1. Alexander Young died in 1806. Search for his marriage to Ellen Douglas, starting from that date.
2. Children to Alexander Young and Ellen Douglas. Jean, Euphemia and John, and possibly others.
3. Marriage of John Young and Agnes Paterson prior to 1838.
4. Children to John Young and Agnes Paterson. Alexander, Helen and Catherine, and possibly others. (Thomas had been born in England.)
5. Deaths of any relevant Young entries.

1. To search for the marriage of Alexander Young and Ellen Douglas, I first found the reference number from the computer index. I filled in an OPR order slip (Illustrations: Fig. 14) to obtain the microfilm for Inveresk, and recorded in my notebook:

OPR Inveresk Co. Midlothian (689/13) Marriages.
  1799   Alexander Young, Wright, & Helen Douglas married at Edinburgh upon the 29th day of January 1799, by the Revd. Dr Grieve, Minister.

2. To search for issue to the above couple I used the computer index to OPR births which shows the names of parents.

OPR Inveresk, Co. Midlothian (689/9) Births/Bapts.

1800   Alexander Young, Wright, Musselburgh & Helen Douglas his wife, their daughter Jean, born 9th bapt. 23 March. Witnesses: John Young and John Douglas.

1802   Alexander Young, Wright, Musselburgh & Helen Douglas his wife, their son John, born 18th July, baptized 5th August. Witnesses: John Young and Alexr. Shaw.

1804   Alexander Young, Wright, & Helen Douglas his wife, their daughter Euphemia born 17th Novr. baptized 2nd Decr. Wits: John Young and John Douglas.

I continued the search for children up to October 1807. Although Alexander Young died in 1806, there may have been a posthumous child.

3. No entry for the marriage of John Young and Agnes Paterson was found in Inveresk. Noted the fact that I had searched these records and the years covered. (The entry was found in Edinburgh.)

4. As the 1851 census return showed two children born in Musselburgh to John Young and Agnes Paterson, I tried to find their birth entries, as well as the entry for Alexander born *circa* 1835. I covered the years 1835 to 1847, and 1854 for late entries, but found no children to John and Agnes registered in Inveresk.

5. In the search for any relevant Young deaths, I confined the search to the names known from the tombstones and census returns.

I had to refer to the OPR paper index list to obtain the necessary reference numbers as no OPR deaths have yet been indexed on computer. Not many parishes recorded deaths and/or burials, but luckily Inveresk did. There is a register of deaths for the years 1750–1854, and entries for the years 1810–1854 are indexed.

OPR Inveresk, Co. Midlothian. (689/14) Deaths.

1806   October 14. Alexander Young, Wright in Mussell was buried in the Southside of Handyside Stone.

The wording of this entry implies that Alexander Young did not have a tombstone of his own, but was buried near the Handyside family. This fact is borne out by the knowledge that the Young family tombstone was erected in later years by Alexander Young's grandson, Thomas. The Handyside stones are still there, the Young stones are next to them.

Also named on the tombstone were Jean (born 1800) and Euphemia (born 1804). As they may have died in infancy I searched the Inveresk death registers from 1800 to 1834, and noted the only other relevant entries during the search.

OPR Inveresk, Co. Midlothian (689/20) Deaths/Burials

1839   Alexr. Young, son of John Young, Wright. Died 1st March aged 3.

1850   Euphemia Young, daughter of Alexr. Young, Wright. Died 26th June, aged 45.

1854   Jean Young, daughter of the late Alexander Young, Wright, Died 22nd May, aged 54.
       Place of death: 84 East Crosscausey, Edinburgh.

I searched the 1851 census return for the Edinburgh address, but there was no trace of Jean Young there. There was no entry in the death register for John Young who, according to the tombstone, died in 1847. He may have died in Edinburgh, but I did not extend the search at this stage.

What next?

Although Thomas Young was born in London, I wished to see if his parents, John Young and Agnes Paterson were married in Scotland. Using the computer marriage index I found that the marriage had taken place in Edinburgh in 1835.

This entry (Illustrations: Fig. 17) showed that John Young was a Wright by trade, so I could visit the National Library for a book on Wrights in Edinburgh; search the apprentice records held in the National Archives of Scotland, in Princes Street (there are some Scottish apprentice records to be found in the NA(E) in Kew, London), and search the *Post Office and Trades Directory*. Any of these places might yield information concerning John Young.

The 1835 marriage entry for John Young showed that he and Agnes Paterson were both residing in Grass Market, New Greyfriars Parish in Edinburgh, but by the 1841 census return they were in Musselburgh, having had a son Thomas in London in 1838. So you see, the farther back the search goes, the more difficult and time-consuming it becomes; but it is all the more satisfactory when the correct entry does eventually turn up!

Now, as far as the Young family is concerned, it should be possible to undertake some more work on Inveresk records to try to take back the line there. A visit to London to the Family Records Centre for the birth entry for Thomas and his children Alexander and Ann would be interesting. Where were they living, and what was the English connection that made Thomas return to the place of his birth?

The drop-line chart for the Young family is progressing. (Illustrations: Fig. 18).

What next?

I decided to turn my attention to the Dudgeon line. Maria Long Dudgeon married Thomas Young in 1859 in Edinburgh, and you will remember that both her father Adam Dudgeon, and her mother Jean Charles were deceased by then.

According to the 1891 census return, Maria was born in Musselburgh, County Midlothian, *circa* 1840. So the first thing to do was to search the 1841 census for Musselburgh for the Dudgeon family:

1841/689/7/29 at Smart's Wynd, Musselburgh, Parish of Inveresk.

Adam Dudgeon	20	Flesher	Y.
Jane Dudgeon	20		Y.
Maria L. Dudgeon	1		Y.
William R. Hayart	6 months		Y.

We do not know who William R. Hayart was, but I imagine that Jane Dudgeon was a wet-nurse; having had her own baby recently, she probably had enough milk to feed little William too.

While winding on the microfilm searching for Adam Dudgeon, I came across another family which may have had a link with Adam (the name Archibald has been handed down into the Young family), so I made a note of it in passing.

1841/689/6/3 at High Street, Musselburgh, Inveresk Parish.

Archd. Dudgeon	65	Flesher J.	Y.
Ann Dudgeon	55		Y.
Archd. Dudgeon	25	Flesher J.	Y.
David Dudgeon	15	Flesher	Y.
Marion Dudgeon	10		Y.

I then extended the search to the 1851 census for Inveresk, and found:

1851/689/2 Musselburgh/43 at Smart's Wynd, Musselburgh,
Parish of Inveresk, Co. Midlothian.

Adam Dudgeon	Head	married	32	Flesher	Born	Inveresk, Co. Midlothian.
Jane Dudgeon	wife	married	31	—	Born	Inveresk, Co. Midlothian.
Marian Dudgeon	daughter		10	Scholar	Born	Inveresk, Co. Midlothian.
Ann Dudgeon			11		Born	Inveresk, Co. Midlothian.
Archibald Dudgeon	son		5		Born	Inveresk, Co. Midlothian.
Jane Dudgeon	daughter		2		Born	Inveresk, Co. Midlothian.

Now I knew the names of more children born to Adam Dudgeon and Jane Charles. The names Jane and Jean tend to be interchangeable. Maria was recorded as Marian and she now had a brother Archibald, which made the Archibald Dudgeon of the 1841 census even more likely to be ours: so I noted the following entry:

1851/689/1/9 at High Street, Musselburgh, Par. of Inveresk,
Co. Midlothian.

Archibald Dudgeon	Head	mar.	79	Flesher	B.	Inveresk, Co. Midlothian.
Ann Dudgeon	wife	mar.	66	–	B.	Inveresk, Co. Midlothian.
Archibald Dudgeon	son	unmar	39	Flesher	B.	Inveresk, Co. Midlothian.

Two members of Archibald Dudgeon's family had either died or moved away; possibly married. David who was aged 15 and Marion who was aged 10 in the 1841 census were no longer with their parents in 1851.

What next?

Adam and Jane/Jean were both deceased by 1859 when their daughter Maria married Thomas Young. Did they die between 1855 (start of statutory registration in Scotland) and 1859?

On searching the computer index for deaths I soon found that Jane Dudgeon (M/S Charles) had died in 1855 (Illustrations: Fig. 19). Such an occurrence is always fortunate for genealogists because an 1855 certificate contains so much more information than that for any other year:

Death of Jane Dudgeon.
    1855   Inveresk, Co. Edinburgh (689/7) on January 8th at Wonder Street, Musselburgh.

Jane Dudgeon.	Aged 36. Born in Inveresk. married to Adam Dudgeon, (Flesher).
Issue	Maria aged 15
	Anna aged 12
	Helen deceased at 10 months in 1847
	Archibald aged 8
	Jane aged 6
Daughter of	James Charles. Shoemaker (deceased) and of Maria Charles M/S Long (deceased)
Cause	Consumption, one year as certified by A. Macdonald Sanderson. Surgeon, who saw deceased 7 Jany. 1855.
Burial place	Inveresk Churchyard. As certified by Robert Gibson, Undertaker.
Informant	Maria Dudgeon. Daughter.

The deaths registers for 1855 have now been digitised to view on computer.

Most of her children's names were listed in the 1851 census return, but now I knew that there was another baby girl, Helen, who died in 1847 aged 10 months. Helen was not born by 1841 and she had died before 1851, so she could not appear in a census. Later death certificates do not list childrens' names so this kind of information about a family is not as easily found after 1855.

The death certificate showed that Jane's parents, James Charles and Maria Long were both deceased by 1855, and that her husband Adam Dudgeon was still alive . . . but was he . . .? These early certificates tend to be a bit suspect; it was odd to find the informant being Maria who was only 15 years old, if her father had been still alive. Adam was deceased by 1859 when his daughter Maria married, so I had only to search the death index from 1855 to 1859. This I did, and as I suspected, there was no trace of the death of Adam Dudgeon. Of course, this does not *prove* that he died before 1855; he may have gone off somewhere, and died out of Scotland, but it is unlikely.

Before leaving the modern (post-1854) records, I decided to see if the deaths of Archibald and Ann Dudgeon could be found, in case they were the parents of Adam Dudgeon. Archibald was aged 79 and Ann was aged 66 in the 1851 census, so I searched the 1861 census return for Inveresk, but could find only their son Archibald; from which I assumed that his parents had died. Once again I was searching in that twilight area of 1856–60 when spouses' names were not recorded in death certificates, and ages were not recorded in the index. I searched the death index from 1855 and found Ann Dudgeon's death in 1858; she was the daughter of James Leckie and Mary Hart. Although her husband's name was not recorded, Ann was recorded as 'widow of a Flesher'; her age at death (74) was correct, her address was correct, and the informant was her son Archibald.

Ann Dudgeon was a widow when she died in 1858, but a search for the death of Archibald Dudgeon between 1855 and 1858 failed to turn up the relevant entry. He must, therefore, have died prior to statutory registration in 1855.

What next?

Having done as much as I could using statutory records from 1855, it was time once again to sit back, review the situation, add a few facts to the chart (Illustrations: Figure 20) and work out what I hoped to find in the Inveresk Old Parish Registers prior to 1855. Before starting to search the registers, however, I listed all the items I hoped to find:

OPR Inveresk, Co. Midlothian (689) Search for:
1. Marriage of Adam Dudgeon and Jean/Jane Charles before 1841. (daughter Marian/Maria aged 10 in 1851 census).
2. Birth of Maria Long Dudgeon, given as Marion in the census return. circa 1840/1841.
3. Births of her brother and sisters, using the list of children from the 1855 death entry of her mother Jane Dudgeon as well as the list of children in the 1851 census return.
4. Birth of Adam Dudgeon aged 32 in 1851 census, therefore born circa 1819. Parents unknown.
5. If found, then search for births of siblings and marriage of the parents.
6. Death of Adam Dudgeon between 1851 and 1855.

1. For the marriage of Adam Dudgeon and Jean Charles, who were married prior to 1841, I obtained the reference number from the computer index (OPR 689/19). This microfilm contains the Inveresk marriage register 1836–54 and an index. In 1839 I found the marriage of Adam Dudgeon and Jean Charles:

OPR Inveresk, Co. Edinburgh (or Midlothian) (689/19) Marriages.
1839   Dudgeon, Adam, Flesher, residing in this Parish and Jean Charles also residing in this Parish gave up their names for proclamation of

banns on 23rd March 1839 Cautioner for the man Alexander Kirk and for the woman Robert Henderson.

Note that this entry is for the proclamation of banns only, and that the actual date of marriage is not stated.

A Cautioner (pronounced cationer as in nation) acted as a surety for the couple to ensure their good behaviour before the wedding date and also to ensure that they married within the stipulated time of forty days after the proclamation of banns.

2 & 3. To search for the birth of Maria Long Dudgeon and her siblings, I again referred to the OPR computer index and found:

OPR Inveresk, Co Edinburgh (689/17) Births/Baptisms.
1840, Dudgeon, Adam, Flesher and Jean Charles his wife, their daughter Maria Long born 25th May and baptized [blank] 1840. Witnesses William Gilkerton and Robert Borthwick.
1842, Dudgeon, Adam, Flesher and Jane Charles, his wife, their daughter Anne, born 11th June baptized 7th August, Witnesses Robert Borthwick and William Smith.
1844, Dudgeon, Adam, Flesher, Musselburgh, and Jean Charles his wife, their daughter Helen born June 26th & baptized Septr 8th 1844. Witnesses John Veitch & Willm. Gibson.

This 1844 birth entry for Helen Dudgeon revealed an inaccuracy in the 1855 death certificate of her mother Jean, where Helen's birth and death dates were recorded as 1846 and 1847. This is not surprising when you remember that the informant was Maria, aged 15 at the time.

I searched extensively but in vain in Inveresk for the birth or baptism entries for Archibald and Jane, who were both listed in the census, and on their mother's death certificate. They may have been born and recorded in Edinburgh, but I did not take time to search for them farther afield.

4. To search for the birth of Adam Dudgeon I again referred to the OPR computer index. My notebook showed:

OPR Inveresk, Co. Edinburgh (689/10) Births/Baptisms.
Searched for the birth of an Adam Dudgeon. Started to search in the year 1819 as he was aged 32 in the 1851 census return, and found the following entry in 1816:
    1816   Dudgeon, Archibald, Flesher, & Anne Leckie, their son Adam born 28th Jany. & bapt. 1st Feby. Wits. David Leckie & Wm. Dudgeon.

Was this our Adam? The only way to make sure was to search for a few more years either side of 1816 to see if the birth of another Adam Dudgeon had been recorded. This I did, covering the years 1820–12, and luckily I did not find the birth of another Adam Dudgeon registered in Inveresk. So his age in the 1851 census should have been recorded as 35 and not 32.

5. Using the names found in the index, I looked them up in the OPR, noting the different volume numbers for different years:

OPR Inveresk, Co. Edinburgh (689/9) Births/Baptisms.
1804 Dudgeon, Archibald, Flesher, & Anne Leckie, his wife, their son George. born 14th & bapt. 26th August. Wits. D. Leckie & G. Dudgeon.
1806 Dudgeon, Archibald, Flesher, & Ann Leckie, his wife, their son James, born July 26 and bapt Augt [blank] Wits. James and John Leckie.

OPR Inveresk, Co. Edinburgh (689/10) Births/Baptisms.
1809 Dudgeon, Archibald, Flesher, & Anne Leckie his wife, their son Archd. born 23rd June & bapt. 7th July. Wits. David & Geo. Leckie.
1818 Dudgeon, Archibald, Flesher & Anne Leckie, their daughter Marion, born 8th & bapt. 18th June. Wits. David Leckie and Wm. Dudgeon.

OPR Inveresk, Co. Edinburgh (689/16) Births/Baptisms.
1820 Dudgeon, Archibald, Flesher, & Anne Leckie, their daughter Margaret, born 4th & bapt. 29th December. Wits David Leckie & James Dudgeon.
1823 Dudgeon, Archibald, Flesher, & Ann Leckie, their son David, born 27th November 1822, & bapt 27th Feby. 1823. Wits. David Leckie & James Dudgeon.
1830 Dudgeon, Archibald, Flesher, & Ann Leckie his wife, had their daughter Menie, born 1st January & bapt. 2nd May 1830. Wits. D. Moodie and Charles Webster.

There are some points to be noted from the above birth entries, Ann was sometimes Anne; the witnesses' names tend to suggest that they were members of the family, perhaps uncles to the children; and the 1823 entry for David showed that he had been born in the November of the previous year, 1822.

Archibald Dudgeon and Anne Leckie had their first child in 1804, so I searched the computer marriage index from that date:

OPR Inveresk Co. Edinburgh (689/13) Marriages.
1803 Dudgeon, Archibald, Flesher & Ann Leckie, both in this parish were married at Edinr. on the 9th May by the Revd. John McClaurin, Minister of the Gaelic Chapel of Glasgow.

This is an interesting entry. Both Archibald Dudgeon and his bride Ann Leckie lived in Musselburgh, Parish of Inveresk, but they were married in Edinburgh, and not only that, they were married by the Minister of the Gaelic Chapel of Glasgow! I wonder what connection they had with the Revd John McClaurin, and why, if he came through to Edinburgh to marry them, he did not go to Musselburgh which is only between five and six miles away.

It is highly unlikely that the Dudgeon family were Gaelic speakers as they lived in the south of Scotland, but perhaps Ann Leckie's family came from a Gaelic-speaking area. It would be interesting to extend the search on the Leckie family for more detailed information.

6. Before leaving Inveresk, I searched the OPR for Dudgeon deaths.

OPR Inveresk Co. Edinburgh (698/20) Deaths.

1845   May 14 Helen Dudgeon, daughter of Adam Dudgeon, Flesher, Aged 1, Died at Wonder Street, Newbigging, Musselburgh.

1853   July 30 Adam Dudgeon, Flesher, aged 34, died at High Street, Musselburgh.

1853   Septr. 18 Archibald Dudgeon, Flesher, aged 84, died at High Street, Musselburgh.

Unlike the Young family, the Dudgeons did not have a tombstone.

This seemed a good place to stop this search in the OPRs – for the time being anyway. There is always more to be done; I could certainly try to take back the Dudgeon line, and the Charles line (Jane Dudgeon who died in 1855 was the daughter of James Charles and Maria Long), and so it goes on . . . and on . . .and on!

What next?

The next step was to visit the National Archives of Scotland to search for wills and deeds to see what could be found for the Young and the Dudgeon families. There is no charge for searching records in the NAS, so it is better to plan your research so as to stay in New Register House until you have used up your search pass there – one day, or one week or for whatever period you have paid.

I searched the index of testaments (wills) and inventories, in the Edinburgh Commissariot, for the Young family. There was nothing for John Young and his wife Agnes Paterson, but I did find wills and inventories for their son Thomas Young and his wife Maria Dudgeon.

'At Edinburgh the First day of March Nineteen hundred and twenty six, the following Inventory of the Personal Estate of Mrs Maria Dudgeon or Young, and Deed relating to the disposal thereof, were presented by Alex. Ross, S.S.C., 108 George Street, Edinburgh: "Inventory of the moveable or personal estate and effects, wheresoever situated, of the late Mrs Maria Dudgeon or Young, wife of and who resided with Thomas Young, at Number 18 Dudley Terrace, Leith, Edinburgh, who died at 18 Dudley Terrace, aforesaid, on the fifth day of February 1926".'

There followed a list of sums of money, cash in the house, cash in the bank, Bonds and the value of her personal effects. In her will she made the following bequests:

'I Mrs Maria Dudgeon or Young, Wife of and residing with Thomas Young at number eighteen Dudley Terrace, Leith being desirous of settling the succession to my means and estate after my death Do Hereby assign and Dispone and Bequeath to my daughters Agnes Paterson Young and Annie Dudgeon Young, my whole means estate and effects heritable and moveable which shall belong to me at the time of my death subject to the following legacies vizt: – To my eldest daughter Agnes Paterson Young, my diamond gold ring; To my youngest daughter Annie Dudgeon Young my diamond gold brooch and gold watch and chain; and any Jewellery, Silver plate, Linen and China equally divided between my two daughters before mentioned: I also bequeath to my daughter-in-law Isabella Paterson Young the sum of Ten Pounds Sterling to be paid after my death free of Legacy Duty: And I nominate and appoint my sons John Young, two Bellevue Crescent Ayr and Thomas Young one hundred and six Comiston Drive Edinburgh and the survivor of them to be my Executors and Executor. In Witness Whereof these presents written on this page are subscribed by me at Edinburgh on the eighth day of June Nineteen hundred and twenty before these witnesses Robert Somervell Campbell, Solicitor Supreme Courts Edinburgh and James Haxton Banks Clerk to Messrs Alexander Campbell and Son, Solicitors Supreme Courts, Edinburgh.'

For Thomas Young, the husband of Maria Dudgeon, I found an inventory and a will. The inventory listed money in the same way as the inventory of his wife, but there was also a value of the house and effects, and an amount due to Thomas by his son Thomas. From the genealogical point of view, the will was more interesting than the inventory.

'At Edinburgh the Seventeenth day of January One thousand nine hundred and twenty eight the DEED herinafter engrossed was presented for registration in the Books of Council and Session for preservation and is registered in the said Books as follows:

I, Thomas Young residing at Number eighteen Dudley Terrace, Leith, being desirous of settling the succession to my means and estate after my death do hereby nominate my sons John Young, Number two Bellevue Crescent, Ayr, Thomas Young, One hundred and six Comiston Drive, Edinburgh, and Archibald Young, Number Seven Cargil Terrace, Edinburgh, to be my Trustees and Executors and I assign, dispone, devise and bequeath to them as Trustees under these presents and the survivor of them the whole means and estate heritable and moveable real and personal wherever situated which shall belong to me or over which I may have the power of disposal at the time of my death in trust for the following purposes videlicet (First) for payments of my debts funeral expenses and the expenses of executing the Trust hereby created (Second) I direct my Trustees to deliver the following legacies (1) to my son the said John Young the portraits of myself and my late wife and also my bureau (2) to my son the said Thomas Young my gold chain and appendages, gold sleeve links and studs and silver watch, and (3) to my son the said Archibald Young, my gold watch

(Third) I direct my Trustees to convey my house and pertinents at Number eighteen Dudley Terrace, Leith, to my son the said John Young and my daughters Agnes Paterson Young and Annie Dudgeon Young equally between them (Fourth) I direct my Trustees to deliver to my daughters the said Agnes Peterson Young and Annie Dudgeon Young the whole household effects belonging to me at the time of my death equally between them (Fifth) I direct my Trustees to convey to my sons the said John Young, Thomas Young and Archibald Young equally between them my heritable properties situated at number Fifty two Maryfield, Edinburgh, and Number Twelve Brunton Terrace, Edinburgh, and to pay to them equally between them the sum of Five hundred pounds Sterling and (Sixth) I direct my Trustees to pay assign or convey the whole residue of my means and estate to my daughters the said Agnes Paterson Young and Annie Dudgeon Young equally between them share and share alike. And I confer on my Trustees all requisite powers for carrying out the purposes of this Trust in particular I empower them to sell any part of my means and estate by public roup or private bargain And I consent to registration hereof for preservation: IN WITNESS WHEREOF these presents written on this page are subscribed by the said Thomas Young at Leith upon the Fourteenth day of April Nineteen hundred and twenty seven before these witnesses Mrs Janet Miller Innes, Twenty Dudley Terrace Leith, and Mrs Mary Agnes Preston, Typist to Alexander Ross, Solicitor Supreme Courts, Edinburgh, (Signed) Thomas Young, Janet M. Innes. Witness, M.A. Preston, Witness.'

I also searched the Register of Sasines and found who had bought the property belonging to Thomas Young. I did not, however, search for apprentice records of John Young. I searched for wills for Archibald Dudgeon and for his son Adam, but could find nothing for them at all. So there I called a temporary halt to the search.

Alexander Young who married in 1799 was probably born about 1775, and Archibald Dudgeon who died in 1853 aged 84, was probably born about 1769. His wife Ann Leckie died in 1858 aged 74, and her parents James Leckie and Mary Hart are Margaret Dudgeon Young's great-great-great grandparents. (Illustrations: Fig. 21).

I did not complete either line, but if I were to continue the search I might find their births and the marriages of their parents . . . and their births . . . and . . . !

This search took me about ten days, working for six hours a day.

Index

Fictitious names used as examples throughout the text, and names found in 'Step by Step' are not included in this index.
FHS = Family History Society